The Transformation of the Woman Suffrage Movement

THE DOUGLASS SERIES
ON WOMEN'S LIVES AND THE MEANING OF GENDER

The Transformation
of the Woman Suffrage Movement:
The Case of Illinois, 1850–1920

STEVEN M. BUECHLER

Rutgers University Press   New Brunswick, New Jersey

Library of Congress Cataloging in Publication Data

Buechler, Steven M., 1951–

The transformation of the woman suffrage movement.

(The Douglass series on women's lives and the meaning of gender)

Bibliography: p.

Includes index.

1. Women—Suffrage—Illinois—History.   2. Illinois—

Social conditions.   I. Title.   II. Series.

JK1911.I3B84   1986   324.6'23'09773   85–2200

ISBN 0–8135–1131–3

To My Parents,
John and Audrey Buechler

CONTENTS

TABLES

This book addresses three interrelated issues. Primarily it analyzes the transformation over its seventy year history of a regional branch of the woman suffrage movement in the United States. By comparing new data from Illinois with secondary data on the national movement this detailed case study also complements our knowledge and refines our interpretations of the national woman suffrage movement. The final task is more speculative: the study advances our theoretical understanding of social movement transformation in general and illuminates some of the distinctive characteristics of women's social movements.

The rationale for such a regional study is that a geographically limited focus provides the strongest illustration and allows the fullest exploration of the connections between social change and movement transformation. A number of general histories of the national suffrage movement already exist, but their broad focus and vast subject matter have precluded the intense scrutiny of movement transformation that a geographically limited study permits. A regional study offers the best opportunity to advance our understanding of the suffrage movement because it provides the historical specificity and concrete examples that are needed to complement our general histories and to evaluate our standard interpretations of the suffrage movement.

I chose Illinois for analysis because most suffrage literature analyzes either the national movement as a whole or the woman suffrage movement in the northeastern United States. Existing knowledge of the suffrage movement is thereby skewed toward national figures and northeastern activism, and relatively little is known about other regions of the country. While I chose Illinois for analysis precisely because it was not part of the northeastern movement, positive factors were also considered in the choice. First, unlike either the far West or the deep South, the Midwest experienced continuous mobilization for the vote from the Civil War period until the national victory in 1920. Second, this ongoing movement for the women's vote in the Midwest has been almost completely ignored in the scholarly literature to date. And finally, Illinois offered especially rich examples of the kinds of social change most important in accounting for movement transformation over time. Given the methodological advantages of a regional study and the particular attractions of Illinois, I decided to confine my primary research to the Illinois woman suffrage movement.

While analyzing the suffrage movement in Illinois is an important and worthwhile task, I have also related the Illinois data to existing knowledge and prevailing interpretations of the woman suffrage movement at the national level. New knowledge from Illinois complements our understanding of the overall movement for the vote by revealing both regional variations and common threads between different branches of the movement. Focusing on the Illinois movement also allows significant testing and refining of various interpretations of the suffrage movement as a whole. Through this process a more inclusive explanation of movement change, strongly supported by the data from Illinois, will emerge. It is an explanation that can be generalized at a suitable level of abstraction to the national suffrage movement as a whole. At various points in the text the case for such a generalization is made, but its limits are also indicated.

While the case for generalizing to the national suffrage movement is documented with reference to both primary and secondary sources, the case for generalizing to other social movement transformations and other women's movements is necessarily more speculative. From the very beginning my research into the Illinois movement has been animated by an interest in the general question of social movement transformation, which for many reasons is an oft-ignored aspect of social movements. While no single study can answer such general questions, I attempt to identify and clarify the implications of my research for the study of other social movement transformations. Researching the suffrage movement also uncovered several striking parallels between the suffrage movement and the contemporary feminist movement. These parallels warrant further and fuller research if we are to move beyond facile comparisons, but my work along with impressionistic evidence from the current movement supports speculation regarding some distinctive features of women's social movements in general.

The organization of the book is meant to facilitate these multiple objectives. The first chapter situates my work relative to existing work on woman suffrage by presenting a brief overview of the national movement, discussing prevailing interpretations, and identifying some unresolved questions about the suffrage movement. The second chapter situates my work relative to sociological theories about social movements by discussing theories of movement change, identifying their limitations, and developing a conceptual framework for studying movement transformation in the woman suffrage movement. The next three chapters present the case study of the Illinois movement based on a periodization of the movement into three phases. Each of these chapters blends evidence and interpretation for a more profound understanding of the links between social change and movement transformation. The sixth and concluding chapter returns to the general considerations of the early chapters, summarizing the conclusions of the case study and discussing their implications for our view of the woman suffrage movement and our approach to the sociological topic of social movement transformation. An appendix presents a brief comparative analysis of the midwestern and the national suffrage movements.

I gratefully acknowledge the many people who made important contributions to this project. Numerous discussions with Mary Solberg helped convince me that this project was worth undertaking. Early drafts of the manuscript benefited from the comments of Lewis A. Coser, Michael Schwartz, Nancy Tomes, and Carole Turbin. Later drafts received the careful attention and helpful advice of Nancy Cott, William O'Neill, and Naomi Rosenthal. By challenging my ideas, refining my focus, and correcting my errors, all these individuals helped make this volume a stronger piece of work.

My research into the suffrage movement was supported by the National Science Foundation under Grant SES 8007152; this support increased both the quantity and quality of the research that informs this book. I was ably assisted by numerous librarians and archivists who directed me to materials I might otherwise have missed. My thanks to Archie Motley and Linda Evans of the Chicago Historical Society, to Harriett McLoone of the Huntington Library, to Elizabeth Shenton of the Schlesinger Library, to Roger Bridges of the Illinois State Historical Society, to Josephine Harper of the State Historical Society of Wisconsin, to Mary Lynn Ritzenthaler of the University of Illinois at Chicago Circle, and to Mary Lynn McCree of Jane Addams Hull House. These individuals and their staffs graciously aided my efforts, above and beyond the call of duty.

At Rutgers University Press, Marlie Wasserman was consistently helpful, knowledgeable, and supportive at every stage in the process of publication;

her professionalism and encouragement provide a model for what a good editor should be. Eileen Finan was very helpful in identifying needed changes and corrections. Kathryn Gohl's meticulous copyediting improved the tone and style of the book. At the University of Wisconsin—Platteville, Connie Cushman and Kelly Spillane typed various sections of numerous drafts with unfailing professionalism.

Finally, I would like to acknowledge the support of Susan J. Scott which has sustained me throughout the writing of this book.

ABBREVIATIONS

AWSA	American Woman Suffrage Association
CFL	Chicago Federation of Labor
CHS	Chicago Historical Society
CPEL	Chicago Political Equality League
CPL	Chicago Public Library
CWC	Chicago Woman's Club
CWM	Catharine Waugh McCulloch
EBH	Elizabeth Boynton Harbert
ECS	Elizabeth Cady Stanton
ERA	Equal Rights Association
ESS	Ella Seass Stewart
GFWC	General Federation of Women's Clubs
HL	Huntington Library
HWS	*History of Woman Suffrage*
IESA	Illinois Equal Suffrage Association
IFWC	Illinois Federation of Women's Clubs
ISHS	Illinois State Historical Society
IWSA	Illinois Woman Suffrage Association
JAHH	Jane Addams Hull House
LC	Library of Congress
NAW	*Notable American Women*
NAWSA	National American Woman Suffrage Association

NL   Newberry Library

NWSA   National Woman Suffrage Association

SBA   Susan B. Anthony

SHSW   State Historical Society of Wisconsin

SL   Schlesinger Library

UC   University of Chicago Library

UICC   University of Illinois at Chicago Circle

WCC   Woman's City Club

WCTU   Women's Christian Temperance Union

WPU   Women's Political Union

WTUL   Women's Trade Union League

The Transformation of the Woman Suffrage Movement

The Woman Suffrage Movement: Unresolved Questions

The social movement to secure the vote for women lasted over seventy years. The longevity of this effort is testimony to the vitality of several generations of women who participated in the movement. It is also a telling commentary on the resistance of American society to efforts to improve the political status of women. The confrontation between activist women and a resistant society was a continuing theme, evident at the very beginning when male abolitionists tried to prevent women from using abolitionist lecture platforms to raise the issue of women's rights. And it was evident at the very end when liquor interests, fearing an alliance of suffragists and temperance advocates, obstructed legislation through legal and illegal means. Like most social movements, the suffrage movement involved ongoing conflicts between different interests, and those conflicts affected the course of the movement in many important ways. Unlike many social movements, the suffrage movement did not succumb to such resistance but rather succeeded in winning what it had come to define as its major goal—the right to vote for women.

As this struggle of competing interests unfolded, the larger society was undergoing dramatic social changes. Between 1850 and 1920 the United States was transformed from an agricultural to an industrial nation; cities grew rapidly; enormous wealth was created; massive immigration occurred; and the nation became a world power. These broader social changes continually altered the social terrain on which the movement sought a firm foothold for conducting its struggle for the vote. These changes did not remain external to the suffrage movement but rather flowed into it in important ways. They affected not only what the movement perceived as possible in the realm of social change, but also what the movement defined as desirable in the struggle to improve the status of women.

This book explores the connections between these broad social changes and a series of transformations in the woman suffrage movement. Most social movements do not afford a good opportunity to study this question because they are too short-lived. Whether they succeed or fail (or something in between), most movements begin and end in a relatively short span of time. The suffrage movement is thus distinctive in its persistence over time and its coexistence with major social changes. While the history of the woman suffrage movement is increasingly well known, interpretations and explanations of the movement's transformations over time remain in dispute. My goal is to offer a new interpretation of transformations in the suffrage movement in a way that sheds light on the suffrage movement in particular and on social movements in general.

This chapter provides a brief, descriptive history of the woman suffrage movement in the United States, thus preparing a foundation for the subsequent discussion of major interpretations of the suffrage movement and its transformations over time. Some important unresolved questions about the suffrage movement are identified as well. The remainder of the book is an attempt to answer these questions.

THE WOMAN SUFFRAGE MOVEMENT: AN OVERVIEW

The origins of the women's rights movement in the United States are typically traced to the Seneca Falls convention of 1848.[1] Although this event was highly significant, the calling of this convention must itself be explained and understood by reference to the sociohistorical context that made such a convention possible. Several factors in the prehistory of the women's rights movement are important in accounting for this event.

The first concerns the existence of women's associations and organizations that dated back into the eighteenth century. This prehistory has been admirably described by Nancy Cott in *The Bonds of Womanhood* (1978). The book's title refers to the dialectic in which the same conditions that bound women down relative to men also bound them together as women, thereby providing a basis for various forms of sisterhood. These bonds provided the foundation for women's involvement in numerous church-based philanthropic and moral reform associations in the early decades of the nineteenth century. While these associations were based on common features of women's social position, the associations did not challenge that position as much as they built on it to extend womanly influence into the public realm and the larger society. In Cott's account, only in the 1830s did these associations develop a critical response to women's social position. This initial response involved wider participation by women in various reform movements as well as demands for better educational opportunities for women.

From the perspective of the development of a women's rights movement, the most important reform effort in which women participated was the abolitionist movement. The history of women in the abolitionist movement reveals a "dialectic of opposition" which recurred throughout the nineteenth century. The pattern was one whereby women sought to join a nonfeminist activity as coparticipants alongside men. In the process, male objection to female participation raised the issue of gender, and in response women had to address this alongside or before the original set of issues. In the case of the abolitionist movement, many women entered the movement as abolitionists and only coincidentally as women. Opposition to them as women and limitations on their activities politicized the issue of gender and necessitated a "two-front war" for many female abolitionists.[2]

In addition to providing an important impetus for a women's rights movement, the involvement of women in the abolitionist movement also provided them with resources for launching such a movement. Through their participation, women became increasingly well versed in the principles of ideology, the arts of rhetoric, the forms of organization, and the methods of agitation—important prerequisites of any successful social movement. Throughout the 1830s and 1840s the abolitionist cause functioned both as an impetus to and a training ground for the women's rights movement, which would become more sharply focused at the end of that decade (Hersh 1978).

It was in this context that Elizabeth Cady Stanton and Lucretia Mott issued a call for a women's rights convention in July of 1848. The Seneca Falls convention resulted in the "Declaration of Sentiments and Resolutions" which cleverly rephrased the Declaration of Independence and explicitly stated the program of the women's rights movement for the first time. As Ellen DuBois has noted, the declaration "anticipated every demand of nineteenth century feminism" (1978, 23); it included but by no means was limited to the demand for the ballot. Several aspects of the context of this convention are worth stressing. First, for all the attention this event has rightly attracted, it is best seen as the culmination of a decade of discussion and debate over women's rights within the abolitionist movement. Second, the convention did not signify a sharp break with the abolitionist movement but rather introduced and partially legitimized the issue of women's rights alongside the abolitionist cause. Third, notable differences existed among the women themselves on the appropriate role for women's issues within the movement. Some wished to minimize the "woman question," while others sought to elevate it to equal prominence with abolitionism. Finally, the Seneca Falls convention was one in a series of conventions that occurred throughout the next decade in many locales. In context, then, Seneca Falls did not represent a sharp break with either past or future, although it was the most dramatic occurrence in this historical sequence of events.

In the 1850s this sequence broadened to include women's rights conventions in Worcester, Syracuse, New York, Cleveland, and Boston; these conventions featured prominent male as well as female abolishionist speakers. Many female abolitionists divided their time between the two causes and often used the same platform to discuss both issues. While the cause of women's rights acquired some grudging legitimacy throughout this decade, there remained tensions within the abolitionist movement and the society as a whole over the status and priority of women's issues in the larger cause of reform. In addition, the entanglement of women's rights and abolitionism now began to exercise a paradoxical kind of restraint on the former:

> Ironically, the Garrisonian politics and abolitionist alliance that had enabled the women's rights movement to develop in the first place were beginning to restrain its continued growth. Like the abolitionists before them, women's rights activists saw themselves as agitators, stirring up discontent. However, they had no way to consolidate the feminist sentiment that their agitation was beginning to create. . . . The movement's close political relationship with abolitionism further restrained its organizational growth, in that its ability to rely on the organizational resources of the American Anti-Slavery Society meant that it did not develop its own. (DuBois 1978, 51)

The complicated connection between abolitionism and feminism—whereby the former both nurtured and restricted the latter—persisted through the end of the 1850s. At that point the outbreak of the Civil War introduced profound changes into the women's rights movement and its relation to the abolitionist cause.

During the war itself, agitation for women's rights came to a virtual standstill. This did not mean that women refrained from political and organizational activity; rather they found ways to connect these activities with the war effort itself. Two important examples are provided by the Sanitary Commission and the National Women's Loyal League. The Sanitary Commission quickly became the "right arm of the Union hospital and medical services" (Flexner 1975, 107) and contributed in important ways to the larger war effort. Organized and run by women, the commission's activities ranged from recruiting nurses and providing medical supplies to running hospitals and locating the relatives of injured and deceased soldiers. The National Women's Loyal League, organized by Elizabeth Cady Stanton and Susan B. Anthony in 1863, collected almost four hundred thousand signatures on a petition calling for a constitutional amendment to ban slavery. Like the abolitionist movement, the Sanitary Commission and Loyal League were important training grounds: "Perhaps one of the most far-reaching effects of the League's work was to accustom the women themselves to the value of organization as a means to accomplish their ends. Their experience in the League, fortified by the many other activities they carried on during the war, acted as a powerful solvent in changing their earlier views that organization could only be constricting and harmful" (Flexner 1975, 111). With the close of the war and the impetus to reform it inspired, women appeared to be in their best strategic position to date for advancing the goals of the women's rights movement drafted almost twenty years before at the Seneca Falls convention.

The emancipation of the slaves during the Civil War raised the question of enlarging the electorate in a dramatic fashion. Nothing appeared more logical to women's rights advocates than to propose and work for the simultaneous enfranchisement of blacks and women as one overall reform toward a more just and equal republic. To the Republicans seeking control of the South, however, nothing seemed more dangerous to the prospects of black enfranchisement (and their own bid for southern hegemony) than to link the two issues. To the dismay of women's rights advocates and the satisfaction of most Republicans, the Fourteenth Amendment introduced into Congress in the summer of 1866 called for enfranchising black males only. The amendment did more than ignore feminist interests; it set them back by introducing the word *male* into the Constitution. If this amendment were adopted, enfranchising women would require a further amendment to the Constitution.

Female abolitionists were thereby presented with a fundamental dilemma. The result was a split in the ranks of the women's rights movement between those who favored the Republican strategy of blacks first and women later and those who saw the issues as one indissoluble reform. Stanton and Anthony, having chosen the latter position, proceeded to campaign against the proposed Fourteenth Amendment for its failure to include the cause of woman suffrage. The dilemma assumed a more concrete form in Kansas in 1867. In that year the state legislature authorized two separate referenda on black and female suffrage. The campaign proved a disaster for both issues as Republicans engaged in antifeminist rhetoric, feminists courted Democratic support, Democrats nurtured the split, and the issues were defined as antithetical; both referenda were ultimately defeated. As a result, women's rights and abolitionism became increasingly divorced, and feminists themselves were increasingly split over their relation to the Republican party and the abolitionist movement.

Tensions were further inflamed by the involvement of George Francis Train. An eccentric, racist, fiercely anti-Republican financier, Train appeared in the midst of the Kansas campaign and offered financial backing to Stanton and Anthony to publish a newspaper under their editorship to be called *Revolution*. To the dismay of all abolitionists and some feminists, Anthony was receptive to the offer and the first issue appeared in January of 1868. The paper and the link it signified between Train and the women's rights movement further split that movement. Of particular importance, these events alienated Lucy Stone and Henry Blackwell from Stanton and Anthony and created a schism in the suffrage movement that persisted for over two decades.

All these matters came to a head in the 1869 convention of the Equal Rights Association (ERA) in New York. The association had been the main organizational link between the causes of abolitionism and women's rights, and Stanton and Anthony hoped to mobilize it as a vehicle for pursuing a sixteenth amendment to enfranchise women. The convention led to a major debate over organizational priorities. Frederick Douglass eloquently argued for the priority of black rights while Stanton and Anthony were equally vociferous on the importance of women's rights. Lucy Stone responded by rejecting the priority debate and arguing that "We are lost if we turn away from the middle principle and argue for one class" (cited in DuBois 1978, 188). It became apparent to most feminists that the ERA could not serve as the organizational basis many felt was necessary for pursuing the cause of women's rights. Out of this impasse women established the first national organization exclusively dedicated to advancing the political rights of women. (Standard usage and descriptive accuracy make this the most appropriate historical moment to change terminology from the *women's rights movement* to the *woman suffrage movement*, though this terminological shift should not obscure the considerable continuity within the movement before and after 1869.)

The National Woman Suffrage Association (NWSA) was formed by Anthony and Stanton—just after the ERA convention in 1869—to pursue a broad range of reforms in the interests of women. It explicitly rejected male leadership, party affiliation, and abolitionist entanglements. Some months later Stone and Blackwell announced the formation of the American Woman Suffrage Association (AWSA) in Cleveland. This group actively sought the support of abolitionist men and Republican leaders while tactically focusing on the single issue of woman suffrage. This organizational split persisted until 1890 when the two associations merged into the National American Woman Suffrage Association (NAWSA) to pursue a more coordinated struggle for the ballot.

Standard accounts of the woman suffrage movement have focused heavily on this split and have exaggerated some of the differences that divided these organizations (see, e.g., Flexner 1975). While they obviously differed on important tactical questions and while these differences were spiced by personal rivalries, the two organizations nonetheless proceeded from a broadly similar analysis of women's subordinate status (see Buechler 1982a, 84–87, 227–230). More important, the attention focused on this split has diverted attention from the larger significance of these events. Ellen DuBois's excellent history of this period (1978) serves as an important corrective by stressing that the events of 1869 signified the first emergence of an independent, organizationally based movement for women's emancipation in the United States. Twenty-one years after the Seneca Falls declaration, the movement had finally established the appropriate organizational vehicles for pursuing its goals. From this point on—to paraphrase Marx—the movement made its own history, even if it did not make that history under circumstances of its own choosing.

Having established its independence, the woman suffrage movement faced further difficulties almost immediately. Three separate events undermined its legitimacy and helped antisuffrage forces discredit the movement, its goals, and its leadership. The first was Stanton and Anthony's continuing association with George Train. The collaboration led to the publication of the short-lived *Revolution*, a major journal expressing the radical ideology of the NWSA under Stanton and Anthony. However, Train's name and political stand continued to alienate many in the women's movement. More lasting material damage was done when Train left the country and defaulted on his financial promises to Anthony, leading to the demise of the *Revolution* in May of 1870 and leaving Anthony with a debt that consumed a decade of lecture fees.

While movement ties with Train alienated most abolitionists and Republicans, movement ties with Victoria Woodhull probably alienated even broader segments of the public. Woodhull was an avid and eccentric reformer who embraced a variety of causes including "free love." Although she had worked closely with Stanton and Anthony and made important contributions to the feminist cause,[3] her unqualified endorsements of free love presented the movement with great difficulties at a time when it was seeking broader social support. Though Stanton remained a friend and defender of Woodhull, most movement participants consciously distanced themselves from both Woodhull and the issue of sexual freedom and sought to restore the legitimacy of the suffrage movement in the eyes of the public.

Woodhull created further difficulties for the movement when she publicized allegations of a love affair between Henry Ward Beecher (former AWSA president) and Elizabeth Tilton, whose husband Theodore Tilton was a prominent feminist and suffrage advocate. Publicity compelled Tilton to sue Beecher, which in turn led to even more spectacular publicity during the jury trial that eventually exonerated Beecher and resulted in Tilton's humiliation. Opponents nonetheless cited the probable affair as conclusive evidence that the suffrage cause signified a broader attack on public morality, to the great discomfort of a majority of suffrage advocates. As a result, movement participants had to devote considerable energy to distinguishing their position on marriage and divorce reform from the public's conception of free love.[4]

While most suffragists were dismayed by these events, they were encouraged that the territories of Wyoming and Utah had granted woman suffrage by 1870. They pointed to these gains as important symbolic victories for the cause, but most historians agree that they resulted more from sectional interests than from feminist agitation. "In Wyoming, the measure was part of an attempt to establish control by 'real' settlers in the face of frontier drifters," while in Utah the measure was enacted "to improve the image and reinforce Mormon control of the community" (Morgan 1972, 17). These seeming victories contained a hidden and more ominous lesson: woman suffrage could be used to serve essentially conservative interests, and the cause could become a tool of intergroup struggle and a means of reinforcing existing structures of social control.

It was in this context of seeming setbacks and apparent victories that the suffrage movement sought a coherent and consistent strategy to advance its goals in the 1870s. Its choices were shaped in important ways by the political events of the late 1860s and the political structure of the United States. As noted earlier, the Fourteenth Amendment, which enfranchised black males, was a major legal setback for the suffrage movement. Introducing the qualification *male* into the Constitution meant that woman suffrage could only be achieved by a further constitutional amendment. While the movement had always considered the ballot an important goal, these events made the struggle for the vote more imperative and more difficult. Hence, the movement came to focus more exclusively on the ballot and to channel its relatively meager resources to this struggle.

In addition to shaping goals, these events also shaped strategies. The major NWSA strategy over the next several years involved a two-pronged constitutional battle. First, it claimed that women already possessed the right to vote and merely needed to exercise that right by registering and voting. This claim rested on the legal arguments that women were citizens of the United States and that suffrage was an inalienable right of citizenship protected by the Fourteenth Amendment. In the early 1870s hundreds of women voted or attempted to vote and carried these arguments into ensuing court battles. In most cases the court denied any such inalienable link between citizenship and suffrage, pointed to other forms of restricted suffrage, and denied the suffragists' claim.[5] The other, more long-standing constitutional strategy was to call for a Sixteenth Amendment whose exclusive aim was the enfranchisement of women on equal terms with men. This demand was ultimately met—not as the Sixteenth Amendment in the 1870s but as the Nineteenth Amendment ratified in 1920.

The political structure of the United States also had an important bearing on movement strategy. This loosely federated structure with overlapping and ambiguous multiple jurisdictions on state and federal levels posed a major strategical dilemma for all social movements that had to confront it. This dilemma was neatly mirrored in the organizations of the woman suffrage movement: the NWSA opted for a national strategy and a constitutional amendment while the AWSA favored a state-by-state approach whose gradual success, it was felt, would eventually deliver a federal amendment in the natural course of events. Thus, if the behavior of the Republican abolitionists contributed to the split within the suffragist movement, the political system of the United States helped nurture that split by providing a basis for legitimate disagreement over movement strategy. This strategical tension between the state and the federal levels plagued the movement to its last days.[6]

By the mid-1870s the strategy of attempting to vote under the Fourteenth Amendment had been exhausted; after many attempts and unsuccessful court decisions, the tactic was abandoned. The major goal of the NWSA became a federal amendment, while the AWSA concentrated on local campaigns. Neither strategy met with much success. No states were won for over a twenty-year period, and little progress was recorded on the national level by even the most optimistic standards. The major events in the movement during this time were the yearly conventions of the two major suffrage organizations. The AWSA convened in a variety of locations, while the NWSA underscored its national strategy by convening in Washington, D.C. These conventions allowed participants to explore and discuss a wide array of movement issues with activists from around the country. Given the lack of concrete progress, the major function of these conventions became organizational maintenance. By continuing to meet annually even in the face of dim prospects, the conventions helped to maintain the motivation of older members and to recruit newer ones, thereby preserving the organizations for a time when they would become more effective in pursuing their goals.

A more specific contribution to movement maintenance was undertaken by Stanton and Anthony in this period. At the end of the 1870s Anthony decided to start writing the history of the suffrage movement. The first volume of *History of Woman Suffrage* (henceforth abbreviated as *HWS*) appeared in 1881, followed by others in 1882, 1886, 1902, and two final volumes in 1922 edited by Ida Harper. The preface to the second volume defended this premature history by arguing, "We feel that already enough has been achieved to make the final victory certain" (*HWS* 2:iv). It is clear that Anthony conceived of *HWS* as both an educational resource and a means of conducting the struggle itself. In this way, even the movement's own history became a resource whose unfinished character helped recruit and motivate new generations of women who joined the movement over subsequent decades.

By the late 1870s the NWSA's strategy of tilling the Washington soil began to bear grudging fruit. In 1878 Senator Sargent of California introduced for the first time what came to be known as the Anthony amendment.[7] A number of women spoke in favor of it, but it received an adverse committee report and never reached the floor. Bolstered by this incremen-

tal progress, the NWSA redoubled its efforts and secured select committees on woman suffrage in both houses of Congress. In 1882 both committees reported favorably on the suffrage amendment, but no further
action was taken. The Senate committee continued to report favorably in
1884 and 1886, and in the winter of 1886–1887 the amendment was debated on the floor of the Senate for the first time. Several dozen women
had arguments read into the *Congressional Record*, although the debate itself was confined to senators. When the resolution finally came up for a
vote on the floor, it was soundly defeated: 16 voted yea, 34 voted nay, and
26 were absent. This clear defeat not only killed the measure in 1887 but
also helped insure that the amendment would not reach the floor of Congress again for well over a decade.

If the NWSA had little to show for its efforts, the AWSA could claim no
better for its strategy. Between 1870 and 1910 woman suffragists conducted dozens of state amendment campaigns and secured fifty-five statewide popular votes on woman suffrage. Behind these efforts were hundreds
of campaigns directed at state legislatures and state party conventions (Kraditor 1965, 3). As of 1910 the total yield was two clear victories (Colorado
in 1893 and Idaho in 1896) and some limited gains in the form of partial
and restricted suffrage.

Even these limited gains provided no lasting momentum to the suffrage
movement. The victories in the West (along with Wyoming's and Utah's
admission to statehood with woman suffrage intact) were not persuasive in
the East and merely served to underscore the peculiarity of the West in this
respect. Victories in limited forms of suffrage contained their own hazards,
as Eleanor Flexner has argued (1975). Even partial suffrage brought women
into party politics, which in some instances meant that they supported
their party's position on the suffrage issue even if the party was opposed to
the measure. In addition, partial suffrage attracted low voter turnouts
among women, allowing opponents to reinforce their traditional argument that women did not really want the vote. Finally, these limited victories mobilized the liquor industry into a highly organized and well-
financed opponent of woman suffrage, believing that once enfranchised,
women would overwhelmingly vote for temperance and prohibition. In
short, the state campaigns began to appear more futile despite occasional
successes:

> In contrast to these small victories was the endless succession of cam-
> paigns to get state legislatures to place the suffrage issue before the

voters, each one involving untold work and expense, and the interminable series of defeats at the polls. Each campaign or vote could serve as an example of the obstacles inherent in the referendum as a weapon to win woman suffrage. (Flexner 1975, 228–229)

In short, the history of the suffrage movement through the 1870s and 1880s involved not a slackening of effort but a marked imbalance in the ratio of effort to gain. Against this backdrop the two national organizations began discussing a merger shortly after the Senate defeat of the suffrage amendment in 1887. According to Flexner (1975), Alice Stone Blackwell (Lucy Stone's daughter) should be given major credit for bringing about the merger, which was consummated at a joint convention in February of 1890 and gave birth to the National American Woman Suffrage Association (NAWSA).

Flexner discusses several factors that facilitated the merger at this time (1975, 222–228). First she claims that healing had occurred with the passage of time, implying that the original split was grounded in personality conflicts. In addition, the major personalities had retreated somewhat from their positions of organizational dominance; Stone was less active in general, Stanton's interests were running in other directions, and a new generation of leaders was playing a more significant role. Third, Flexner suggests that the NWSA had become more moderate in tone and temper by 1890. With such moderation, a merger was easier to achieve than it would have been earlier. Finally, Flexner argues that the new generation of leaders included "more professionals, writers, and women of substantial means" (1975, 223). Hence, a younger and more like-minded generation of professional women at the head of each organization was primarily responsible for unifying the major movement groups of the day.

The year 1890 brought to a close a second phase in the history of the suffrage movement. The first phase had ended around 1870 when the movement had formed independent suffrage organizations to pursue the goal of women's emancipation. The second phase ended with the merger of these separate organizations in 1890. Suffragists entered the third and final phase of the movement with the hope that organizational unity and strategic coordination would be more effective in achieving the goal that had eluded them throughout the 1870s and 1880s.

If the merger was facilitated by a younger generation of suffragists, they nonetheless displayed respect for their elders by electing Elizabeth Cady Stanton and Susan B. Anthony as the first two presidents of the new suffrage organization.[8] However, these popular choices did not prevent intra-organizational conflicts which resulted from the merger. One set of conflicts was primarily ideological and involved long-standing differences between the old National and American associations' approaches to reform. The former had traditionally included issues beyond the vote, while the latter had favored a narrow focus on the vote. The more narrow and conservative orientation eventually came to predominate in the NAWSA, but not without some internal conflict and struggle.[9] Another set of conflicts involved organizational policy; the merger translated old interorganizational differences into new intraorganizational disputes. The issue concerned whether the appropriate focus of agitation should be on the state or federal level. The NAWSA sought a compromise between the two strategies by directing its resources to whichever campaigns seemed most promising at a given moment.[10] While this compromise strategy initially helped to unify the new organization, it later paralyzed it, thereby promoting rival suffrage organizations exclusively oriented to the federal level.

By coincidence, the first full woman suffrage state appeared in the year of the NAWSA merger: in 1890 Wyoming was granted statehood with its (territorial) suffrage plank intact. In 1896 Utah similarly was admitted to the Union. Two more significant victories were recorded when voters enfranchised women in Colorado in 1893 and Idaho in 1896 as a result of carefully conducted suffragist campaigns. While these victories appeared to support the state-by-state strategy, their gains must be evaluated in the context of efforts expended. From 1870 through 1910 there were 480 campaigns in 33 states to submit the issue to the voters; only 55 actually led to popular votes, and only 2 won. Hence, the list of suffrage states in 1910 had not expanded beyond the four western states that had been won as of 1896 (Kraditor 1965, 3).

These western victories were due in part to the meticulous organizing efforts of Carrie Chapman Catt. Through the 1890s Catt worked within the NAWSA to replace informal and idiosyncratic agitation with more organized approaches that utilized movement resources more efficiently. Catt's organizational skills made her an important asset to the suffrage cause, reflected in Anthony's support of Catt for the presidency of the NAWSA when Anthony retired in 1900.[11] Catt presided from 1900 to 1902 and then temporarily retired for personal reasons; later she returned to work for the NAWSA, regaining the presidency in 1915 and guiding the organization to its ultimate victory in 1920.

As of 1906 no suffrage states had been won in a decade, and no immediate prospects were in sight. In the eyes of Harriot Stanton Blatch, (Elizabeth Cady Stanton's daughter), the suffrage movement was in an interminable rut, confined to old ineffective methods (see Flexner 1975, 258). Blatch's perception was shaped by her experiences in the British suffrage movement and her observation of the earlier stages of that movement's tactical militance. In an effort to overcome the listlessness and ineffectiveness of the NAWSA, Blatch organized the Equality League of Self-Supporting Women (soon renamed the Women's Political Union [WPU]) in 1907. Unlike the NAWSA, the WPU actively solicited support from working women, organized labor, and trade unions. It also introduced tactical innovations, including suffrage parades and outdoor public meetings. By the next year the WPU membership had climbed to nineteen thousand women. During the same period Carrie Catt was building a power base in New York State which led in 1909 to the Woman Suffrage party. While neither effort was immediately successful, both laid the groundwork for more effective suffrage agitation during the last decade of the movement.

The next concrete sign of progress occurred in 1910. In that year suffrage referendums appeared on the ballot in two western states. The measure lost in Oregon but succeeded in Washington, thereby adding a fifth state to the suffrage column after a fourteen-year hiatus. The next year a suffrage referendum also passed in California. In the case of both victories, campaign organizers had received their training within Catt's Organization Committee of the NAWSA, and the success of these campaigns vindicated her emphasis on steady, methodical organization as the key to legislative success. The California victory was particularly significant for two reasons. First, the liquor industry had mounted a massive campaign effort against the sufferage referendum, fearing a female prohibition vote if the measure passed. The California victory, signaling the fallibility of business and liquor opposition, came at an opportune moment for inspiring similar campaigns in other states. The California campaign also witnessed the first widespread use of new tactics in a suffrage campaign. Blatch's WPU had taken the first step in this direction in 1910 when they organized the first woman suffrage parade in New York City; the 1911 California campaign expanded the tactical repertoire to include billboard advertising, high school essay contests, and plays and pageants. Rather than educating and proselytizing small numbers in an intense way, these new tactics relied on reaching large numbers of people with brief messages. From this point on, the movement increasingly adopted the methods of mass marketing and advertising to get its positions across to the general public.

In 1912 six states were slated for woman suffrage referenda, including the politically important states of Ohio, Michigan, and Wisconsin. In Wisconsin and Ohio extensive lobbying by the liquor industry defeated the measure by large margins. In Michigan the vote was close enough that it required ballot tampering to block the victory of the suffrage referendum. These defeats put the West Coast victories in a different light. Rather than being the first steps in a state-by-state victory march, it became clear that the major function of these victories had been to awaken, mobilize, and coordinate the opposition to suffrage referenda in other states. Rather than drawing the obvious conclusions, however, the NAWSA under Anna Howard Shaw's ambivalent leadership continued to vacillate between state and federal strategies. A coordinated plan for winning a federal amendment was not developed until the return of Carrie Catt to the presidency late in 1915.

Washington, D.C., once again became the focus of suffrage agitation in 1913. In April of that year, Alice Paul and Lucy Burns organized a parade of five thousand women to march on the day before Wilson's inauguration.[12] The march generated considerable publicity and some sympathy for the cause when marchers were beaten by onlookers and the police chief lost his job for his mishandling of the event. Shortly thereafter, Paul organized the Congressional Union as a NAWSA committee to develop federal-level strategies. When the NAWSA refused to support an all-out federal campaign several months later, Paul split from the organization and established the Congressional Union as an independent suffrage organization. Contributing to the NAWSA's ambivalence were Shaw's weak leadership, the organization's concern over the allegiance of southern suffragists, its commitments to upcoming state campaigns, and its overall size and diversity— all of which immobilized the organization in times of critical decision making. By contrast, the CU was a small, tightly knit organization with a clear strategy and strong leadership.

This organizational split was soon accentuated by another strategical dispute. The CU adopted British movement tactics by taking an explicitly partisan approach to party politics—blaming the party in power for failing to pass the suffrage measure. The policy was implemented through the formation of the Woman's party in all states where women already had the vote. The party's goal was to punish recalcitrant incumbents by voting them out of office at the next election. This policy contrasted sharply with the NAWSA's strictly nonpartisan stance, and this dispute continued to divide the two organizations until the very end of the suffrage fight.

The debate over state versus federal routes to suffrage came to a head in 1914 in the form of the Shafroth-Palmer Resolution (named after its congressional sponsors). In effect, the measure would have made it easier to place state referenda on the ballot, and its implications for orienting the movement toward a state strategy were clear to all involved. In keeping with its federal strategy, the CU rejected the measure immediately. The NAWSA, on the other hand, experienced bitter internal struggles over this issue. Providing lukewarm support for the measure for almost a year, it then rejected the measure as too divisive and damaging to the long-term interests of woman suffrage.

This decision was finally reached at a NAWSA convention in December of 1915. The same convention issued a summons asking Carrie Catt to once again assume the presidency of the organization. She accepted, though with full awareness of the difficulties that lay ahead for the organization and the cause. The NAWSA's dominance of the movement had been considerably undermined by the CU, which had succeeded in bringing the Anthony amendment up for congressional consideration for the first time in over twenty years. In addition, the CU had organized in all forty-eight states and was proceeding with a tactical flair that further underscored the ineffectiveness of the NAWSA. At the same time, the overall cause of suffrage had suffered major setbacks when referenda were defeated in the politically crucial states of Massachusetts, New Jersey, New York, and Pennsylvania. Catt's incisive analysis of the movement's difficulties at this time deserves lengthy quotation:

> A serious crisis exists in the suffrage movement. A considerable number of women in the various states have turned to the Federal Amendment as the most promising avenue. The victory of the Federal Amendment especially appeals to the women of those states with constitutions which make a successful referendum well-nigh impossible. A considerable number of women in the South are dead set against the Federal Amendment. The first anti-suffrage organization of importance to be effected in the South has been formed in Alabama with the slogan: "Home Rule, States Rights, and White Supremacy." A considerable number of other women wish to work exclusively for suffrage within their own states. The Congressional Union is drawing off from the National Association those women who feel it is possible to work for suffrage by the Federal route only. Certain workers in the South are being antagonized because the National is continuing to work for the

Federal Amendment. The combination has produced a great muddle from which the National can be freed only by careful action. (Cited in Flexner 1975, 284)

One indication of Catt's careful leadership was that the NAWSA increased its membership twentyfold in the next two years, from one hundred thousand to two million.

The history of the last four years of the suffrage movement divides into two major parts: how the NAWSA developed into an effective mechanism for political and legislative struggle under Catt's leadership and how the rival organizations complemented each other's efforts in a largely unplanned but generally beneficial manner.[13] With the next major political event the 1916 presidential election campaign, the CU convened the Woman's party in Chicago just before the Republican convention and advocated bloc anti-Democratic voting by women voters and other interested parties. This threat failed to materialize, but the failure allowed the NAWSA to argue that Wilson owed a favor to his female electors in the form of a federal suffrage amendment.

As woman suffrage acquired new political legitimacy at the national level, more detailed strategical coordination of the overall campaign became possible. After a year of rebuilding, Catt presented a "Winning Plan" to the board of the NAWSA, providing a blueprint they followed to the end of the campaign. The plan targeted the thirty six states most likely to ratify a federal amendment; the ultimate goal was to ensure that a woman suffrage plank would be found in the platform of whichever party won the 1920 election. The plan even included a timetable for ratification designed to win acceptance of the amendment by 1 April 1922. The only major deviation from the plan was that exogenous events speeded up the timetable. During this period Catt was also successful in attracting back into the NAWSA fold a number of splinter groups that had departed earlier under Shaw's organizationally ineffective leadership. The major exception to this was the CU, which remained outside the NAWSA and merged with its offspring (the Woman's party) to become the National Woman's party in 1917. It was this group that sent the first woman suffrage pickets to the White House gates on 10 January 1917, carrying placards demanding the vote for women.

United States involvement in the First World War presented a major dilemma for the NAWSA. On the basis of both strategic considerations and nationalist sentiments, the NAWSA leadership supported the war effort.

At the same time, many suffragists feared the potential subordination of the suffrage issue, which had plagued the movement so many times before. Catt's reading of the political realities led the NAWSA to endorse the war effort, but with as little reduction in suffrage activities as possible. The WPU took a different stance. Reflecting its heavily Quaker-based membership, it rejected the war effort, criticized the NAWSA for its support of the war, and continued its tactics of militant agitation. The WPU also played on nationalistic rhetoric by proclaiming that while the United States was making the world safe for democracy, it was denying a political voice to its female citizens. In the context of the war, both the public and the government were less receptive to CU tactics, and pickets began to be arrested and jailed on a fairly regular basis with ambiguous effects on public support for the movement. The NAWSA emphatically denied any connection with the CU and its tactics and criticized the organization publicly, thus allowing Catt to portray the NAWSA as the calm and reasonable arm of the movement to President Wilson and congressional leaders. While the CU was picketing the gates of the White House, Catt was ushered in the front door with formal presidential appointments; she used these occasions to ply political leaders with eminently reasonable arguments urging their support of the suffrage movement.

The NAWSA's bargaining power was increased immeasurably by a stunning string of state victories in 1917. In a three-month period, carefully orchestrated campaigns won the vote for women in North Dakota, Rhode Island, Nebraska, and Arkansas, as well as the politically more significant states of Ohio, Indiana, and Michigan. Perhaps most important, suffragists won the state of New York later in the year, culminating a decade-long effort that went back to Catt's organizing work in that state. By December of 1917 the NAWSA could speak with the cool tone of organizational power and mount a creditable threat:

> If the Sixty-fifth Congress fails to submit the Federal amendment before the next congressional election, this association shall select and enter into such a number of senatorial and congressional campaigns as will effect a change in both Houses of Congress sufficient to insure its passage. The selection of candidates to be opposed is to be left to the Executive Board and to the boards of the states in question. Our opposition to individual candidates shall not be based on party considerations. (Cited in Flexner 1975, 301)

The next month—precisely one year after the first pickets appeared at the White House—the House of Representatives approved the Anthony amendment by a one-vote margin. The vote in the Senate was almost as close but unfavorable; the measure fell short of the required two-thirds majority by two votes.

In the election of 1918 the Republicans gained control of Congress and approval of the amendment was almost a foregone conclusion. Lame-duck Democrats attempted to pass the measure before being unseated, but without success. As the Sixty—sixth Congress was seated, it was deluged with over five hundred resolutions from civic, church, labor, and educational groups urging passage of the amendment. In the interim, six more states had approved suffrage referenda. The Republican party then made good on a promise it had made fifty years ago to the suffrage movement: it helped secure passage of the amendment by a large margin in the House on 20 May 1919; the Senate followed suit on 4 June. There followed a three-month ratification campaign that contained its own minidramas (including the fierce opposition of southern suffragists), but the amendment was ratified on 26 August 1919. On that day, twenty-six million women of voting age across the United States won the right to vote. Suffragists were grateful to issue a call for the last suffrage convention, which met in Chicago for a six-day celebration in February 1920 and began the process of dismantling the NAWSA and converting it into the League of Women Voters.

INTERPRETATIONS OF THE WOMAN SUFFRAGE MOVEMENT

The story of the woman suffrage movement is increasingly well known. However, most histories of the movement have focused on important individuals and dramatic events, paying less attention to patterns of continuity and change that linked these individuals and events over the entire course of the movement. In addition, most standard histories abstract the movement out of its social and historical context, thereby ignoring important forces that shaped the movement throughout its history.[14] As a further result, histories often fail to answer systematically the questions that most interest students of social movements. What were the movement's ideology, tactics, strategies, social base, organizational forms, and resources? How did they change throughout the course of the movement? In short, most accounts of the suffrage movement fail to offer an interpretation of the events they describe.

There are at least three noteworthy exceptions to this pattern where authors have moved beyond narrative history to offer explicit interpretations of some aspect of the movement. These interpretations merit brief discussion here because they help pose the questions that this study investigates. In many ways the present analysis extends and deepens the analyses offered in these earlier studies of the suffrage movement, while also suggesting important modifications for these prior works.

Aileen Kraditor: Changing Ideology

Aileen Kraditor describes the changing ideology of the movement (1965). She argues that throughout most of the nineteenth century, pro-suffrage arguments were based on political principles derived from Enlightenment philosophy, the doctrine of natural rights, and the Declaration of Independence. Basing their arguments on a principle of justice, suffragists insisted that the United States political system, ideological traditions, and revolution demanded the extension of suffrage to women. When women raised these demands, opponents were forced to construct a specific counterideology to justify and legitimize existing practices.

Antisuffrage ideology was thus a new, reactionary response to prosuffrage arguments. It was also a response based on an old cultural tradition that advocated separate spheres and highly differentiated sex roles for women and men. Although antisuffrage arguments contained many contradictory premises, they nevertheless contributed heavily to defining the contours of the ensuing debate over woman suffrage. When suffragists sought to counter every antisuffrage argument, their own arguments came to involve contradictory premises as well (e.g., sexual equality versus the moral superiority of women). While indicating how these debates shaped positions on both sides, Kraditor is less helpful on the question of earlier tensions within feminist thought because her book focuses on the period from 1890 to 1920. A more detailed investigation into the earlier strains of feminist thought thereby promises to shed additional light on the ideological shifts within the movement over time.

Kraditor nonetheless detects a consistent conservative premise below the convoluted surface of antisuffrage thought. This premise involved seeing the family as the fundamental social unit in civil society. From this premise flowed the idea that the family needed only one political representative to defend its interests and that this duty logically fell to the male head of household. Behind all the argument and counterargument, then, was a more fundamental conflict between a conservative stress on families as the building blocks of society and a classically liberal premise of individual rights and duties. To a true conservative, woman suffrage represented not merely a quantitative change in the size of the electorate but a qualitative change in the nature of society toward a more atomized and anomic form of social life. In somewhat paradoxical fashion, later opponents of the movement shared with its early proponents a sense that the ballot implied a whole series of changes in the status of women, though the groups differed diametrically on the desirability of these changes.

In Kraditor's account, the justice argument for the vote prevailed until roughly 1900. After that, suffragist ideology was increasingly couched in terms of expediency. That is, rather than construing the vote as a natural and inalienable right, expediency arguments cast the vote as a subordinate means to some larger end. In one version, expediency arguments demanded the vote as a tool that women could utilize for further reforms, including protective legislation for female and child labor. Other versions were shaped by the audience to which the appeal was directed and invoked explicitly racist, nativist, and elitist themes. Whereas earlier arguments said, in effect, share your political power because it is just, later arguments directed to southern whites and northern Anglo-Saxons said, in effect, double your political power because it is in your interests. Suffragists also began advocating educational or literacy requirements for the vote, thereby shifting the goal of the movement from merely enlarging the electorate to selectively rearranging it. The extent to which these arguments rested on tactical concessions versus the extent to which they reflected a complex suffragist worldview shaped by factors of social class, race, and ethnicity remains to be clarified.

At various points (see especially 1965, 43–57ff.), Kraditor suggests five distinct reasons for the justice-expediency shift in suffragist ideology: (1) justice arguments were devalued in an era of declining faith in democracy; (2) the shift reflected the entry of "socially conscious women" into the movement; (3) the interpenetration of household functions and municipal services in an increasingly urban society allowed women to demand the vote in keeping with their traditional domestic role; (4) a new breed of reform-minded politicians provided an audience for expediency arguments; and (5) past progress reduced the need for arguments to legitimate the cause and increased the need for arguments to tactically advance it.

These reasons shed light on the causes of ideological shifts within the suffrage movement, but they invite further questions and require more detailed answers. For instance, Flexner (1975) also mentions the increasing role of "socially conscious women" in the movement as a factor in ideological change, but neither author consistently explores the role of such women and the changing nature of their impact on the movement over time. Further investigation into these areas promises a fuller understanding of the nature of movement transformation.

William O'Neill: Brave Failure

William O'Neill locates the movement in a broader context of social change by focusing on the "woman movement" in the widest sense, including almost all organized public activities engaged in by women in the later nineteenth and early twentieth centuries. To help organize this multifaceted phenomenon, O'Neill makes a useful distinction between social feminism and hard-core feminism. Those organizations that saw political change toward sexual equality as minor or secondary compared to other reform causes are *social feminists*. *Hard-core feminist* describes those groups for whom political equality constituted the main priority. By tracing the relations between these two orientations as well as the larger society from Victorianism through the Progressive Era, O'Neill anchors the suffrage cause in its social surroundings and renders some of the processes Kraditor describes more understandable. At the same time, the very breadth of O'Neill's approach precludes a detailed and specific analysis of movement transformation in the suffrage cause itself.

Several noteworthy themes in O'Neill's eclectic work are relevant to an interpretation of the suffrage movement. First, O'Neill concurs with other interpreters who perceive a fundamental radicalism in the early stages of the movement. In his view, this radicalism derived from the early movement's direct challenge of the family, thereby questioning the whole range of Victorian attitudes on relations between the sexes. On the other hand (and this constitutes a second theme), the early movement even at its most radical could not completely escape the pervasive Victorian ethos it criticized. It incorporated some of those notions (e.g., the moral superiority of women), thus making the ideology of the movement a paradoxical hybrid of conflicting values and beliefs.

O'Neill thereby illuminates a tension in the orientation of the early movement that nicely complements Kraditor's attention to the later movement.

At the same time, this dualistic view of clashing values obscures the possibility that at least some women may have embraced Victorian stereotypes for their own political purposes. Examples may be found in the seemingly prudish beliefs that men should become as sexually chaste as women were supposed to be and that sexuality should be limited to reproductive functions. In more politicized terms, these were two major ways for women to maximize reproductive self-determination to an extent well beyond what could be achieved with the existing technology and politics of birth control. The early temperance cause provides another example of a seemingly moralistic and ascetic issue that may initially have had as much to do with the politics of the family—that is, women's lack of both economic independence and legal recourse in the face of domestic violence—as it did with Victorian prudery run amok. While most women may not have conceptualized their Victorianism as a political stance, the probability that at least some women did requires a more nuanced reading of these tensions in the early movement.

These issues are relevant to understanding two additional themes that O'Neill discusses. The first involves the way the earlier critique of domesticity eventually faded, leaving a one-issue movement narrowly focused on the vote. The other theme, resulting from this narrow focus, involves the way the later movement "overburdened" the vote and its power by presenting it as the necessary and sufficient condition for all other reforms that women might seek to accomplish. There can be little doubt that these changes occurred within the suffrage movement, and O'Neill offers two reasons for these shifts. One is the social control and negative sanctions that society imposed on the movement's radicalism, while the second is the inadequacy of the movement's own analysis and self-understanding. Both factors are important pieces of a puzzle that nonetheless remains incomplete.

The role of social control in taming the movement's radicalism is important, but it is complicated enough to warrant further investigation and analysis than O'Neill's broad focus allows him to provide. In the first place, there were noteworthy efforts to socially control the movement's radicalism throughout its history, but these efforts largely failed before 1870 and only began to succeed toward the close of the nineteenth century. The differential success of social control thus stands in need of explanation. It can be argued here that social control efforts intensified throughout the nineteenth century and that this accounts for their ultimate success, but this argument raises a second issue regarding the timing of these changes.

The key question here is whether increasing social control really preceded movement change or whether both processes occurred in tandem as part of a larger social transformation. A final complication in the social control explanation revolves around the relative weight of external forces and internal pressures in producing movement change, and the extent to which the movement tamed itself over time as well as responded to social control efforts from outside its ranks. Hence, the exact nature and relative importance of social control as a factor in movement change requires further investigation and analysis.

O'Neill's second explanation of movement change also points to an important factor while inviting further investigation. He argues that the early movement's analysis of women's subordination approached but ultimately failed to conceptualize the economic key to women's position and thereby contained the seeds of its own dissolution in later periods. This conceals rather than reveals the extent to which different historical conjunctures gave rise to different analyses of women's position (rather than merely diluted versions), as well as the extent to which there may have been struggles within the movement over its proper ideology (rather than a simple evolution of views).

Taken together, these two explanations of movement change—social control and inadequate analysis—constitute an ex post facto and defeatist reading of the events. On one hand, the movement is portrayed as not consistently radical enough to achieve its professed goals because of its inadequate analysis. On the other hand, the movement is portrayed as more than radical enough to ensure its demise at the hands of various agents of social control. In this interpretation, the failure of the movement to achieve its early goals seems predestined. Without denying the role of either social control or movement analysis in producing movement transformation, further exploration into these complicating factors is warranted.

Ellen DuBois: Early Radicalism

Ellen DuBois concentrates on the earliest stages of the women's rights movement in the United States (1978). By virtue of her limited chronological focus (1848–1869) she provides more detailed information about the movement than either Kraditor or O'Neill, but does so for only a small—albeit important—part of the history of the movement. DuBois's work develops two major themes of interest for our purposes. The first is a more detailed specification of the radicalism of the early women's rights movement, while the second traces the organizationally and ideologically tortuous route the movement followed before establishing itself as an independent women's movement in 1869.

DuBois cites three distinct reasons why the demand for the ballot in the early women's rights movement should be construed as a radical demand (1978, 40–47ff.; also see DuBois 1974, 1975, 1979). First, the social position of women in the mid-nineteenth century was fundamentally structured by the complete legal subordination of women's political and economic interests to those of their husbands or fathers. As a result, women's legal relationship to the public sphere was at best institutionally mediated by male heads of household. To raise the demand for the ballot in this context was to directly challenge this mediation and subordination by seeking to establish a direct link between individual women and the broader public and political community. Implicit in the demand for the vote, then, was a challenge to the notion of separate spheres and sex-specific rights, duties, and obligations.

Second, DuBois points out that in classical liberal theories of democracy, the right of suffrage had always been linked to an independent social status. This was the rationale for traditionally denying the vote to those in some form of dependent status, including slaves, servants, and those without property. The ballot demand thus asserted a claim about a group's independent social status. In the case of woman suffrage, this claim posed a further challenge to the ideology of separate spheres, the cult of domesticity, and the general social subordination of women to men.

Third, DuBois claims that participants, observers, and opponents of the women's rights movement all perceived the ballot as the single most radical demand of the early movement. Of all the resolutions to change women's legal status discussed at the Seneca Falls convention, only the demand of the ballot did not pass unanimously. The resolution passed with only a narrow majority because many perceived the demand as too radical. While DuBois's claim that "we are obliged to honor the perceptions of the historical actors in question" (1974, 63) ignores the thorny problem of "false consciousness," it sensitizes us to the historical context in a way that is essential for an adequate understanding of this phase of the movement.

The other major theme in DuBois's work concerns the significance of the independent status that the women's rights movement finally achieved after the Civil War. Her history traces how the movement before 1869 was either allied or seeking alliances with other groups in ways that subordinated women's demands to those of other groups. Before the Civil War this pattern was evident in the relations between women's rights and abolition-ism. Immediately after the war the pattern became more pronounced as the Republicans embraced the "Negro's hour" in setting their priorities for reform. The initial response of the movement was to seek alliances with labor in general and women workers in particular. Once again, however, these potential alliances raised the specter of women's demands being sub-ordinated to other demands. In DuBois's account, these real and potential entanglements eventually convinced women's rights advocates that the movement must first establish its independent status in an organizational form, and they acted to do so in 1869. This tension between the need for organizational independence and strategic alliance is one that deserves to be investigated throughout the history of the suffrage movement.

The combined efforts of these historians provide important analytical and interpretive foundations for all future research into the woman suf-frage movement. At the same time, their work leaves a major gap in our knowledge and understanding of the movement. DuBois provides an in-tensive examination of the early movement, but one that ends just as the organizationally independent movement for suffrage began. Kraditor picks up some important threads in the story, but her focus is on the twenti-eth century with only brief allusions to the movement before this point. O'Neill includes the entire history of the suffrage movement, but includes so much more that his comments on the suffrage movement do not go be-yond speculative insights about the topics he addresses. This study com-bines O'Neill's time frame with Kraditor's and DuBois's explicit attention to the suffrage movement. This focus reveals a fascinating series of social movement transformations which existing knowledge helps us to describe but does not yet allow us to explain.

UNRESOLVED QUESTIONS ABOUT THE SUFFRAGE MOVEMENT

The history of the suffrage movement in the United States reveals a series of major changes and transformations in the ideology, goals, and program of that movement. This is clearest when one contrasts the early movement (just after the Civil War) with the movement after the turn of the century. As we have seen, most historians and interpreters depict the early movement as broad based and raising multiple issues. During this time the movement demanded not just the vote but a series of fundamental changes in the economic, social, political, and marital status of women.

The ballot was an important part of this program for change, but its importance derived precisely from its organic connection with the other changes the movement envisioned. Because of this connection, the demand for the vote took on the symbolic connotation of a challenge to every aspect of women's subordination. In this early phase the ballot demand thereby conveyed a challenge to separate spheres, to sex-specific rights and duties, to cultural constructions of sex roles and gender-specific personality traits, and to all social institutions and cultural ideas that contributed to women's subordination. One useful way to gauge the nature of this program is through a thought experiment. If by some miraculous means the articulated goals of the early movement could have been simultaneously and fully implemented, what would have been the impact on American life? Historically informed responses to this imaginative question might differ in details but would have to agree that an implementation of this early program would have resulted in profound changes in many aspects of American society.

A parallel analysis of the ideology, goals, and program of the woman suffrage movement in the early twentieth century reveals sharp contrasts with its earlier stance. Most historians and interpreters agree that the later movement was considerably more limited in its orientation to social change and could arguably be described as conservative in its ultimate implications for American society. The later movement largely restricted its goals to the vote alone. Thus the demand for the ballot was detached from an organically related set of demands for changes in the position of women. Once this occurred, the vote was attached to a series of other goals that had little relation to the original feminist impulse behind the vote. In the most dramatic cases, the ballot was construed as a means of reinforcing and strengthening traditional social arrangements. One example of this reversal may be seen in "municipal housekeeping" arguments for the vote. These arguments began from the premise of traditional sex roles and separate spheres, consciously endorsed those arrangements, and proceeded to construct an argument for the vote on this basis.

The contrast between the earlier and later movements becomes most evident through a parallel thought experiment. If the articulated demands of the later movement had been accomplished, what would their impact have been on American life? In this case our answer is less speculative for the Nineteenth Amendment enfranchising women accomplished the articulated goals of the later movement. Once again, historically informed opinion may differ in details but in broad outlines it is indisputable that the impact of this change on American society was relatively minimal. This is certainly clear relative to the imagined impact of the earlier movement's program for change and is even evident relative to the inflated expectations of later suffragists active in the final stages of the movement. (See Chafe 1977 for a reasoned assessment of the impact of winning the suffrage.)

These sharply contrasting pictures of the same movement at different points in time imply the major unresolved questions about the history of the suffrage movement. Most simply, these questions revolve around two basic issues. First, what happened to the suffrage movement over the course of its history? Second, why did it happen? The first question is both a descriptive and a conceptual question; the second is essentially an explanatory question. The interpretations discussed above shed some light on both questions and suggest the direction for further work.

With respect to the first question, DuBois has helped clarify the early posture of the movement while Kraditor and O'Neill have suggested some of the important departures from this early posture. Building on these efforts, a more theoretically refined version of our first question would be How can we adequately conceptualize the nature and types of changes in movement ideology, goals, and program over time? A desirable conceptualization of these changes would be one that brings order and coherence to the evidence of movement change over time, accurately captures the specifics of changes in the suffrage movement, and is potentially generalizable to other movements and patterns of movement change. In the next chapter, such a conceptualization of movement transformation is developed.

Existing interpretations also help illuminate our second question involving the reasons for movement change over time. Both Kraditor and O'Neill have identified important elements that help account for this change. Building once again on these earlier accounts, a more general framework for investigating the reasons for movement change is offered in the next chapter. This framework identifies those changes in the movement's broader social context that affected its course, describes the mechanisms by which these broad changes influenced movement orientation, and analyzes the relative role of various factors in producing movement change over time. Once this conceptualization of movement change and this framework for analyzing its causes have been established, we will explore these questions through a case study of the Illinois woman suffrage movement.

T W O

Issues in the Sociology of Social Movements

The history of the woman suffrage movement in the United States provides a rich source for those interested in the more general study of social
movements. It is unusual, therefore, that no sociologist has yet offered any
detailed analysis of this movement, despite sociologists' claim to having a
distinctive approach to and body of theories about the nature of social
movements.

Several reasons exist for this continuing disjunction between theoretical
and empirical knowledge. For one, until recently sociologists have been inattentive to the study of history in general. In the search for generalizable
theory, sociologists have tended to abstract social events and processes out
of historical context and to analyze them as if they existed in a temporal
vacuum. Only in the last decade or so have sociologists developed a new
appreciation of historical knowledge, and such appreciation has begun to
influence the nature of their theories once again.[1] Alongside this general
inattentiveness to history has been a more particular inattentiveness to the
history and sociology of women. To borrow Sheila Rowbotham's phrase,
women have long remained not only hidden from history (1976) but hidden from sociology as well. This tendency may be changing, although the
bulk of sociology's interest in questions of sex and gender seems confined
to the study of contemporary sex roles.

Alongside these general points is a more specific reason for the lack of
any in-depth analysis of the suffrage movement from a sociological perspective. In theoretical terms, the most intriguing and important feature of
the woman suffrage movement is the transformation it underwent during
its considerable history. Yet the topics of movement dynamics and transformation over time are perhaps the least developed aspects of sociological

theories about social movements. In one assessment of such theories, Wood and Jackson (1982, 141) approvingly cite John Wilson's remark that "the data presently available on the transformation of social movements are not adequate to provide the basis for any convincing generalizations about the circumstances under which transformation typically takes place and of what specific processes it actually consists" (Wilson 1973, 334; see also Marx and Wood 1975, 349). Hence, the suffrage movement poses a theoretical problem that existing theories of social movements are ill prepared to answer, which also helps explain why no sociological analysis of the suffrage movement has yet been presented.

This book seeks to remedy this shortcoming by developing a sociological analysis of transformations in the woman suffrage movement. The overall project has a dual focus. On the one hand, I adopt a sociological perspective to deepen our understanding of the nature of the suffrage movement and its transformations. On the other hand, I use the suffrage movement to underscore the shortcomings of contemporary theories about social movements and, more positively, to suggest some fruitful directions for the future development of those theories.

This chapter develops the sociological approach that will guide the case study of the suffrage movement in Illinois. In the first section I discuss and evaluate those sociological theories that appear to have the greatest applicability to the problem of movement transformation in the suffrage movement. I conclude that none of these approaches is fully adequate to an interpretation of that movement. The next two sections build on sociological knowledge, offering tentative answers to the two major unresolved questions identified in the previous chapter. In response to the conceptual question of what happened to the movement, I develop a movement transformation concept to describe the process. In response to the explanatory question of why this transformation occurred, I suggest an explanatory model that relates movement processes of transformation to major patterns of social change in American society during the period of the suffrage movement. In subsequent chapters this conceptualization and explanatory model guide the case study of the Illinois movement toward the ultimate goals of a better understanding of the suffrage movement and a stronger theoretical approach to the problem of social movement transformation.

SOCIOLOGICAL THEORIES ABOUT MOVEMENT TRANSFORMATION

While sociology does not possess a generalizable theory of social movement transformation, some work has been done in this area. Sociologists have offered some theoretical analyses of the possible ways in which movements may be transformed over time (e.g., Zald and Ash 1966) as well as some detailed empirical studies of particular transformations in given movements (e.g., Schwartz 1976; Piven and Cloward 1977). While varying in their particulars, virtually all proposed explanations of movement transformation may be roughly divided into two categories. The distinction rests on whether an explanation primarily stresses internal processes within social movements and their organizations or whether the predominant accent falls on external factors that influence movement orientation. Obviously, both factors are likely to be relevant to the explanation of a particular change in a specific movement, but the two arguments are analytically distinct and may be initially discussed as separate types of explanation.

Internalist Arguments

The classical roots of internalist explanations of social movement transformations are found in the work of Robert Michels ([1915] 1962). In his well-known study of the German Social Democratic party, Michels concluded that political parties are subject to an iron law of oligarchy that operates regardless of the participatory ideals and democratic intentions of party members and leaders. In Michels's view, the need for organization creates an inevitable tendency toward oligarchy: "It is organization which gives birth to the domination of the elected over the electors, of the mandataries over the mandators, of the delegates over the delegators. Who says organization says oligarchy" ([1915] 1962, 15). Michels's argument on the inevitability of oligarchy rests on both structural and psychological considerations. In structural terms, the emergence of oligarchical leadership is seen as an inevitable response to increasing size and complexity, the development of functional specialization and expertise, and preexistent or emergent differences between leaders and members in terms of age, class background, and other social characteristics. These structural tendencies toward oligarchy are reinforced in Michels's scheme by psychological tendencies of followers, including apathy, hero worship, and general incompetence. As a result, the need for organization inevitably brings oligarchy in its wake (Michels [1915] 1962; Zeitlin 1981).

Once oligarchy occurs, Michels suggests, it is followed by equally inevitable tendencies toward goal displacement, organizational maintenance, conservatization, and other movement transformations. Common to all these changes is that they promote the interests of the oligarchical leadership as distinct from and frequently as opposed to the interests of the membership and broader following of the party. In this account, then, organizational processes internal to political parties account for why they change their orientation over time. From this analysis of political parties it is a relatively short step to the analysis of organized social movements. If Michels's argument works for political parties, it should also work for social movements that assume an organizational form and thereby become subject to similar sets of organizational dynamics.

Michels's provocative argument, as discussed in the most recent social movement literature, remains controversial. Piven and Cloward have invoked a version of it to account for the failures of poor people's movements in the United States once they assume an organized form (1977). Others have sought to identify weaknesses in Michels's logic that convert his dramatic "iron law" into a more routine "tendential law" of organizational dynamics. For instance, Zeitlin (1981) argues that Michels points to the need for leadership of some sort but does not demonstrate the inevitability of oligarchy. Zald and Ash argue that goal transformation, organizational maintenance, and oligarchization are contingent rather than inevitable outcomes, that they occur only under certain specifiable conditions, and that oligarchization does not necessarily lead to greater conservatism (1966). Schwartz, Rosenthal, and Schwartz (1981) argue that neither oligarchy nor goal displacement are inevitable and that leaders may act to the detriment of movement organizations if and when it serves their larger interests. The combined force of these criticisms has not led to a rejection of Michels's argument as much as it has limited its applicability in certain ways. It remains a possible and potentially plausible means of explaining particular movement transformations over time.

One particular version of this explanation has been implicitly suggested as one reason for changes in the suffrage movement by Mari Jo Buhle and Paul Buhle (1978).[2] In a discussion of the merger of the National and American Woman Suffrage associations which occurred in 1890, they analyze patterns of organizational change that produced a more conservative national suffrage movement. These included more orchestrated conventions, less delegate representation, the elimination of spontaneous discussion and debate, and an overall reduction of member input into the shaping of organizational policy. As a result of these changes, they argue, the organizational leadership of the national suffrage movement became a self-conscious elite advocating a narrow political philosophy and exercising increased control over the movement as a whole.

This argument fits neatly into the larger logic of Michels's analysis of organizational dynamics and the inevitability of oligarchy. It also has considerable empirical validity for understanding the posture of the national suffrage movement after the turn of the century. However, if this explanation is to be effective with respect to the entire history of the suffrage movement, it must fulfill an important temporal condition. Simply put, the organizational changes cited by Michels and the Buhles must precede transformation in organizational ideology, goals, and program for change if this explanation is to work. In other words, if a movement undergoes substantial changes in its ideology, goals, and program before it experiences these organizational dynamics to any significant degree, then this explanation of movement transformation is ruled out because the sequence of cause and effect suggested by the internalist argument does not apply.

To anticipate our analysis of the Illinois suffrage movement for a moment, I will argue that major patterns of movement transformation occurred in Illinois before any significant signs of these organizational dynamics and changes were in evidence. While it is true that the leadership of the Illinois movement was also becoming a self-conscious elite through the 1890s, major patterns of movement transformation had already been occurring throughout the 1870s and 1880s. If these changes occurred before increasing bureaucratization, oligarchization, top-down control, and the like, then the latter cannot be invoked to explain the former. In short, the sequence of changes in the Illinois case precludes this internalist explanation of movement transformation. Hence, this sociological approach to understanding movement transformation has limited utility in the case of the woman suffrage movement examined here.

Externalist Arguments

More recent analyses of movement transformation have utilized an organizational approach that locates movements and their organizations within their larger situational context and social environment. For these approaches, movement transformations are to be understood more on the basis of external factors and relations than strictly internal processes. For Zald and Ash (1966), the most important external influences affecting movement orientations and transformations are the ebb and flow of supporting sentiments in the larger society, the possibilities for success and failure, and the nature of a movement organization's relations with other organizations that may be pursuing roughly similar goals. Depending on how these external factors combine in any particular case, movements will experience a variety of outcomes and changes over the course of their growth and development. Zald and Ash offer a number of propositions about how these different variables will combine to produce specific outcomes, though few of these hypotheses have been tested in any systematic fashion.

The subsequent development of the resource mobilization approach to the study of social movements has also promoted externalist explanations of movement orientations and transformations. In the words of McCarthy and Zald, "The resource mobilization approach emphasizes both societal support and constraint of social movement phenomena. It examines the variety of resources that must be mobilized, the linkages of social movements to other groups, the dependence of movements upon external support for success, and the tactics used by authorities to control or incorporate movements" (1977, 1213). In this approach, external factors loom larger than internal processes in accounting for movement transformations. In some cases, internal processes are themselves seen as governed by external relations, as when the goal of mobilizing resources from the environment mandates a particular organizational form to achieve this result. Externalist approaches have thus sought to subsume Michels's argument in a double sense: by seeing oligarchy as one possibility among others and oligarchical tendencies as themselves contingent on external factors.

An important variation of the externalist approach has been suggested by Schwartz, Rosenthal, and Schwartz (1981). They argue that movements often involve tensions and conflicts between leaders and followers, a premise consistent with Michels's argument. However, Schwartz, Rosenthal, and Schwartz add that many of these tensions arise from leaders and followers occupying distinctly different positions in the larger social structure of their society. Thus the choice of strategies by movement leaders is often influenced by their occupancy of these external positions and the larger interests associated with them. On this basis, they suggest, leaders may pursue strategies (including movement transformations) that are unrelated or actually detrimental to the movement as a whole and the needs of its members and constituents in particular, but which are consistent with the larger structural interests of the movement leadership.

In these ways, externalist approaches seek the roots of movement orientations and transformations in a movement's situational context and larger social environment. As such, they offer a second distinctive way of accounting for particular transformations in specific movements over time. At the same time, many externalist approaches—those most closely associated with the resource mobilization perspective—have deflected attention away from some important aspects of these transformations by arguing that the nature of movement grievances is relatively unimportant in accounting for social movement processes. More important for this perspective are such things as the availability of resources to mobilize a movement, the shifting balance of opportunities for actually organizing such resources, and external influences on possibilities of success and failure. At the extreme, the resource mobilization perspective has argued that prior grievances are irrelevant to the generation of a social movement and that such movements are often created by professionals and movement entrepreneurs to advance their own interests (McCarthy and Zald 1973).

While this view provides an important corrective to earlier approaches that stressed discontent and grievances to the virtual exclusion of other factors, the more extreme versions of resource mobilization theory themselves require a corrective by reestablishing the relative importance of discontent and grievances. If these factors are underemphasized, the question of changes in movement ideology, goals, and program will also be slighted, and an important aspect of movement transformation will be ignored.

Whereas Buhle and Buhle (1978) have provided one version of an internalist argument to account for changes in the suffrage movement, the major externalist argument advanced to explain changes in the suffrage movement has been provided by William O'Neill (1969; also see chapter 1). To briefly reiterate, O'Neill suggests that one major factor contributing to changes in the suffrage movement involved social control efforts by the larger society. O'Neill's account neatly fits the logic of externalist arguments by highlighting the relations between the movement and the larger society of which it was a part and by seeking an explanation for change in these relations. However, as already noted, complications with this explanation require further investigation. It appears that social control had a differential effectiveness in different periods of the movement; it was ineffective in taming early radicalism but was considerably more influential during the later stages of the movement. In part, this was because American society in general became more subject to various forms of social control toward the end of the nineteenth century. In the case of the suffrage movement the important follow-up question is Can it be demonstrated that this increasing control clearly preceded movement change?

I will argue in my analysis of the Illinois case that substantial changes in movement orientation occurred either before or alongside increasing social control. Thus while both occurred, their relative timing makes it difficult to explain the former on the basis of the latter. In this respect the Illinois movement may have differed from the national movement, making it a particularly good case study for identifying other processes that, alongside social control, contributed to movement transformation.

Neither internalist nor externalist accounts, in their general sociological formulations or their specific applications by prior analysts, provide sufficiently detailed and theoretically compelling explanations of transformations in the woman suffrage movement. In both cases, the relative timing of the events in question makes it difficult to adequately account for movement change because that change—at least in the Illinois case—either preceded or accompanied the processes that have been proposed to explain it. While there can be no doubt that internal organizational processes and external social opposition reinforced and added momentum to the process of movement change, a search for other causal factors is warranted.

PATTERNS OF TRANSFORMATION IN THE SUFFRAGE MOVEMENT

An adequate account of movement change requires a clear conception of the actual changes. Most analysts of the suffrage movement describe its early program as broad in scope. For our analysis we need a detailed and precise specification of that breadth. Once this is established, subsequent changes in movement ideology, goals, and program may be conceptualized as a process of movement transformation.

The concept of movement transformation is being used to suggest the extensiveness of the changes the suffrage movement underwent. I intend this concept to connote a change not only in the public demands of the movement leaders but in their private hopes as well. This contrasts with many of the sociological conceptions of movement transformation reviewed above. For many of those accounts, movement transformation is primarily a result of tactical considerations in the face of various factors beyond the control of the movement. In this scenario, movements strategically moderate their demands while privately hoping for more extensive changes than those demands imply. My reading of the suffrage movement suggests a more fundamental redirection: many movement leaders not only moderated their public demands but also experienced a change in their worldview of the relations between the sexes. In sum, transformation in the suffrage movement involved a change not only in what leaders perceived as possible in a tactical sense but also in what they defined as desirable in a normative sense. The concept of transformation is thereby meant to suggest changes on both of these levels over the course of the suffrage movement.

Scope in Social Movements

Sociologists have paid relatively little attention to the question of social movement scope (one important exception here is Gamson 1975). While movements are sometimes described as broad or narrow, few systematic attempts have been made to identify what distinguishes a broad social movement from other types of movements. The concept of movement scope proposed here rests on three general points. First, scope is conceived as a variable feature that refers to the relative breadth of a movement's program. Analyzing scope as a matter of degree allows instructive comparisons between the stances of different movements at a single point in time and between stances of the same movement at different points in time. Second, scope refers to a movement's ideology, goals, and program for social change. These are important, independent objects of analysis aside from the resources mobilized to pursue them and the strategies deployed to achieve them. Third, scope is defined in relation to some particular structure of power that a given movement confronts and challenges. This implies that a movement should not be characterized as broad or narrow in general; rather it should be characterized vis-à-vis the system of power relations that the movement identifies as a problem and seeks to change in some fashion. In sum, movement scope may be conceived as a variable feature of movement ideology, goals, and program in relation to the system of power the movement confronts.

Given these points, a broad social movement may be defined as one whose ideology, goals, and program pose a wide challenge to some existing system of power, while a narrow movement is one whose ideology, goals, and program pose a more tangential challenge to an existing system of power. This distinction implies that revolutionary movements are inher-

ently broad by virtue of their wide challenge to social order, but that reform movements may be either broad or narrow depending on the extensiveness of the challenge they present to a particular system of power. The
evolution of reform movements thus raises the possibility of movement
transformation over time, where such transformation is conceived as a
shifting orientation along the dimension of scope from broad to narrow or
vice versa. With these conceptual reference points, we shall turn to a more
detailed analysis of the orientation of the early suffrage movement.

The Breadth of the Early Suffrage Movement

The proposed conception of scope in social movements underscores the
relation between a given movement and the power structure it confronts.
In the case of the woman suffrage movement in the United States, the
power structure the movement confronted was a patriarchal one, systematically privileging men over women in many spheres of social life. An assessment of the breadth of this movement thereby requires an analysis of
how wide a challenge the suffrage movement presented to this set of power
relations. I will argue that the early suffrage movement (from the 1840s
through the 1870s)—better described as the women's rights movement—
posed a relatively broad challenge to this system of power and that subsequently the movement underwent a process of transformation.

If breadth may initially be defined in this context as challenging the multiple roots of a male power structure, then the breadth of the early movement was evidenced in four interrelated ways. First, as a function of the
historical context in which it sought the vote the movement had an inherently broad scope. Second, this broad character was expressed in the wide
variety of legal rights it demanded for women. Third and most important,
the breadth of the early movement was expressed in its critique of the sexual division of labor and the manner in which women's social position in
both the public and private spheres reinforced their subordination in each.
Finally, the breadth of the early movement was evidenced by an ideology
and analysis of women's subordination that linked their status to other subordinate and dispossessed groups and led to calls for greater justice and
equality for all those groups. Each of these dimensions merits further
discussion.

The manner in which the sociohistorical context of the early movement
contributed to its broad scope has already been identified by Ellen DuBois
(1974, 1975, 1978, 1979) and described in the previous chapter. Accord-

ing to DuBois, women's virtually complete legal subordination, the traditional association between voting and independence, and the perceptions of movement participants all combined to make the ballot demand itself a wide challenge to women's inequality in mid-nineteenth century America.

However, the breadth of the early movement did not derive exclusively, or even primarily, from the historical context and social perceptions surrounding the demand for suffrage. To capture the full extent of this breadth we must move beyond DuBois's arguments on the ballot demand itself. A second indicator of early movement breadth was its articulation of multiple grievances which were translated into demands that women be given a wide variety of legal rights available to men. Some of these demands were primarily economic in nature, including the right to inherit property and the right to control and dispose of one's own wages. Other demands addressed women's access to the public sphere: the right to enter into contracts and other legally binding agreements as independent individuals, the right to serve on juries, and the right to enter professions and occupations typically closed to women by legal statute or longstanding custom. Finally, some demands addressed women's position in the family, including a liberalization of divorce laws and a provision for joint guardianship of children. These demands, along with suffrage, called for dramatic changes in the social, political, and economic status of women relative to men, with implications for "separate spheres" and women's overall subordination which were not lost on participants, opponents, or casual observers of the movement. This wide-ranging focus and its implications for women's overall status provide a second way of conceptualizing the breadth of the early movement (Kraditor 1965; Flexner 1975).

The third and most substantial aspect of the early movement's broad scope was evident in its critique of the sexual division of labor. These protests analyzed the manner in which women's domestic, marital, and economic subordination reinforced each other, thereby structuring women's overall social inequality. These interrelated grievances were expressed in detailed criticisms of the cult of domesticity, the notion of separate spheres, women's economic dependence on men, women's lack of reproductive self-determination, the contribution of religion to women's subjection, and the role that marriage and the family played in the oppression of women. The plight of single women—whether unmarried, divorced, or widowed—seems to have been especially important in crystallizing this analysis. Their situation dramatized for many the vicious circle of economy and family in which economic dependence forced women into marriages which in turn perpetuated that dependence and still provided no assurances of humane treatment, lasting support, or escape through divorce if opposed by the husband (O'Neill 1969).

Elizabeth Cady Stanton was perhaps the most eloquent of the numerous women who stated these grievances. In a remarkable speech delivered in 1870,[3] Stanton called for a womanhood "as dignified and independent as manhood" which would be rooted in economic self-sufficiency and would thereby provide a more voluntary and more authentic basis for entering into marriage (Davis [1871] 1970, 63). That these issues loomed larger than the ballot was evident from one of Stanton's articles in Anthony's paper *Revolution*:

> The ballot is not even half the loaf; it is only a crust—a crumb. The ballot touches only those interests, either of women or men, which take their root in political questions. But women's chief discontent is not with her political, but with her social, and particularly her marital bondage. The solemn and profound question of marriage is of more vital consequence . . . than any such superficial and fragmentary question as woman's suffrage. (Cited in O'Neill 1969, 19–20)

This critique of the sexual division of labor which focused on the need for both economic independence and marital equality stands as one of the most profound illustrations of the breadth of the early movement in the immediate post–Civil War period.

A fourth and final dimension of early movement breadth completes this picture. The final dimension concerns the extent to which the early movement envisioned itself as part of a larger reform movement to alleviate the plight of all disadvantaged and dispossessed groups. The historical ties between abolitionism and feminism were complemented after the Civil War by attempts to ally with the nascent labor movement and its grievances (see, e.g., DuBois 1975, 261ff.). While the attempted alliances with workers and the labor movement eventually foundered, the vision of a reform movement working on behalf of all disadvantaged groups contributed in important ways to the broad scope of the early movement.

These various dimensions of early movement breadth were not without limits nor without internal contradictions. But on balance, the ideology, goals, and program for change that characterized the early movement constituted a fundamental challenge to male power in the mid-nineteenth century. As such, the movement's early orientation conforms well to our general conception of movement breadth as involving a wide challenge to a structure of domination.[4] This multidimensional conception of early movement breadth not only clarifies the stance of the early movement but also provides a clear baseline for comparisons with the stance of the suffrage movement at later points in its history. It is this question to which we now turn.

Indicators of Movement Transformation

The ideology, goals, and program of the later movement to enfranchise women form a sharp contrast to the early movement's breadth. By whatever benchmark one chooses, the later movement was not only more tame and timid in style but narrower in its overall analysis and identification of the roots of women's subordination and the problems derived from that condition. In terms of our typology of social movement orientations, the suffrage movement changed from a broad to a narrow reform movement because its challenge to patriarchal power changed from a wide to a relatively tangential one. The flavor of this contrast may be conveyed by briefly comparing the later movement on each of the dimensions identified above.

One contributing factor to the transformation of the movement concerned its changing historical context as well as the participants' changing perceptions of themselves. In the intervening decades, women gained through several routes a partial and grudging entry into the public sphere while still being denied the vote. As a result, the suffrage demand no longer connoted the same symbolic challenge to patriarchal power it had conveyed earlier. Defusing this symbolic challenge allowed a large and confusing array of other reasons to be advanced in support of the vote for women. The variety of expediency arguments that Kraditor (1965) has documented came to replace earlier and less ambiguous justice arguments for the vote. Among these expediency arguments, several were unrelated to or actually at odds with the original feminist impulse that had animated the earlier phase of the movement.

Also evidence suggests that movement participants themselves no longer perceived the suffrage issue as involving the same breadth of scope. One example is provided in the contrast between the Seneca Falls convention of 1848 which only narrowly approved a suffrage resolution because it was too radical and the 1896 convention of the National American Woman Suffrage Association. At the latter convention, suffrage had become routine, normal business, but members drafted and passed a resolution explicitly repudiating Stanton's privately published *Women's Bible* and its critique of religious orthodoxy (Kraditor 1965, 68–69). While obviously done with an eye toward public relations, this action illustrated how the ballot had become detached over the intervening decades from a larger agenda of social change.

This changing historical context is important for understanding changes in the movement, but it remains a background factor in the actual transformation. Even in the new context the movement could have retained a broad orientation in other dimensions, and it is these other dimensions that must be examined to really capture the meaning of transformation. The second dimension of breadth concerned the early movement's many demands for legal changes that, taken together, constituted a wide challenge to the prevailing social, economic, and political roles of women. The later movement, in contrast, underwent a process of goal transformation whereby it increasingly focused on the vote to the exclusion of other issues. In part this transformation was eminently logical in that women did achieve some legal gains although the vote was still withheld. However, many other legal demands were not granted, partially granted, or granted and then revoked, and it is these that largely disappeared from the movement's analysis and concern as it became a one-issue movement for the vote.

Closely related to this process of goal transformation, the vote shifted its locus in the movement's analysis from being considered one reform among others to being touted as the major solution to women's problems. Thus, although women remained interested in problems other than securing suffrage, movement ideology increasingly presented the vote as both a necessary and sufficient condition for achieving all other goals. The claim of necessity denied the efficacy of all other forms of political activity, while the claim of sufficiency resulted in a dramatic overburdening of the vote. As a result, an amazing and almost unlimited set of benefits (to both women and society at large) were portrayed as inevitable once the franchise was secured. These patterns of goal transformation created a distinctively narrower movement in at least two ways. First, reduction to a single issue detached the vote from what had previously been an organically related set of demands to change women's overall social position. With this detachment, the single demand could be and was accommodated to many aspects of women's still subordinate position. Second, insistence on giving the vote this priority constricted support for other solutions that might have had a more fundamental and lasting effect on women's condition.

The most dramatic and compelling evidence of the transformed nature of the later movement is found in the fate of its earlier criticisms of the sexual division of labor and its identification of women's domestic, marital, and economic status as the root of subordination. In a word, these analyses and orientations faded away and ultimately disappeared over time. The process of goal transformation thus occurred not only with respect to legal demands but also with respect to the deeper and more structural analyses that once relegated the vote to a relatively minor and less important role in the movement's conception of desired changes. As this critical orientation to fundamental aspects of social organization faded, the demand for the vote was again detached from a program calling for basic structural change and was put forward as having no particular implications for these larger issues.

Indeed, the shift was even more striking because the later movement constructed arguments for the vote that assumed and endorsed the prevailing sexual division of labor. To take brief examples, after the turn of the century women in urban areas began to argue that their traditional domestic and maternal duties required the vote because the home had become linked up with the larger municipality in various ways. To properly execute their domestic duties, these arguments claimed, women required municipal suffrage so they could exert control over sanitation, food inspection, waste removal, and the like (Kraditor 1965, 53–54). At about the same time, women began to endorse traditional sex roles and gender-specific personality traits in a more uncritical and one-dimensional fashion. On this basis, they proceeded to argue that the solution to political corruption resided in enfranchising women, who would then introduce a beneficial and specifically feminine influence into political life. In these and other ways the later movement took for granted aspects of the social order that had previously attracted the earlier movement's most incisive and critical attention. And the later movement constructed arguments for the vote that endorsed, legitimized, and reinforced those aspects.

A final way of conceptualizing the transformation of the woman suffrage movement involves the erosion of its earlier vision of a broad reform movement on behalf of disadvantaged groups. In many ways it became a less democratic movement, no longer seeking increased participation for a number of groups but instead seeking to advance its own interests to the exclusion and sometimes the disadvantage of others. In the South, where all political questions were focused through the lens of race, the task of woman suffragists became one of demonstrating numerically how enfranchising women would reinforce white supremacy. However, this procedure was not merely a southern strategy. In 1895 Elizabeth Cady Stanton published an article on "educated suffrage" that proposed to deal with the "ignorant foreign vote" by increasing already existing restrictions: "Instead of repealing the educational law in some states . . . I would draw the line a little higher, at intelligent *reading* and *writing*" (emphasis in original).[5] The ultimate goal was no longer to introduce sweeping changes into the social order for a more just and equal republic; rather, the goal became one of preserving existing institutional arrangements and relations of power, with woman suffrage as one means of advancing toward that goal. Thus a movement born in ferment and agitation for broad social change eventually matured into a movement seeking one narrow reform that was, at times, portrayed as serving the conservative goals of social preservation and social control.

These two pictures of the same movement to enfranchise women offer dramatic illustrations of the pattern of movement transformation. As the challenge the suffrage movement posed to patriarchal power became more tangential, the reform movement simultaneously became narrower. Having depicted the movement at two different points in time, it should be acknowledged that the contrasts described here are, in one sense, exaggerated. These pictures stress the differences and downplay some of the common features of the movement over time. This exaggeration is deliberate because it focuses attention on movement transformation as a topic of investigation.[6] This exposition has provided a tentative answer to the first unresolved question about the suffrage movement: what happened to the movement over its seventy-year history was a complex pattern of transformation from a broad reform movement to a narrow reform movement.

SOCIAL CHANGE AND MOVEMENT TRANSFORMATION

The second unresolved question involves the reasons for the movement's transformation. The earlier discussion of prior analysts of the suffrage movement and of standard sociological approaches to social movements underscored the need for a more inclusive and comprehensive explanation of movement transformation. On one hand, this requires a more extensive investigation of the involvement of socially prominent women in the movement, the operation of social control mechanisms, and the like. On the other hand, this requires a sociological framework that acknowledges both internal processes and external pressures while paying particular attention to the relative timing of these various forces vis-à-vis movement transformation. This section describes an "explanatory schema" that has the potential to provide a more inclusive and comprehensive explanation of movement transformation. The schema accentuates the role of broad patterns of social change in American society that made important contributions to movement transformation. As these patterns of social change unfolded, they set in motion a series of internal and external processes that culminated in a transformed movement.

A Framework for Explaining Movement Transformation

It is a widely accepted principle that social movements are shaped and patterned in important ways by the larger social context in which they take place (see, e.g., Oberschall 1973; Schwartz 1976; Useem 1975). It would seem a plausible corollary of this principle that as that larger social context changes in major ways over significant amounts of time, the social movements that survive these changes will register their effects in a number of ways. This corollary is less familiar and less tested precisely because most social movements do not survive broad social changes. Many are simply too short-lived. Of those with the potential for longer life, most succumb in the face of broad social changes that drastically alter the fragile combination of conditions needed to sustain a movement. Consequently, those social movements that survive over time and alongside major social changes offer a unique opportunity to explore the effects of broad changes in social structure on particular transformations in social movements. The woman suffrage movement is a prime candidate for this approach and thus has important implications for our more general understanding of the nature of social movements.

The period from 1850 to 1920 witnessed fundamental and far-reaching changes in the social structure of the United States. Many of these changes were promoted by the process of capitalist industrialization which created and concentrated massive wealth, transformed most workers into wage laborers, and greatly accelerated patterns of urbanization and immigration. Within this fundamental process of societal transformation, six interrelated changes are particularly important for a fuller understanding of transformations in the woman suffrage movement.

First, this period witnessed the transition from an agriculturally based to an industrially based class structure. This transition drastically changed the relative importance of a number of class groupings and sectors. Farmers, artisans, and small-business owners declined in relative importance while wage laborers, owners of large amounts of capital, and the white-collar sector increased in importance. This trend was roughly indexed in the 1870 census, the first to find more persons working for others than self-employed. In general terms, this period involved the rise, development, and crystallization of a modern class structure shaped by industrial capitalism and including a permanent industrial proletariat as a result of the increasing concentration and centralization of capital. The latter also increased the overall range of inequality as the distance between the upper and lower levels of the class structure grew in this period (Wiebe 1967).

During this same period, a corresponding rise in class consciousness occurred as these groups began to articulate and act upon consciously defined and partially conflicting class and sectoral interests. The representatives of industrial capital, perhaps in the best structural position to see the shape of things to come, acted on these perceptions in a number of ways, including rapidly incorporating what had previously been individual or partnership businesses and prevailing on the state to serve business interests in a wider variety of ways (Wolfe 1977). In the working classes, numerous solutions to new problems were attempted. These groups gradually converged on an understanding of their role in this new economic order while continuing to disagree on the best political strategy for advancing labor's interests. Finally, in the middle classes there was an increased cultural perception of the role of social class, as optimism increasingly gave way to anxieties over roles in this newly emerging society. Such anxiety was warranted on the part of the small-business sector in terms of their own, narrowly defined self-interest. But in addition to this narrowly defined interest, many indicators among the middle classes showed an increased concern over the shape of society in general, and numerous attempts were made to deny or minimize the role of class warfare in favor of a more organically harmonious social system (Leach 1980).

Having alluded to these broad trends in class structure and class consciousness, it is appropriate to focus on the implications of these changes for the middle class in particular and for women in general. The second half of the nineteenth century initiated important changes in the nature of the middle class(es)—changes summarized in the distinction between the "old" and "new" middle classes. The basis of the old middle class was self-employment, whether running a farm or a small business or engaging in a professional occupation. The new middle class consisted of those employed by others in a wide variety of forms of mental labor. Within this new middle class there developed an increasingly marked bifurcation between those who performed professional and managerial tasks on a salaried basis and those who were engaged in clerical and sales tasks for which they received an hourly wage.[7] While the old and new middle class existed side by side throughout this historical period, their relative size and specific weight underwent a marked change over time. Both sectors of the new middle class expanded while the old middle class contracted under the impact of capitalist industrialization. To the extent that this occurred, the referent of the term *middle class* is by no means identical in, for example, 1860 and 1910. By implication, the notion of a "middle-class movement" is equally simplistic and must be rethought in light of the distinctions drawn above.

If we turn our attention to the impact of these processes on the situation of women, we can hypothesize that as this new class structure emerged and crystallized, it differentiated women by social class to a greater extent than in earlier periods (see Chafe 1977). Substantiation of this claim requires consideration of two processes. The first involved the way various opportunities and resources became available to women as a result of industrialization throughout the second half of the nineteenth century. The second process involved women's increasingly differentiated ability to take advantage of these new opportunities and resources. Consideration of these processes allows a refinement of this notion by acknowledging that while women have always been differentiated by social class, until the mid-nineteenth century they differed largely through their relation to husbands who occupied various positions in the class structure. After this point, by virtue of class-mediated access to new resources and opportunities women became increasingly differentiated on an individual basis as well as through their husband's class location. As this new process of class-based gender differentiation occured, it eliminated some of women's cross-class commonalities that had typified the earlier period.

The example of education will illustrate this overall process. In the first half of the nineteenth century a small number of middle-class women were able to acquire advanced formal educations in female seminaries and girls' schools, but this education was inferior to men's and was restricted to a minute percentage of women. In the latter half and especially the last quarter of the nineteenth century, educational opportunities for women steadily increased both through the founding of women's colleges and through increasingly equal access to institutions formerly restricted to men. Education thereby became one of the bases that increasingly differentiated women from one another (as mediated by social class) toward the end of the nineteenth century. To the extent this example is paradigmatic of other spheres of social life, including increasingly differential access to certain occupations, to the existing technology of birth control, to medical care, to changes in household technology, to leisure time, and to participation in voluntary organizations, we have a basis for conceptualizing the increased differentiation of women's life-styles, situations, and experiences by social class throughout this period.

One other factor that differentiated women (as well as men), during the last two decades of the nineteenth century in particular, concerns the increased flow of immigrants representing a wide diversity of cultural backgrounds. These immigrants brought with them deeply embedded and highly distinctive cultural traditions, customs, rituals, and work patterns that differed sharply from prevailing Anglo-Saxon tradition and persisted well into the present century (Gutman 1977). This seemingly exogenous factor that differentiated women is connected to our themes above in at least two ways. First, immigration was prompted in part by American industrial capital's need for cheap and relatively unskilled labor. Second, the bulk of these immigrants, especially southern European peoples, entered American society through the lower levels of the working class. Immigration thereby increased the heterogeneity of a class that was itself increasingly differentiated from other sectors of the society.

A final change that requires consideration concerns the impact of capitalist industrialization on the sexual division of labor. In preindustrial systems of production the household was often the center of economic production, and women occupied well-defined and socially recognized productive roles within this system. With the onset of industrialization, the household lost much of its technically productive status, the market increasingly intervened between home and work, and women who remained within the household lost their economically productive roles as a result. Once this stage was reached a noticeable separation between privatized households and socialized production became evident, and the major economic function of the household became the production and reproduction of labor power for the growing industrial economy (Strasser 1977, 1982).

As capital increasingly permeated all forms of production, especially the realm of consumer goods, the economic function of the household continued to change. From a unit of production and then a locus for the reproduction of labor power, the household increasingly became a unit of economic consumption (Strasser 1977). And thus a new economic role for women materialized: responsibility for the procurement of consumer goods at the level of the individual household. Whereas early industrialization was responsible for separating the spheres of home and work, later industrialization partially overcame this separation by articulating the home back into the economic system as a unit of consumption. The re-integration did not provide new productive roles for the majority of women, but it did represent a definite change from the intermediate period. The domestic role was upgraded and legitimized as an economically useful one in which women concretely mediated the connection between production and consumption.

All of these trends and patterns of change—in class structure, class consciousness, middle-class composition, women's differentiation, ethnic diversity, and sexual division of labor—constituted major threads in the sociohistorical fabric of nineteenth and early twentieth century America. All are valuable for understanding the transformation of the woman suffrage movement.

A Periodization of the Suffrage Movement

The next task is to weave the suffrage movement and its transformations into this larger pattern of social change and specify some of the connections between the two. This can best be accomplished by a tentative periodization of the suffrage movement that suggests the major impact of these social changes on movement transformation. The periodization of historical events is always a hazardous and potentially misleading practice. In this case, however, the theoretical benefits outweigh the methodological dangers if three caveats are kept in mind. First, the precise beginnings and endings of any particular period are obviously somewhat arbitrary since they impose artificial boundaries around fluid events. Second, the value of any periodization lies in its utility for highlighting particular problems for analysis and investigation; it is a way of asking questions rather than providing answers. Finally, any periodization must be treated as a sensitizing and heuristic device subject to modification or even abandonment as new information is brought to bear upon it. With these provisos, the following model is useful for initially conceptualizing the impact of broad social changes on transformations within the woman suffrage movement.

1840–1870: The Early Movement

This initial period was historically conducive in several respects to the development of a broadly oriented movement among certain middle-class women. First, the decline of family production meant that the economic status of middle-class women underwent a decline relative to that of middle-class men. Second, the legal status of women differed sharply from that of men, thereby emphasizing and underscoring a number of cross-class similarities in women's situation both on the formal, legal level as well as on the level of social practice, cultural norms, opportunity structures, access to the public realm, and the like. Third, a few middle-class women were nonetheless attaining public, political roles which provided both an impetus and an opportunity to protest this situation; this occurred primarily in the abolitionist movement, although the issue of women's rights was raised somewhat more tentatively in the temperance and moral reform movements as well.

Out of this mixture of declining economic status, cross-class legal and social restrictions, and involvement in the rhetoric and goals of the abolitionist movement, certain middle-class women developed a broad analysis that went beyond legal rights to the interaction between economic dependence and familial subordination as the root of women's oppression. This analysis, in turn, was put forward by movement leaders as representing the interests of all women in fundamental social change. This claim to universality was simultaneously an expression of some important, extant, cross-class similarities and an exaggeration of those commonalities for the sake of mobilizing large numbers of people into a feminist movement. The related questions of exactly how this analysis was generated, how widely it was accepted, and how accurate the claim to universality was, remain to be clarified.

1870–1890: Patterns of Transformation

This intermediate period is striking in two important respects. On the one hand, most of the social changes outlined above began to produce effects throughout the social structure; on the other hand, the movement became relatively quiescent. Among the changes that account for the quiescence and were crucial for subsequent events were the development of a new class structure and the increasing differentiation of women.

This process of differentiation was initiated by the elimination of some legal restrictions (with occasional reversals) on women's activities, which reduced some cross-class commonalities and simultaneously brought social-class bonds into the foreground as a basis for differentiating groups of women. As industrialization produced new opportunities and resources, social class became increasingly important in determining who would take advantage of them. And it served to further differentiate women on the basis of their educations, occupations, social activities, leisure time, health care, domestic labor, and the like. Finally, as the changing class structure sorted itself out, increasingly distinct and partially antagonistic class interests began to separate women and their goals more sharply than had previously been the case. As a result of these changes the movement entered a state of drift and uncertainty wherein the older, broad-based analysis began to break down but nothing equally definitive emerged to take its place.

1890–1920: A Specialized Movement

This final period was considerably less conducive to the persistence of a broad suffrage movement. Moreover, it contained a number of structural features that contributed precisely to the transformation of the suffrage movement. A new industrial class structure was crystallizing with a number of important effects: the range of economic inequality increased, capital-labor emerged as the major axis of this new structure, class interests became more defined and more antagonistic, class consciousness intensified as a result, and southern European immigration increased the heterogeneity of the working class in particular and of society in general. However, the trend of legal change continued: women were increasingly (though hardly completely) "free" to be "determined" by their increasingly differentiated class position.

These interrelated changes contributed to movement transformation by increasing the extent and salience of class differences between women while simultaneously decreasing the extent and salience of gender commonalities among women. From yet another angle, the newly emerging economic role of household consumption for women took hold during this period. This role remained both a domestic and a nonproductive economic role; yet it was consciously promoted, upgraded, and legitimized (often in scientific and technical terms) as the most important and respected economic function of women in the new industrial society. This further contributed to transforming the movement by providing a new and powerful variant of the separate spheres argument, which partially integrated women into economic processes (mediated through family and household), but in a way that failed to substantially alter their economic dependence on men or their subordinate position in the family.

Corresponding to this very different social context was a distinctly different suffrage movement. It largely jettisoned its critique of domesticity, economic dependency, and their implications for maintaining women's subordinate role in the family. It presented the vote as a tool of middle-class reform rather than a political right of all women. It reduced its political program to the single issue of winning the vote. It suggested ways of rearranging the franchise to favor white, native-born, middle-class women to the disadvantage of other groups and sometimes other women. It presented the vote as the major key to changing women's condition. And, somewhat paradoxically, it began to emphasize distinctive traits by gender as an argument for the vote (just as Victorian pressures in this direction were perhaps beginning to lessen). The result was a distinctive and unprecedented blend of one-issue reform, nativism, social control, and class/feminist consciousness.[8]

Notes on the Logic of Explanation

This tentative periodization offers a way of initially conceptualizing the relations between broad social changes and particular transformations in the woman suffrage movement. It also provides a way of advancing and testing competing explanations of the transformation of that movement. Before proceeding to that task in the case of the Illinois suffrage movement, a few words of clarification about this explanatory schema are in order.

The first clarification concerns why a new explanation of movement transformation is needed in the first place. The reasoning is as follows: Some of the transformations in the woman suffrage movement must obviously be understood on the level of tactics and strategies. They represented a pragmatic shift from what was defined as desirable by early leaders to what was perceived as possible by later leaders. However, other transformations represented changes not only in what was perceived as possible but also in what was defined as desirable by movement leaders. It is this level that requires closer scrutiny of the broad social context of the movement, how that context changed over time, and how this changing context contributed to movement transformation.

This distinction may be further elaborated by noting the respective types of evidence that support each of these views. If the changes in the suffrage movement were primarily tactical, we should be able to find evidence demonstrating a disjunction between public demands and private desires in the later movement. If it could be shown that movement leaders privately adhered to radical goals but publicly presented more moderate demands, tactical changes would be considered the major form of movement transformation. If the changes in the movement were more substantial (as I contend), we should be able to find evidence demonstrating a relative consistency between public demands and private desires. If it could be shown that movement leaders adhered to moderate goals on both public and private levels, the notion of a substantive transformation of the suffrage movement would be supported. The bulk of the evidence presented below supports this second interpretation, which is part of the reason why an expanded explanation of movement change that links social change and movement transformation is needed.

A second clarification concerns how these explanations are to be derived. The framework outlined above is no more than an "explanation schema" because it merely suggests possible causal factors in a highly abstract fashion. Converting this schema into an authentic explanation of movement change requires identifying mediating links between broad societal causes and particular movement effects. This is necessary if the resultant explanation is to acknowledge but not reify the impact of processes like class formation, industrialization, and the like. At the outset, three types of mediating links between social change and movement transformation may be proposed for closer scrutiny.

The first mediating link involves a number of factors and processes related both to social class and to changes in those factors and processes over time. Class background is obviously important, but one cannot simply read off changes in the movement from changes in class background. Of greater importance is the more fluid notion of class situation. Assessing class situation sensitizes the analysis to what a given class background meant in a particular historical moment, how involved participants perceived their own class situation, what forms of class consciousness predominated, how people saw their relation to other classes, and the like.

Such a procedure will shed new and needed light on the truism that the woman suffrage movement was a middle-class movement. Given the vagueness of the term as well as the changes in that class over time, this truism obscures more than it reveals about who participated, in what proportions they participated, how class consciously they participated, who led and who followed, and how all of these changed over time. Of particular interest here are the relations between the old and new middle classes, their different prospects in the newly emerging social order, and how this may have influenced the orientation of the movement. Finally, consideration must also be given to the role of other classes in this movement and its direction. While this requires attention to the episodic involvement of working and working-class women in the movement, it also requires attention to the later influx of truly upper-class women into the leadership ranks of the movement.

A second mediating link between social change and movement transformation involves organizational processes and factors. The standard sociological literature on movement transformation has its greatest relevance here by suggesting competing or complementary processes (alongside class factors) that may have contributed to movement transformation. In keeping with our earlier discussion, these factors may be divided into primarily internal and external forces that affected movement orientation. Within suffrage organizations themselves, two areas worthy of investigation are conflicts over appropriate movement goals and changes in organizational structure. While I have already argued that such internalist approaches are not adequate to explain the overall pattern of movement transformation, such factors may nonetheless be important in accounting for particular turning points in movement orientation. In addition, such factors may indicate more precisely how class-related factors were translated into a changing movement orientation as class-based interests shaped organizational dynamics within the suffrage movement.

In addition to intraorganizational dynamics, interorganizational relations provide a further mediating link between social change and movement transformation. It is well known that throughout its history the suffrage movement became allied or entangled with other reform causes. What needs to be more systematically clarified are the effects of these relations on movement orientation. In tracing these connections, particular attention must be paid to the social-class base and ideology of these other organizations. Alliances with conservative movements already playing a social control function (which seems likely, e.g., with the later temperance movement) may be especially important in interpreting movement transformation.

A third and final arena for seeking mediations between social change and movement transformations involves changes in the movement's analysis and ideology. Use of these sources is likely to be analytically hazardous without certain important distinctions. First, changes in movement ideology have already been used to document the process of transformation which stands in need of explanation. However, a careful scrutiny of movement analysis and ideology may tell us more than just *that* they were transformed; it may provide clues as to *how* and *why* as well. It will do so if we can detect, alongside an altered rhetoric, traces of the hypothesized factors above that led to the transformation. For example, support for our explanation would be provided if we could find evidence that at the same time the movement became less broadly oriented it also became more (middle) class conscious, perceiving its audience as differentiated in ways that called for building bridges across social classes on a single-issue foundation. By keeping these two aspects of ideological shifts analytically distinct, it may become possible to trace how, as women became more differentiated by social class, the movement was compelled to narrow and focus its attention on a single, formal issue while more substantive cultural and economic demands fell by the wayside.

The need for a second distinction—between analysis and ideology—is prompted by the realization that the movement's publicly proclaimed ideology may have shifted for tactical reasons (such as mobilizing larger numbers) that had little to do with the factors I am proposing. Such tactical shifts doubtless occurred, but I am making the stronger claim that the movement's actual analysis, in addition to its strategically constructed public face, underwent significant changes toward a narrower posture. On the empirical level, these two changes will be mixed in various combinations, but the conceptual distinction between the two remains crucial if we are to distinguish different types of explanations for movement transformation.

The three mediating links of class factors, organizational processes, and ideological shifts will be used to map the interconnections between broad patterns of social change and specific processes of movement transformation. In so doing, the formal and static explanatory schema sketched earlier will be converted into a more fluid and dynamic explanation of the process of transformation within the suffrage movement.

THREE

The Early Movement, 1850–1870

While traces of feminist activity can be found in Illinois as early as the 1840s, it was not until after the Civil War that a fully articulate and autonomous movement for women's rights became established. This chapter describes the emergence of the women's rights movement in Illinois, with an emphasis on the broad scope of that movement in this early phase. Guided by the multidimensional conceptualization of movement scope described earlier, this depiction of the orientation of the early movement provides a baseline for examining subsequent processes of movement transformation in Illinois.

The chapter opens with an overview of movement activity up to the Civil War; the most notable finding for this period is that there was little antebellum activism for women's rights in Illinois by absolute or relative standards. This began to change after the war. Through comparative biographies I illustrate the diversity of routes by which women eventually came to agree on the need for a broad women's rights movement. The next section describes subsequent efforts to mobilize and organize women around the cause of women's rights and examines the conflicts that emerged both among women and their organizations over the most effective methods for pursuing the goal of women's rights. The fourth section distills from various sources the major themes of the early movement's orientation to social change in the immediate postbellum period, when organization building and movement conflict was at its height. The final section analyzes this early movement breadth in its social context and examines some of the connections between that context and the broad posture of the women's rights movement in this period.

WOMEN'S RIGHTS ACTIVITY THROUGH THE CIVIL WAR

Compared to the women's rights movement in the northeastern United States, the Illinois movement was relatively inactive before the Civil War. (See the appendix for a more detailed exposition of regional variations in the suffrage movement.) In contrast to the eastern seaboard, there were no major women's rights organizations or conventions in Illinois in the antebellum period. The earliest reference I found to women's rights activity described the contributions of a Peoria woman, Mary Brown Davis, to the writing and editing of a family newspaper. During the late 1830s and 1840s she wrote articles on abolition, temperance, prison reform, women's rights and dress reform (Wheeler and Wortman 1977, 25). During the 1850s women's rights became a standard topic for local and national speakers on the lecture circuit. For example, in 1853 Lucy Stone spoke on "the Bible position of woman and on social and political disabilities of woman" (see Cole 1919, 211–213, 438–439; Cole 1920, 319–320; Wheeler and Wortman 1977, 36). Despite these events, the activity of the 1850s never reached the critical mass required to call a major convention or initiate a formal women's rights organization. The only exception occurred in the hamlet of Earlville where the first local suffrage association in Illinois was formed in 1855. According to one account, this organization was formed by Susan B. Anthony at the home of her cousin Susan Richardson (ISHS, J. Ward Smith Collection; see also Beldon 1913, 4–5, and *HWS* 3:560). The Earlville society illustrated a broader point: much of the early activism in Illinois was imported from the outside, either in the form of national speakers on tour or relocated easterners who became active after settling in Illinois.

The abolitionist movement provided an impetus to involvement in the nascent women's rights movement in Illinois. Women formed Illinois's first Female Anti-Slavery Society in 1844, and they were instrumental in two spurs of the underground railroad in Quincy and Galesburg. As in the national movement, most Illinois women who became involved in women's rights did so after first working in the abolitionist movement. Their initial interest in feminism appears to have been a generalization from their analysis of slavery and their correlative commitment to work for the elimination of that institution. In the Midwest the biographies of women like Prudence Crandall, Jane Swisshelm, and Mary Livermore illustrated these important connections between abolitionism and feminism in the genesis of a women's rights movement.

Another factor relevant to the generation of a women's rights movement was the growth of female seminaries and academies throughout this period. From 1830 to 1860 twenty-seven such seminaries were chartered in Illinois, many of which were entirely run and organized by women. These seminaries facilitated the entry of local women into teaching positions, but the supply of seminary graduates was not sufficient to the demand for new teachers. In response to the shortage, the Illinois Education Society began recruiting eastern women in 1847. As a result, the number of male and female teachers in Illinois doubled by the end of the Civil War. These seminaries were important not only because they supplied some of the leaders and followers of the women's rights movement, but also because they encouraged the migration of educated eastern women to the state, making them available to participate in the Midwestern movement (see Wheeler and Wortman 1977, 33–35ff.; Cole 1920, 317).

An important predecessor of the organized women's rights movement was women's involvement in humanitarian and philanthropic organizations. A partial listing of such organizations indicates their diversity and extensiveness: in Chicago they included the Ladies Benevolent Association, organized in 1843 to raise money for the poor; the Chicago Relief Society, organized in 1850 to systematize care for the destitute; the Chicago Female Guardian Association, organized in 1853 to "reclaim abandoned females and promote the cause of moral purity"; the Chicago Asylum and Reform School, organized in 1855 to care for juvenile offenders; the Illinois Woman's Kansas Aid and Liberty Association, organized in 1856 to support free staters in Kansas; the Chicago Relief and Aid Society, organized in 1857 to supply fuel and procure employment for the destitute; the Chicago Home for the Friendless, organized in 1858 to find employment for women and homes for children; the Chicago Nursery and Half Orphan Asylum, organized in 1859 to provide child care for working mothers; the Home for Aged and Indigent Females, organized in 1861 to care for elderly women; the Erring Woman's Refuge for Reform, organized in 1863 to care for female lawbreakers; and the Ladies Relief Association, organized in 1865 to distribute clothing to the needy (Pierce 1937, 2:441–447). While the goals of these organizations were often consistent with traditional relations between the sexes, they nevertheless provided women with an early training ground in forming organizations and achieving tasks in the public realm.

On the eve of the Civil War, women's rights activity focused on the legal status of married women. In 1859 a modest victory was recorded when the legislature passed a law permitting women to reclaim their maiden names after divorce. Throughout 1860 Hannah Tracy Cutler and Frances D. Gage worked for a married woman's property bill that would allow women to own and dispose of their own property; this passed in February of 1861. A year later similar efforts were made to secure joint guardianship of children and easier access for widows to deceased husband's property, but these bills made no progress through the state legislature (*HWS* 3:562ff.). Women's rights activists thus won some gains before the war in the absence of a major suffrage organization. Other gains that might have been forthcoming were overwhelmed by the war and the nation's preoccupation with it. Though it halted women's rights activity in the short term, the war set in motion certain processes that led to a more effective and better organized women's rights movement by the end of the decade.

The most important impact of the war on the women's rights movement in Illinois occurred through women's participation in the Sanitary Commission. Eleanor Flexner has sketched this history for the national movement (1975); the organization was especially important in Illinois. The Chicago branch of the Sanitary Commission was formed in October of 1861; its first fund-raising effort that winter yielded a modest $675 to support the Union's war effort. By 1863 Mary Livermore and Jane Hoge had turned the Chicago commission into a well-organized and highly efficient fund-raiser: the Sanitary Fair that summer raised $86,000 in support of the war effort. Less than two years later the Chicago commission staged a three-week fair that became a truly national event and netted a quarter of a million dollars for the National Sanitary Commission (see Flexner 1975; Wheeler and Wortman 1977). Virtually all the work of the organization at local, state, and national levels was carried out by women. As Flexner has persuasively argued, the Sanitary Commission was an important training ground for women in how to build and run organizations in the name of a larger cause, and this was particularly true of the Chicago branch of the Sanitary Commission.

The participation of women in the Sanitary Commission was a logical extension of their earlier involvement in relief and aid societies, but it differed from these earlier involvements in two major respects. First, the scale, scope, and intensity of the effort was qualitatively greater than any of the earlier humanitarian ventures (for detailed accounts of the Chicago Sanitary Commission, see Andreas 1884, 2:310–324, and Livermore 1897, 469–479). Second, and more important, women's involvement in the Sanitary Commission occurred alongside a period of major social change and institutional reorganization that encouraged many different reforms. It was just after the Civil War that women in Illinois began systematically to apply their organizational skills and resources to the mobilization of a local women's rights movement. Before detailing this history, it is instructive to consider some of the routes that individual women traveled in the immediate postbellum period in Illinois on their way to participate in an organized social movement seeking women's emancipation.

THREE PATHS TO FEMINISM

People do not join social movements for identical reasons (Schwartz 1976), and thus it is particularly striking when movements are able to attain considerable unanimity despite the differing backgrounds, experiences, and motivations of their participants. In the case of the suffrage movement there was no single path to participation. This section briefly examines the biographies of three leaders of the midwestern suffrage movement. These biographical sketches serve three purposes: they illustrate the diversity of paths that women traveled to participate in the movement; they indicate that leaders nonetheless came to a general agreement on the type of movement, ideology, and action needed to emancipate women; and by examining the rhythm of individual lives as they were shaped by events in the larger society, the sketches provide some sense of why an active movement emerged when it did.

Mathilde Franziska Anneke arrived in Milwaukee with her husband in 1849; both were political refugees from the unsuccessful German revolution of 1848. Anneke had already arrived at a radical feminist perspective in Germany, and these views led to her active participation in the women's rights movement in the Midwest and the National Woman Suffrage Association formed by Stanton and Anthony in 1869.

Anneke's feminism grew out of an unhappy prior marriage that had terminated in a lengthy legal battle to gain custody of an infant and regain her maiden name. During this battle she penned articles for the *Kolnische Zeitung* on women's rights, and in 1847 she published *Woman in Conflict with Social Conditions*. The book gained her a national reputation and was instrumental in changing some existing laws governing marriage and divorce. That same year she met and married Fritz Anneke, a Prussian officer involved in radical political activities. Both participated in the revolution of

1848, and when that effort failed the Annekes fled to Switzerland, then France, and ultimately to the United States.

These dramatic changes brought no cessation in political interest or activity on Anneke's part. Almost immediately she set out on a career that eventually included writing and lecturing on politics, art, literature, and drama; founding and editing a number of newspapers and periodicals; and organizing and running a German girls' school in Milwaukee known as the Tochter Institute. In all these activities Anneke remained faithful to the radical political principles she had developed in Germany. It is difficult to tell whether her radically democratic politics grew out of her feminism or vice versa, but clearly both nurtured each other through a lifetime of political concern and activism.

Shortly after settling in Milwaukee Anneke began publishing *Deutsche Frauenzeitung*, "a radical, free-thinker's journal dedicated to the complete emancipation of women" (*Notable American Women* 1:51; henceforth abbreviated *NAW*). In 1852 she participated in a major women's rights convention in New York, and from that point on she corresponded and regularly worked with Stanton and Anthony on women's rights issues.[1] She was present at the founding convention of the National Woman Suffrage Association in 1869, where she delivered a major speech that *History of Woman Suffrage* (1969) reprinted in full. The same year she founded the Wisconsin Woman Suffrage Association, which claimed her involvement and allegiance up to the moment of her death in 1884.

The most distinctive feature of Anneke's feminist ideology was its combination of equal rights arguments based on justice and natural rights with an equally strong stress on personal liberties and freedom of choice. This combination led her to actively eschew some of the causes entangled with the women's rights movement of this period. Her rejection of the temperance cause exemplified this general point: "Many sad mistakes have been made . . . by woman suffragists who seem to think they must prop up *human rights* with their pet little idiosyncrasies concerning certain measures such as prohibition, Sunday restrictions, and the like, and who cannot raise their voice for *justice*, without much seasoning of religious 'cant'" (SHSW, Anneke Papers; emphasis in original). Anneke's rejection of causes that infringed on personal liberty was grounded in principle, but she stressed its strategic value as well. In her view much resistance or apathy toward woman suffrage was grounded in fears that enfranchising women would lead to restrictive statutes: "The truth is, that there are hundreds of thousands of intelligent *voters* in the United States who concede women's rights *in principle*, but who either maintain a *passive* attitude towards our movement, or oppose it in practice, simply because they fear that women . . . would . . . institute a despotic police government *subversive of genuine personal liberty*" (SHSW, Anneke Papers; emphasis in original). On both principled and strategic grounds, advancing women's emancipation for Anneke meant eschewing temperance, empty moralism, and religiosity, and insisting instead on the straightforward principles of justice and equality as the basis for women's rights.

Mathilde Anneke's radical feminism resonated well with the broad scope of the early movement in general and the orientation of Stanton and Anthony in particular. In fact, her background led her to draw an even sharper distinction between political justice and moralistic reform than was found in most circles of the early women's rights movement. By contrast, Susan B. Anthony began her career as a temperance reformer and never abandoned this cause, although her priorities shifted considerably in the direction of political equality for women. Elizabeth Cady Stanton was perhaps the most radical suffrage leader and eventually published her own critique of organized religion; yet Stanton periodically resorted to elitist, racist, and nativist arguments for the vote when the cause became especially frustrating. Due to her involvement in German revolutionary movements and her status as an immigrant in the United States, Anneke's feminism consistently remained free of sentimental moralism and various popular prejudices.

Anneke's path to feminism began with the personal difficulties of an unhappy marriage and a contested divorce. Seeing the political in the personal, she publicized the social subordination of women and eventually developed a much broader political philosophy, which she then transplanted into the U.S. context. Anneke remained faithful to that philosophy, and over the decades it made her one of the most consistent and principled advocates of a radical women's rights movement in the United States.

Myra Colby Bradwell led a much more settled life than Mathilde Anneke, but one that also culminated in intensive involvement in the women's rights movement. In Bradwell's case, a family tradition of abolitionism combined with involvement in the Sanitary Commission set the stage for her feminist activism, while her blocked ambition to practice law pushed her onto that stage. In the end, Bradwell also became an important leader of the midwestern women's rights movement, but she arrived at that point through a decidedly different route than Anneke.

Bradwell's abolitionist parents settled the family in Elgin, Illinois, in 1843, where Myra Colby completed her education at the recently established Ladies Seminary of Elgin. After teaching for several years, she met and married James Bradwell, an English immigrant interested in the study of law. They moved to Chicago in 1854, and the next year he was admitted to the Illinois bar and established a law firm with one of Myra's brothers. In 1861 he was elected county judge of Cook County and was well on his way to a successful and lucrative career. During the early years of their marriage Myra studied law under her husband's tutelage and acquired an interest in practicing law herself. Her next step was the founding of a legal newspaper *Chicago Legal News* whose first issue appeared on 3 October 1868. It rapidly became a major resource for the legal profession and a testimony to Myra Bradwell's competence and ability in this field: "From the first issue, she was in charge of the content, makeup, production and financial operation of the paper . . . [It] quickly became the most important legal publication west of the Alleghenies . . . known for its broad and judicious coverage of the legal news of the entire country. . . . [It] did much to mold opinion in the legal profession of the Midwest for twenty-five years" (*NAW* 1: 224).

The next year Bradwell applied for admission to the bar. Although she passed the bar examination, her application was blocked by the Supreme Court of Illinois on the grounds that a married woman could not enter into contracts and would therefore be unable to practice law even if admitted to the bar. This ruling led to a protracted and complicated legal confrontation between Bradwell, the state court, and the state legislature; the case was eventually argued (unsuccessfully) before the U.S. Supreme Court in December of 1872. Bradwell publicized the case and summarized the issues in the 5 February 1870 edition of *Legal News*. She argued that when the state constitution used the pronoun *he* in reference to attorneys it was an indefinite reference to either sex and that she could not be prevented from practicing law on constitutional grounds.[2] The Illinois Supreme Court responded by referring to the "disability imposed by your married condition" that is, married women's inability to enter into contracts. Bradwell replied that in denying her application on such grounds, the court struck "a blow at the rights of every married woman in the great State of Illinois who is dependent on her labor for support." She concluded her defense by arguing that "what the decision of the Supreme Court of the United States was in the Dred Scott case was to the rights of negroes as citizens of the United States, this decision is to the political rights of women in Illinois— annihilation" (*Chicago Legal News*, 5 February 1870, 147).

After her application was denied by the U.S. Supreme Court, Bradwell never resumed her fight for admission to the Illinois bar,[3] in part because the *Legal News* had become a full-time occupation. But Bradwell had also become more interested in the generalized struggle for legal equality than in her own individual goal of practicing law. One interpreter has suggested that these were her motives from the beginning: "It is clear that Mrs. Bradwell was more interested in attaining equal rights for women than she was in personally practicing law" (Spector 1975, 238). Further evidence of Bradwell's motives was provided by the fact that about the time her case was lost before the U.S. Supreme Court, Illinois passed a law against sexual discrimination in occupations and admitted its first woman lawyer to the bar in June of 1873. Had Bradwell still been seeking a career in law, these developments would most likely have led to a new application and court appeal on her part.

Bradwell's generalized interest in women's rights was evident in her organizational and leadership roles in the Illinois movement as of 1869. She was particularly interested in all aspects of women's legal status, with an emphasis on how discriminatory legislation made it more difficult for women to earn their own livelihood and thus indirectly pressured them into marriages that institutionalized their economic dependency on men. From the late 1860s until her death in 1894, Bradwell continued her involvement with the legal profession through her paper, and she remained an active participant in the women's rights movement.

Bradwell's path to feminism was more typical than Anneke's in two respects. First, her exposure to and support of abolitionism provided her with a language, vision, and ideology of emancipation, as it did for virtually all feminists in this period. Second, her involvement in the Sanitary Commission (see *NAW* 1:224) provided training in organization and involvement within a network of politically active women, as it did for large numbers of women's rights activists. The distinctiveness of Bradwell's path was the way in which an initially individual ambition to practice law was transformed into a broader and more explicitly political position over time. Identifying when this transformation took place is less important than the overall process itself. The concept of a dialectic of opposition described in an earlier chapter fits this case. When Bradwell's pursuit of a nonfeminist goal was blocked on the basis of gender and marital status, she developed an analysis that generalized from this experience to the legal status of all women and the problems of economic and occupational discrimination. Through this route Bradwell arrived at the same point of regional prominence and organizational leadership as Mathilde Anneke.

Mary Ashton Rice Livermore followed a third path to feminism. Livermore also had an abolitionist background and played the leading role in the Chicago Sanitary Commission during the Civil War. Yet Livermore opposed woman suffrage up to the time of Civil War. She changed her position, however, and by the end of the 1860s had arguably become the most important figure in the Illinois women's rights movement.

Livermore's antebellum antisuffragism is easily documented. According to one account, "I visited Chicago early in January '63, met Mrs. Livermore who was then editing the New Covenant and found her very much opposed not only to woman suffrage but to women meddling in politics or otherwise getting out of their sphere" (HL, EBH Papers, Swisshelm to Harbert, n. d.). Livermore's autobiography recorded a general interest in improving women's educational and economic opportunities but a specific rejection of the vote: "I believed that all these things could be accomplished without giving them the ballot" (Livermore 1897, 497). The change in her views occurred during the war, through her work with the Sanitary Commission: "During the war, and as a result of my own observations, I became aware that a large portion of the nation's work was badly done, or not done at all, because woman was not recognized as a factor in the political world" (Livermore 1897, 497). A more contemporary account of Livermore's conversion was contained in an 1867 letter to Susan B. Anthony. In it Livermore stated that she had always believed the ballot would naturally come to women after the right to work and wages, but that she had recently concluded the ballot must come first and other goals would then follow on the achievement of the suffrage (see ISHS, Cornell Collection, Livermore to Anthony, 22 March 1867).

Compared to Anneke and Bradwell, Livermore's relation to feminism in general and the vote in particular was more instrumental. That is, Livermore often argued that women needed the vote to accomplish reforms that were morally and religiously inspired.[4] This is essentially the interpretation of Robert Riegel, when he writes: "Civil War experiences changed Mrs. Livermore's attitude toward her own sex. . . . Now she became convinced that the only way women could fight evils like poverty, drunkenness and prostitution was to become active in politics" (*NAW* 2:412). The purpose of the vote, in this view, had less to do with achieving sexual equality and more to do with imposing moralistic reform on society. There can be little doubt that this described one dimension of Livermore's worldview and her conception of the vote. Such a view was readily evident in the following passage from Livermore's autobiography: "The work that I have undertaken for temperance and for woman suffrage, although the two organizations are entirely distinct, has nevertheless more or less intermingled. It is difficult to advocate one, without encroaching on the boundary of the other" (Livermore 1897, 583). There could not be a sharper contrast than between Livermore's and Anneke's views on women's rights and temperance, and this passage nicely illustrates Riegel's interpretation of Livermore's feminism.

However, seeing Livermore as a moralistic reformer instrumentally interested in the vote is a one-dimensional caricature of the complexity of her views—one especially insensitive to variations in her positions over time. Livermore also made powerful natural rights arguments for the vote, casting the ballot as the centerpiece in women's struggle for political equality: "Under a republican form of government, the possession of the ballot by woman can alone make her the legal equal of man, and without this legal equality, she is robbed of her natural rights. She is not allowed equal ownership in her minor children with her husband, has no choice of domicile, and is herself the legal property of her husband, who controls her earnings and her children" (Livermore 1897, 480). There were thus two Livermores: one interested in the vote as a tool for reforming society and another interested in the vote as a step toward women's emancipation.

A closer look at Livermore's career reveals that the more politicized and egalitarian Livermore came to the fore in the late 1860s. This was a period of great agitation for women's rights in Illinois, and Livermore was directly involved in this activity. The charged atmosphere brought out the more politicized side of Livermore's feminism while supressing the moralistic aspect of her orientation, as is evident in two speeches she composed during this period (and subsequently delivered hundreds of times). Both speeches—"What Shall We Do with Our Daughters?" and "Superfluous Women"—stressed the importance of economic independence for women and the education of young girls for such independence. Once accomplished, women would not have to marry out of economic dependency, nor would they be in such precarious positions if husbands were lost through death or divorce. In short, Livermore struck directly at the interrelation of family and economy in these speeches, thereby sounding one of the most profound themes of the early women's movement (see Livermore 1897).

Livermore also brought a more strategic orientation to the early movement in Illinois. Her strategical sophistication sometimes went hand in hand with a blithe insensitivity to the raison d'être of the movement. In a letter to Mathilde Anneke about the problem of getting signatures on petitions Livermore argued: "Getting the signatures of men has this advantage. . . . Women become willing to sign when they see that the men are doing it. Women wait everywhere to know what is the pleasure of men. So in order to get the women, we must first get the men" (SHSW, Anneke Papers, Livermore to Anneke, 12 July 1869). This was a plausible strategy, particularly if Livermore was correct when she claimed "there are more men willing to sign the petition than there are women." Yet for many activists the fundamental problem was precisely that "women wait to know what is the pleasure of men"; it was this pattern of deference they sought to change rather than use in achieving their goals.

Livermore's path to feminism—and her feminism itself—was the most complex of the three we have sketched here. It involved a change from anti-suffragism to prosuffragism and an uneasy mixture of expediency arguments, natural rights, and strategic considerations. While it is tempting to identify this mix as simply contradictory, Livermore did not regard it in that way; she changed perspectives depending on the context, situation, and general climate of the movement. In the late 1860s that climate called forth the most political aspects of Livermore's feminism. As a result, Livermore arrived at the same point as Mathilde Anneke and Myra Bradwell, though each traveled a distinctly different route. Each path brought all three to play major roles in the creation of an organized and autonomous movement for women's emancipation in the Midwest.

MOBILIZATION, CONFLICT, AND ORGANIZATION

One of the earliest women's clubs formed in the United States was Sorosis, founded by Jennie Croly in New York in 1868.[5] In June of that year, a women's association of the same name was organized in Chicago. Among the leading figures at the founding meeting were Catherine Waite, Cynthia Leonard, and Mary Livermore (all of Chicago), as well as a Mrs. Burleigh from the New York Sorosis. The goals of this new organization were described as follows: "to increase the social relations of woman and mankind, and to advocate anything that will, in any way, tend to promote the welfare of both sexes—the female sex especially" (*Chicago Tribune*, 19 June 1868).

From the beginning, women's rights was a major topic of discussion in Sorosis, and vague plans for a suffrage convention emerged from these early discussions. Late in 1868, however, a dispute over organizational matters precipitated a split that led to two rival groups claiming the name *Sorosis*. One faction, headed by Cynthia Leonard and Delia Waterman, continued to be known as Sorosis; the other faction, headed by Mary Walker and Mary Livermore, dropped its claim to the name.[6] Plans for a suffrage convention continued within both groups, and both eventually issued calls for Chicago's first woman suffrage convention to be held in February 1869 to coincide with an already scheduled appearance by Anna Dickinson.

When these parallel plans became evident, Mary Livermore suggested a reconciliation of the two groups. She proposed a committee of seven—three from each group and an independent—to effect a merger. The very elaborateness of this procedure implied that substantive issues were at stake, and subsequent events exposed the nature of some of those issues. Livermore's merger offer was described by the *Tribune* as follows: "The only condition of union that was imposed was that the discussions should be confined to the woman suffrage question, and that no outside issue should be brought into the convention" (5 February 1869). The Sorosis group found this condition unacceptable: "It was found to be impossible to harmonize the two movements. The Chicago Sorosis would listen to no proposition for union that would not place the whole matter in their hands. As the preparations of both parties were nearly completed, there had seemed to be only one course open to both—to go forward and hold their respective conventions" (5 February 1869). Three days later the *Tribune* printed a lengthy letter from Delia Waterman defending the Sorosis organization. The letter denied that Sorosis had insisted on "total control" and accused the Livermore group of various subterfuges concerning the proposed merger.[7] While it is impossible to evaluate the validity of each claim and counterclaim in this dispute, it is possible to describe the differences between the groups as these were publically discussed in the Chicago dailies.

The 7 February 1869 issue of the *Chicago Times* contained numerous letters and articles from members and sympathizers of the Sorosis group which clarified their position. The *Times* described the two groups in this way: "A call signed by Mrs. Livermore . . . invites all who favor the extension of suffrage to the women of Illinois to meet in Library Hall. . . . There is another call which is issued to those who are in favor of universal suffrage. The signers of this call favor, not particularly women's rights, but what they call human rights" (*Chicago Times*, 7 February 1869). A letter by Sorosis member Sarah Mills provided a detailed look at how that organization viewed the differences between the groups. According to Mills, the Livermore group wanted to bar controversial figures and wider perspectives whereas Sorosis advocated "*Universal Suffrage* and *Equal Rights* for all *The People*, without regard to nationality, color, religion, education or sex" (emphasis in original). Mills described the upcoming Sorosis convention in this way:

> We desire this convention to be in every sense *The People's Convention.* Our deliberations will not be confined to the suffrage question. But the pregnant questions of capital and labor, industrial [illegible], and other equally important questions will be brought before it. We want no self-appointed leaders. The demands of the hour and the age will develop them. . . . Working men and women, remember, this is no women's quarrel. It is the old, world-wide question, only in a milder form, of the People versus the Aristocracy. (*Chicago Times*, 7 February 1869; emphasis in original)

Delia Waterman described the Sorosis position as follows: "We claim to be thoroughly radical on the question of suffrage, taking a broad, expansive view, embracing universal suffrage to all who are amenable to law, casting aside entirely the distinctions of male or female, black or white, rich or poor, learned or unlearned" (*Chicago Times*, 7 February 1869). Finally, a letter simply signed "Progression" supported the Sorosis position and characterized the Livermore group in the following terms: "The 'Livermore' party, it seems, wish [*sic*] to make property and education the test of qualification in a voter, and are, hence, catering the favor and cooperation of the aristocracy and have much to say about the respectability, wealth and position of the callers of their convention" (*Chicago Times*, 7 February 1869).

It is unfortunate that no equally explicit statements were made by the Livermore group. This may have been because they had already gained the upper hand in the struggle for a legitimate claim over the women's rights movement. For instance, the Livermore group had secured Library Hall for their convention and thus tied their proceedings to Anna Dickinson's scheduled lecture. The Livermore group had also arranged for other nationally prominent figures (e.g., Elizabeth Cady Stanton, Susan B. Anthony, and Edward Beecher) to participate in their convention (see Pierce 1937, 2:456). For whatever reason, the Chicago papers contained no specific responses to these charges by the Sorosis group.

At least two sorts of issues divided the groups. The first was the status and priority of women's rights in the program of each group. For the Livermore group, this was the only issue they wished to pursue. For the Sorosis group, women's rights were subsumed under a broader conception of universal rights which included "negro suffrage and other political issues" (Beldon 1913, 12). Second, the Sorosis group appears to have been a broader, more diverse group of reformers than the Livermore group. Indeed, according to one report the diversity of the Sorosis group bordered on chaos: "It would be difficult to give anything like a connected or correct report of the meeting, for there was nothing very connected or correct about it. It worked on a unique principle known only to itself" (*Chicago Tribune*, 14 January 1869). The *Tribune* reported that "no important business was transacted" although a series of rambling and disconnected speeches were delivered on woman suffrage, spiritualism, political economy, and a variety of other topics.[8] The differences between the two groups became clearest at their simultaneous but separate conventions held in Chicago on 11 and 12 February 1869.

The Livermore group convened in Library Hall, where Livermore was promptly elected president of the convention. The morning session featured a summary of the history of the women's rights movement presented by Anthony and supplemented by Stanton.[9] The afternoon session established a commission to work in the state capital for changes in laws relating to women's status. The evening session was devoted to an address by Stanton that introduced the controversies around the enfranchisement of blacks and women and set the stage for debate the next day. Stanton proposed three resolutions whose clear targets were the Fourteenth and Fifteenth amendments and what she saw as the Republican party's "treachery and duplicity" in supporting them.[10] She then presented a series of arguments against male aristocracy, in support of the idea that "manhood suffrage is national suicide and woman's destruction," and in support of the simultaneous enfranchisement of women and blacks. The speech was described in *History of Woman Suffrage* as "able and eloquent, though directly in opposition to the general sentiment of the convention, which was mainly Republican" (*HWS* 3:566–567). This sentiment became evident in discussions during the second day of the convention.

Two prominent figures throughout the convention were Judges Waite and Bradwell, husbands of women's rights activists Catherine Waite and Myra Bradwell. On the convention's second day, Judge Waite offered resolutions supporting woman suffrage, its inclusion in the new state constitution, and the elimination of legal impediments to women's activities in "every department of social, civil and political life." Waite and Bradwell were instrumental in proposing a state suffrage organization, and by the close of the day the Illinois Woman Suffrage Association (IWSA) had been founded with Mary Livermore as president and Myra Bradwell as corresponding secretary. Other procedural matters included the appointment of Livermore, Myra Bradwell, and Kate Doggett as representatives to the Equal Rights Association convention to be held in May and passage of a resolution (submitted by Judge Bradwell) endorsing the stance and goals of Anthony's recently founded *Revolution*. The major business of the day involved discussion of Stanton's proposed resolutions. Judge Waite, speaking in support of one of his resolutions, spiced that upcoming debate when he remarked, "If there was to be any question as between universal and female suffrage, let the latter take the preference. Not that we love the negro less, but that we love the woman more. If, however, the nation is to be placed on a lasting basis, it must be upon the basis of equal rights to all" (*Chicago Tribune*, 13 February 1869).

The debate over Stanton's resolutions had a historical significance that has yet to be acknowledged, for it anticipated virtually all of the key issues debated at the Equal Rights Association (ERA) meeting in May in New York. The result of that more well-known meeting was the dissolution of the ERA organization and the formation of the National Woman Suffrage Association by Stanton and Anthony. The Chicago convention made it clear that the basic differences were already firmly in place by February of 1869. In the Chicago convention—as they did later in New York—Stanton and Anthony argued that black and female enfranchisement had to be treated as inseparable and that support for such "impartial" suffrage was the only defensible position reformers could take. Since the Republicans were already on record with their "Negro's hour" position, Stanton and Anthony withdrew their support from the Republicans. As in the upcoming ERA convention where Frederick Douglass would play the role, the most interesting counterarguments came from blacks who sought to acknowledge the historic support of the Republican party and to provide their own rationale for the "Negro's hour" strategy.

In Chicago this position was supported by William Brown. Brown argued that the roots of women's oppression were to be found not so much in the lack of the ballot as in their subordinate position in domestic and social realms. He also suggested that the lack of widespread female support for woman suffrage distinguished it from the cause of black enfranchisement, requiring a strategy of education among women before pressing the demand for the vote. Stanton and Anthony probably agreed with Brown's premises, but it was imperative for them to challenge his conclusions if they were to salvage their position. The following brief exchange gives some idea of how the debate unfolded between these two sides:

BROWN: Thousands of women feel that the ballot will unsex them and deprive them of the attention and love which the men now bestow upon them.

ANTHONY: That's just what the old slaveholders used to say.

BROWN: Yes, but the master could restrain the slave by the lash. (*Chicago Tribune*, 13 February 1869)[11]

BROWN: The objection lies deeper than the ballot. It is talked on the streets and in the domestic circle that woman does not get her rights from the husband. Is the ballot going to set that right?

ANTHONY: Yes, sir.

BROWN: I say to Miss Anthony, you have to go deeper than the ballot. This question has got to go home. . . . [Women] must impregnate their husbands with the idea of giving women their rights socially and in the home circle. For while the ballot does a great deal for the negro, and gives him a great deal of power and respect politically, if you depend upon the ballot to bring you up, you will never come up. (*Chicago Times*, 13 February 1869)

The Stanton/Anthony position was in the minority at this convention. Anthony acknowledged as much when she reintroduced the Stanton resolutions, noting it was for discussion only and conceding that they would not pass the convention.[12] If they were merely floating a trial balloon, the Chicago convention must have deflated their hopes. Judges Waite and Bradwell were closer to the prevailing sentiment when they spoke against the resolutions. Bradwell was adamant, claiming that passage of these resolutions "would set back the cause of woman suffrage 10 years" (*Chicago Times*, 13 February 1869). Waite, who had earlier implied some guarded support for female enfranchisement before black enfranchisement, nonetheless spoke against the resolutions, claiming that he did not wish to offend any parties to the discussion (i.e., the prevailing Republican sentiment) nor to contradict his own committee on resolutions which had argued that each state must decide this issue for themselves.

On the local level the Library Hall convention was immensely significant. It established the first state suffrage organization in Illinois, which remained in existence until the suffrage battle ended in 1920. The convention also connected local activism with the national movement and its leaders, introducing Chicago to issues that would shortly split the national movement into rival organizations. Finally, the Library Hall convention handed Stanton and Anthony one of their earliest defeats on their national amendment strategy and foreshadowed events and consequences that unfolded later in the year.

During the same two-day period, the Sorosis organization headed by Delia Waterman held its convention at the Crosby Music Hall. The generally hostile *Times* paid some very backhanded compliments when it opined: "The appearance of the convention was the best argument for woman suffrage in the world, the men being ladylike and effeminate and the women gentlemenly-looking and masculine. All the force of character was on the female side, as were also all the good speeches. It was a strange combination of spiritualists, of Fourerites, of free-loveites, and of hobbyists generally" (*Chicago Times*, 12 February 1869). Sarah Mills's opening remarks clarified the reason for separate conventions by reiterating the universal interests of the Sorosis group as compared with the personal ambitions and narrow interest of the Livermore group. In a later speech she commented on two proposed resolutions; the first called for the franchise to be granted to all persons regardless of color, race, or sex while the second specified that "the only disqualifications of voters should be ignorance and an immoral character" (*Chicago Tribune*, 12 February 1869). Mills spoke in favor of the first resolution while rejecting the second. She defended immigrants and workers as part of "the people," arguing that "it was useless to draw any line of demarcation because of ignorance. The ballot must be given the same as railroads—for all the people, and not leave education to manufacture suffrage. In America, we cannot draw any line" (*Chicago Tribune*, 12 February 1869). The convention endorsed her sentiments by passing the first resolution while rejecting the second.

There followed another series of resolutions that called for universal suffrage and general political and legal equality between men and women. One rebuked the U.S. Congress for its endorsement of the exclusion of women: "Resolved, that the late action of congress in amending the constitution by continuing to exclude women from participation in the duties and responsibilities of government, is an error of judgment, and a great source of practical evil to all concerned" (*Chicago Times*, 12 February 1869). Although the language of this resolution is milder and not explicitly anti-Republican, the message is largely the same as the Stanton resolutions that were resoundingly defeated at Library Hall. In Crosby Hall, however, this resolution passed and was adopted by the Sorosis group. There were several ironies in this development. It is likely that the more strongly worded Stanton resolutions would have passed the Sorosis convention as well, and Stanton and Anthony may have received a better reception of their strategy had they participated in this convention. However, it is not clear they were aware of the Sorosis convention, and even if they had been, they may still have preferred the Livermore group because it was larger and more socially influential.

The second day of the Sorosis convention was an eventful one. The morning session featured a debate on "affirmative action:"—certainly one of the earliest on record. The debate arose around the appointment of postmasters and a resolution claiming it was the duty of supporters of universal suffrage "to select some able, intelligent, and competent woman as the nominee of the people." (See the *Chicago Times* and *Tribune* of 13 February 1869 for accounts of this debate.) The morning and afternoon sessions also involved ongoing debates about educational qualifications for the vote as well as the traditional argument that the vote should only be extended to those willing and able to militarily defend the country. In the midst of these proceedings the convention organized its own suffrage organization (the Universal Suffrage Association of the State of Illinois), drafted a constitution and bylaws, elected a slate of officers, and issued a declaration of principles that reaffirmed the orientation of the Sorosis organization as the official stance of the new suffrage organization.

The afternoon session was interrupted by the appearance of Judge Bradwell and a small delegation from the Livermore group who invited the Sorosis group to join the proceedings at Library Hall. Bradwell announced that several prominent members of Sorosis were interested in such a move; his remarks created considerable confusion and heated debate among those assembled in Crosby Hall. Delia Waterman opposed the invitation and Professor Toohey charged Bradwell with deliberately attempting to disrupt the Sorosis proceedings. Cynthia Leonard and Sarah Mills, on the other hand, were receptive to the invitation. Amidst general confusion, a motion carried to join the Livermore convention. After Leonard and Mills (among others) left to do so, Toohey declared the vote null and void, and the Sorosis convention reconvened, issuing its own invitation for the Livermore group to join them in Crosby Hall if they were really interested in a reconciliation. In the meantime, Bradwell returned to Library Hall to announce the union of the two groups, and Sarah Mills spoke of her own rejoicing that a reconciliation had been achieved. Unbeknownst to Bradwell and the others, the convention at Crosby Hall continued its proceedings. The group composed several letters to the press to inform the public that the Sorosis organization had not "committed suicide" by joining the opposition, that the last subterfuge of the opposing forces had failed, and that the press had been unfair in its coverage of events by suggesting that such a union had actually been implemented (*Chicago Times* and *Tribune*, 13 February 1869).

By the end of these eventful days, two statewide suffrage organizations had been established to lead the movement for women's rights in the state of Illinois. The strength of the Livermore group—established before the convention and increased by the presence of Stanton and Anthony as well as the defection of some Sorosis members—was mirrored in the Illinois Woman Suffrage Association's (IWSA) persistence without interruption throughout the fifty-year struggle for the vote. The relative weakness of the Sorosis group, further weakened during the convention, was similarly mirrored in the Universal Suffrage Association's fading from the political scene within the year.

As the Chicago conventions closed, activity shifted to the state capital in Springfield where the legislature was in session. By 21 February the legislative committee of the IWSA (including Mary Livermore and the Bradwells) was already lobbying for a bill that would allow married women legal control of their own wages. Their efforts were quickly rewarded; the Illinois state legislature passed the bill into law on 24 March 1869. Although it acted quickly, the legislature was careful to acknowledge the sexual division of labor with a provisionary clause attached to the bill: "A married woman shall be entitled to receive, use and possess her own earnings, and sue for the same in her own name free from the interference of her husband or his creditors; Provided, this act shall not be construed to give to the wife any compensation for any labor performed for her minor children or husband" (*HWS* 3:570; Beldon 1913, 18). While in Springfield the IWSA committee was joined by Stanton and Anthony, and the group was received by Governor Palmer at a meeting in the Opera House.

Stanton and Anthony continued their tour of midwestern states during February and March, including stops in St. Louis, Toledo, Madison, and Galena, before returning to New York in May for the annual Equal Rights Association meeting. The events of this tour were recorded in an interesting series of letters written for publication in *Revolution* and reproduced in *History of Woman Suffrage* (3:368–378). The letters were full of praise for local workers, and they were particularly complimentary to Mary Livermore. The letters also suggested that although sentiment for women's rights developed later in the Midwest, it took hold and spread faster than in other areas. For example, on 21 February 1869 Stanton wrote from Springfield:

> The telegrams are flying in all directions for us to come here, there, everywhere. Western women are wide awake today. The question of submitting an amendment to the constitution to strike out the word "male" is under consideration. The poor "white male" is doomed. (*HWS* 3:371)

On 3 March Anthony wrote from Galena:

> The women all over the West are wide-awake. Theodore Tilton had just preceeded us, and some ladies laughingly told us that Theodore said they would *certainly* vote in *twenty years*!! Let our cold-blooded Eastern reformers understand that ideas, like grains, grow fast in the West, and that women here intend to vote now. . . . The editor of the *Independent* may talk of twenty years down on the Hudson among the Rip Van Winkles in Spookey Hollow . . . but never to Western audiences. (*HWS* 3:376; emphasis in original)

While these letters were obviously intended to inspire as well as inform, they conveyed the spirit of optimism and the sense of possibilities so typical of the movement during this early period.

THE NATURE OF MIDWESTERN FEMINISM

These same letters brought news of a companion paper to the *Revolution* to be published in the Midwest under the editorship of Mary Livermore. In Anthony's words, Livermore intended to produce a paper that was "nothing more or less than the twin sister of The *Revolution*, whose mission is to turn everything inside out, upside down, wrong side before.

With such intentions, she felt the 'Agitator' was the only name that fully matched the 'Revolution.' All the women present echoed her sentiments, eschewing the 'rose bud' dispensation" (*HWS* 3:373). The first issue of the *Agitator*—published weekly with Mary Walker as associate editor—appeared in Chicago on 13 March 1869. It proved to be short-lived. In 1870, much to Anthony's consternation, Livermore returned to Boston, declared her support for Lucy Stone's rival American Woman Suffrage Association, and merged the *Agitator* with the *Women's Journal*. Nonetheless, during its brief tenure in Chicago the *Agitator* became a nationally recognized voice for women's rights and a major organ for expressing feminist sentiment in Chicago and the Midwest.

The *Agitator* fulfilled its goal as a companion to the *Revolution*.[13] The major difference between the two papers was that the *Revolution* carried numerous articles not related to feminist issues whereas the *Agitator* confined itself to women's rights and topics of especial interest to politicized women. In this sense the *Agitator* was more exclusively a women's rights paper than was the *Revolution*.[14] Their coverage of women's rights issues was similar, however, and little distinguished their approaches to women's rights beyond their differing regional emphases.

In the first issue of the *Agitator* Livermore set forth the goals of the new publication in a lead editorial. The rhetoric located the paper in the mainstream of the women's rights movement of the day:

Nothing less than admission in law, and in fact, to equality in all rights, political, civil, and social, with the male citizens of the community, will answer the demands now being made for American women. Their protest against the unjust legislation and social tyranny of the past is daily increasing in volume and intensity. . . . The *Agitator* . . . will aim to discuss the "woman question" in all its bearings and aspects. (*Agitator*, 13 March 1869, 4)

Yet in the same piece Livermore drew back from the full implications of this statement and sought to establish the legitimacy and respectability of the new paper:

The *Agitator* plants itself squarely on high moral and Christian ground. No assaults upon Christianity will ever be made through its columns. . . . Recognizing the sacredness of the home and the family, which underlie all other institutions, it will aim to render itself worthy of admission to the Christian fireside, and aspires to take rank with religious and educational journals of the highest type. (*Agitator*, 13 March 1869, 4)

Livermore's editorial succinctly summarized a major tension within the movement between the pursuit of a broad analysis wherever it might lead and a priori declarations that certain areas were off limits for such an inquiry.

One of the most consistent themes of the paper concerned the relation of women to work and wages. The situation of married women received considerable attention and provoked demands for the complete legal equalization of married men and women. For example, one issue carried an article by Lucy Stone arguing that despite some improvements, women were still better off legally if they remained single because they forfeited so many of the rights of a *femme sole* upon entering marriage (*Agitator*, 15 May 1869). The paper also recognized that marriage was not the exclusive cause of economic discrimination against women. The lead article of the first issue related the story of a democratically elected female postmistress whose confirmation was under challenge by an ad hoc committee of men who were interested in the position. The paper speculated that their motives centered on the good salary the position carried and concluded with a call for united action by women to "make for a wider sphere of work and better pay." Every issue carried stories of unequal pay and restricted job opportunities for women. It was clear from the tone and the frequency of such articles that the editors of the *Agitator*—and presumably its readers—regarded economic independence and equality as one of the keystones in achieving female emancipation.

A second major theme in the paper involved "antisphere" arguments that pointed to the harmful effects of cultural norms that restricted women's activities to the domestic realm alone. Connecting the economic and antisphere arguments, Anna Dickinson argued that "What is wanted, is that woman shall have a chance to do well-paid, as well as ill-paid work. . . . Women were never accused of abandoning their sphere, so long as they did servile and poorly paid work" (*Agitator*, 13 March 1869, 2). An article in a later issue underscored the necessary connection between breaking out of woman's sphere and establishing the equality of the sexes: "If men will not, or cannot recognize woman's equality while she remains in her 'sphere,' what *can* she do but get out of it? For man and woman *are* co-equal powers in the world, and recognition of this fundamental fact must be attained in some way" (*Agitator*, 15 May 1869, 4; emphasis in original). A final example from an article by Henry Ward Beecher addressed women opposed to the movement and claimed that rather than forcing rights and obligations on women, the goal was to expand the range of choice available to them. In this regard, Beecher said: "All we ask is this: While we accord to you the right to stay at home . . . to work as you will, where you will, and when you will; as we give you plenary personal liberty, do you, in like manner, give every other human being the same plenary, personal liberty" (*Agitator*, 5 June 1869, 3).

A third *Agitator* theme involved criticism of prevailing pressures on women to marry. Dickinson identified ideological, economic, and social factors that, in combination, motivated too many women to enter unwisely into marriage: "The encouragement of this false idea of woman's sphere is constantly forcing girls to marry without love. They go to the altar, not because their hearts force them, but because the exigencies of their pockets, and the sentiments of society compel them" (*Agitator*, 13 March 1869, 2). An article entitled "Too Much Marrying" addressed the problem of divorce by suggesting that the real problem resided in too frequent and overly casual marriages. The article legitimized singleness as an option: "It is not in the facility with which people get divorced, but in the facility with which they get married, that the mischief inheres. . . . We make too much of marrying and being married, until it is thought by many people somewhat of a disgrace for a woman to pass through life alone" (*Agitator*, 15 May 1869, 3).

Through the predominance of these three themes—women's relative exclusion from renumerative employment, their confinement to the domestic sphere, and the quasi-compulsory nature of marriage—the *Agitator* challenged some of the most basic material and ideological underpinnings of the sexual division of labor. Many of these themes were synthesized in an article by Helen Starrett which placed women's work in historical context and anticipated themes that Charlotte Perkins Gilman articulated some twenty years later in *Woman and Economics* ([1890] 1966), her analysis of the evolution of male and female economic roles:

Our system of housekeeping is wasteful and unphilosophical. There is no more reason why our cooking, washing and ironing should be done in our houses than that our shoes, our linen or our pins should be made there. Men, by their machinery and combinations, have taken from us our carding and spinning by which we were made really valuable producers; and unless women arouse and do it themselves, and reap the profits, they will soon take all our domestic labor, and do it by wholesale. . . . The theory is that man is the provider, the bread-winner; and upon that theory is based the present constitution of society. To this it may be replied that comparatively a small proportion of the women of a community are actually supported by men; but even if it were altogether true, it is radically wrong. Women should be producers and breadwinners. (*Agitator*, 13 March 1869, 2)

These were the most important and the most consistent themes in the columns of the *Agitator* during its brief period of publication. Minor themes were evident as well. With the exception of purely factual stories, virtually all the remaining material in the *Agitator* fell into the following, more or less distinct, categories.

1. The "female superiority" theme. Several articles exemplified a broader contradiction in movement ideology by stressing the moral superiority of women over men—a theme that often contradicted and sometimes jeopardized the arguments for equality with men in all spheres. It was variously argued that, because of their superiority, women had an important role to play in uplifting men, purifying politics, saving the race, and the like. Related to this theme was an article that discussed the complementarity of the sexes, suggesting that while it outfitted men and women for different tasks, those tasks should nonetheless be regarded as equal in importance. Again such arguments introduced a definite tension into movement ideology from which it could easily lapse into assumptions of separate spheres arguments. (See *Agitator*, 13 March 1869, 1; 15 May 1869, 1, 5; 22 May 1869, 2.)

2. The question of sexual interests. Another movementwide debate represented in the columns of the *Agitator* concerned the underlying interests of men and women as unequal social groups. Both sides of this debate were represented in the *Agitator*. Some articles presumed that men and women represented distinct conflict groups, that men benefited from existing arrangements, and that they would lose out if greater equality were achieved. Other articles assumed that the long-term interests of men and women were identical and that greater equality would benefit both groups and lead to a general improvement of "the race." (See *Agitator*, 13 March 1869, 3; 15 May 1869, 4.)

3. The forms of profeminist argumentation. Virtually all prosuffrage arguments in the *Agitator* appealed to natural rights and equal justice as the ideological basis for women's rights. When expediency arguments appeared, they were used merely to augment conclusions already reached by rights and justice arguments. In addition, several arguments on the basis of sex role differences adopted scientific and environmental explanations for these differences; the implication was that changing social conditions would also change the majority of these sex role differences. A similar point was made explicit in an article that attacked biological explanations for these differences and the support such explanations provided for prevailing stereotypes. (See *Agitator*, 15 May 1869, 2; 22 May 1869, 1; 29 May 1869, 1, 2; and 5 June 1869, 5.)

4. The theme of sexual politics. Some of the above arguments were elaborated to draw conclusions about sexual politics and changing relations of domination between the sexes. One article called for a "monostandard" of sexual fidelity which would apply equally to men and women. A second called on males to assume responsibility for controlling and regulating their own sexuality. Such arguments drew upon environmental theories of sex differences and made explicit the idea that male sexuality was socially shaped and changeable, not biologically determined. A third article connected movement demands with sexual politics by arguing that women needed the ballot and education if they were to escape their current condition of being the "sexual prey" of men. (See *Agitator*, 22 May 1869, 3; 29 May 1869, 4; and 5 June 1869, 4.)

5. The specter of free love. Like much feminist writing at the time, the *Agitator* was careful to distinguish its critique of contemporary marriage and divorce practices from an advocacy of free love. The first issue, in responding to an attack on the woman suffrage movement by the *Chicagoan*, drew a sharp line between calls for marital reform by "noble and Christian" women and advocacy of infidelity and free love. A later issue contained a similar response to an attack on the *Agitator* itself. Such charges, and the felt need to respond to them unequivocally, were a consistent theme within the movement at this time; a year later the issue achieved national prominence with Victoria Woodhull's advocacy of free love and her association with the woman suffrage movement. Whatever they may have thought privately, Elizabeth Cady Stanton was the only prominent suffragist who came close to defending free love publicly, and this was a relatively minor part of her larger effort to defend Woodhull from an al-

most universally hostile press and public. (See *Agitator*, 13 March 1869, 5; 5 June 1869, 4.)

6. Nativist and racist themes. On three occasions the *Agitator* carried articles that ranged from a moderately nativist account of German anti-suffragism to an overtly racist description of Chinese immigrants. The former responded to articles in the *Illinois Staats Zeitung* opposing women's rights. The *Agitator's* rejoinder distinguished between "cultivated" pro-suffrage Germans and Germans who opposed suffrage, but quickly lapsed into sweeping generalizations and stereotypes about the inherent inability of the "speculative German mind" to conceive of women as anything more than a beast of burden and a breeding animal. The reference to immigrants quoted a minister who condemned the Fifteenth Amendment's enfranchisement of "100,000 bestial Chinamen importing their lust by the shipload" while denying women even the protection of the ballot. (See *Agitator*, 13 March 1869, 3; 22 May 1869, 4.)

7. Women's rights and labor's interests. Two *Agitator* articles dealt favorably with the question of labor and labor's interests. One was a rather abstract tribute to "Labor," extolling the virtues of hard physical work as an important foundation of the nation. The second presented a radical argument against the evils of "class legislation" and discussed the parallel evils of "sex legislation" against women. (See *Agitator*, 13 March 1869, 4; 15 May 1869, 1.)

8. Women's rights and religion. The relation of religion and women's rights was explicitly addressed in two articles. One contradicted Livermore's editorial promise by claiming that women had always occupied the status of slaves under Christianity. The second article claimed, to the contrary, that Christianity was the only religion consistent with equality between the sexes. (See *Agitator*, 13 March 1869, 6; 22 May 1869, 4, 6.)

Despite its brief tenure, the *Agitator* was an important part of the movement for women's emancipation in the Midwest. It brought readers information about women's rights issues, reports on national conventions, and articles by nationally prominent movement leaders. The *Agitator* was an editorial success as well, and it regularly reprinted endorsements from other papers and reformers around the country. Significantly, the *Revolution* was lavish in its praise of the *Agitator* and its role in Chicago. The general press was also impressed with the *Agitator's* overall contribution to journalism, as the following examples indicate:

We have no hesitancy in pronouncing the *Agitator* the best journal of its kind now published anywhere. (*Detroit Herald*)

I do not hesitate to pronounce it the ablest paper published in Chicago. (Professor Haven, suffragist)

The *Agitator* is proving itself by far the best paper of its class yet made. (*Boston Christian Register*; see *Agitator*, 15 May 1869, 8)

Further insight into midwestern feminism can be gained by examining the relations between the local movement and the national movement as the latter split into two organizations in 1869. The 22 May issue of the *Agitator* reported on the Equal Rights Association convention in New York that precipitated the split in the feminist ranks. Livermore's report to the paper noted that the predictable alliance had emerged: Stanton and Anthony had spoken against the Fifteenth Amendment for its exclusion of women's rights, while Livermore and Stone spoke in favor of the amendment.[15] The next issue reported the formation of the National Woman Suffrage Association (NWSA) by Stanton and Anthony. The report was quite favorable, noting that many women felt the need of a society specifically devoted to the advancement of women's rights. Two critical notes were sounded, however. The first questioned the "illiberal, inconsistent plan of excluding males, and making the society a purely female one"—a proposal put forward by Stanton and Anthony but rejected by the group as a whole. The report also identified the most serious drawback of the founding meeting as the "absence of so many we could wish to have seen there," including Livermore, Anneke, and Stone. The report was intentionally ambiguous on the motives of those who did not appear: "Some, no doubt, had left the city, others perhaps—who knows?—had purposely 'withheld themselves.'" The report nonetheless concluded on a supportive note: "Yet, let us hope that no personal or private dissensions will prevent their working with and for this new society, wherever they may be" (*Agitator*, 29 May 1869).

The same issue carried a long, discursive letter by Mary Livermore stressing two practical points of the debate over the Fifteenth Amendment. The first was that a large majority of women in the suffrage movement had also been active in the antislavery cause and believed that the needs of blacks were more "immediate and pressing" than those of women. Therefore, Livermore claimed, the potential basis of support for the Stanton/Anthony position was too small to be politically effective. Second, she noted that "Negro suffrage is almost *un fait accompli*," the implication being that it was folly to oppose a virtually assured outcome and that such a course could only gather more enemies. From Livermore's perspective, the best course was to begin agitation for a Sixteenth Amendment to enfranchise women. This suggestion by Livermore was intriguing because it shortly became the preferred approach of the NWSA under Stanton and Anthony. In addition, this approach implied a commitment to working on the federal rather than the state level to enfranchise women. In other words, Livermore endorsed the two leading NWSA strategies in May of 1869, even though by the end of the year she would declare her affiliation with Stone's rival American association.

The Livermore letter also detailed how and why women became frustrated working for their goals within the ERA. Historians have stressed the rift between abolitionists and some feminists, but Livermore underscored the sheer number of causes the ERA supported and its resulting weakness in concretely pursuing any one. Her description of this point merits lengthy quotation:

> There is no "National Woman Suffrage Association,"[16] only one for the obtaining of "Equal Rights," whose platform is so broad, that every interest under heaven can get a foothold upon it, and a hearing from it. Negro suffrage, the interests of working-men and women, the subjects of labor and capital, land monopoly, marriage and divorce, temperance, the wrongs of the Indian, dress reform, womanhood suffrage—there is hardly a subject, or a topic, that concerns the human family, that does not come legitimately under the surveillance of an "Equal Rights Association." While there are great principles involved in each of these subjects, and while all of them challenge the gravest and most serious consideration of thinkers, legislators and reformers, there is, manifestly, no hope of considering more than one at a time, at a two day's meeting. (*Agitator*, 29 May 1869)

The heterogeneity of the ERA's goals frustrated all of its constituents, including feminists: "Thus closed the two days' session of the 'Equal Rights Association' in New York. We doubt if they realized anybody's expectations. . . . The mistake lay in our hoping to do one special thing, through an organization formed to do everything" (*Agitator*, 29 May 1869).

Given this organizational impasse, Livermore advocated a separate suffrage association and claimed that this was the preference of virtually all suffragists. At three separate points in her letter, she emphasized the same theme:

> The feeling was unanimous among all women, that a National Woman Suffrage Association must be formed immediately—but there was opposition towards merging the present "Equal Rights Association" in any other. . . .
>
> . . . If we had convened for the purpose of forming a "National Woman Suffrage Association," and had kept close to the business legitimately growing out of that, we might have accomplished something for woman. All of the women present desired this, and regretted that it had not been done. We shall do better another time. . . .
>
> . . . before another May, we hope an organization will be formed through which women can work safely for themselves. For ourself, we have solemnly resolved, never again to be mixed up in the *olla podrida* of an Equal Rights Metting. (*Agitator*, 29 May 1869)

This account implies that no matter how bitterly divided women may have been over the Fifteenth Amendment, they were in agreement as of May 1869 that a new organizational framework was required to pursue the goals of the women's rights movement. These common sentiments, in fact, produced just such an organization that very month. Only toward the end of the year did it become evident that although suffragists agreed on the need for an organization, not all were comfortable with or willing to accept the organization that emerged under Stanton and Anthony's leadership.

The next statement of Livermore's position was a letter to Lucy Stone dated 9 August 1869. The letter described an ongoing discussion Livermore was conducting with Susan B. Anthony over merging the *Revolution* and *Agitator*. Livermore was favorably inclined, but eventually rejected the merger on the advice of friends and husband.[17] Livermore also commented on Stone's proposal for a new suffrage organization to challenge Stanton and Anthony's NWSA. For strategic reasons if no others, Livermore spoke against such a move. Her reasoning was that Stanton and Anthony had worked hard and were very popular in the West and that no organization could expect much success without their active participation. Livermore concluded that a new organization would do more harm than good, and she recommended a strategy of "boring from within" to change the orientation of the NWSA. She approvingly quoted Theodore Tilton on this strategy: "You have got to take things as they are, and if you find an organization in the field, even if it is not what you want, it is better to take it and remodel it, than to have the discord and disturbance that would result from getting it out of the way, and getting another in its place" (LC, NAWSA Papers, Livermore file, Livermore to Stone, 9 August 1869). In support of this strategy, Livermore claimed that Anthony was willing to moderate her stance on the Fifteenth Amendment and would "make great concessions to effect a cooperation of all the forces." Livermore agreed, saying she would be willing to "endure much" if the suffrage forces could be harmonized. She concluded that she would rather renounce any organizational affiliation than experience another quarrel like the May ERA convention and that local agitation would continue without any national affiliation if that became necessary.

In the space of about two weeks Livermore's position changed dramatically. In the interim Stone apparently had declared her intention to proceed with a new organization despite Livermore's advice. Faced with an actual proposal, Livermore supported Stone's plan for a rival association. As a more concrete indication of this support, she offered the *Agitator* to Stone to parallel the role of the *Revolution*, which had become the organ of the National Woman Suffrage Association.[18] Expressing satisfaction that Stone's plan would "open up the way for a peaceful inauguration of the American Association," Livermore underscored the need for concerted effort if the new association was to succeed. With respect to organizing the West, Livermore emphasized the necessity of Stone's appearance at an upcoming suffrage convention in Chicago in September to offset the appearance of Anthony and to demonstrate Stone's interest in a genuinely national organization (LC, NAWSA Papers, Livermore file, Livermore to Stone, 24 August 1869).

These plans culminated in the formation of the American Woman Suffrage Association (AWSA) in Cleveland in November of 1869. The Illinois delegation at this convention included some of the most prominent figures of the Illinois movement. Among them were the Judges Waite and Bradwell (elected vice-president and executive committee representative from Illinois respectively), Mary Livermore (elected one of eight vice-presidents-at-large), and Myra Bradwell (elected corresponding secretary). The editors of the *Revolution* were gracious enough to publish the convention call for this rival organization, but felt compelled to editorialize:

Where are those well-known names, Susan B. Anthony, Parker Pillsbury, and Elizabeth Cady Stanton? Not one of them appears. In fact, it is clear that there is a division in the ranks of the strong-minded, and that an effort is to be made to ostracise the *Revolution*. Can it be possible that a National Woman's Suffrage Convention is called without Susan's knowledge or consent? Whether the meeting will be legitimate without her sanction is a serious question. A National Woman's Suffrage Association without speeches from Susan B. Anthony and Mrs. Stanton will be a new order of things. The idea seems absurd. (*Revolution*, vol. 4, no. 17, 28 October 1869, 265–266)

Among the midwesterners who actively rejected the AWSA, Mathilde Anneke was the most vociferous. Anneke had sided with Stanton and Anthony at the ERA convention in May and had already forged an alliance with the NWSA faction. Livermore nonetheless wrote to Anneke urging her to attend the Cleveland convention. The letter was a clumsy invitation at best; it began by insisting that Anneke appear at the convention because they had already advertised her appearance. Further, it implied that Anneke was instrumentally needed to soothe fears and recruit recalcitrant foreigners: "The Germans are wholly against us, and you have the power to make an impression on them that no one else can" (cited in Heinzen 1940, 211).

An exchange of letters between Anthony and Anneke implied that even a diplomatic invitation would not have persuaded Anneke to attend the AWSA convention. Anthony's letters to Anneke described Livermore as an intriguer and the AWSA as an unholy alliance between Livermore and Stone in which the former sought financial salvation for a troubled paper while the latter sought support in the West through Livermore. According to Anthony, some members of the Boston group had already "seen through" Livermore, including one who commented that "to throw Susan Anthony overboard and take in Mrs. Livermore would be jumping out of the frying pan into the fire" (cited in Heinzen 1940, 212). Anneke concurred with Anthony's judgment and expressed her view of these issues in a letter to her husband: [19]

As to the Cleveland Convention, I knew how to evaluate the whole swindle correctly right from the first, and did not sign the so-called Call, in spite of all requests which were addressed direct to me personally. I also do not recognize at all this "After-Nat. Association" because a well organized Nat. Assoc., founded in May of this year, exists. . . . This Assoc. contains elements too radical for the nativistic churches and temperance leagues to be able to conform to it, so it happened that the split arose. The Cleveland organization will be the prevailing one for a while. . . . Livermore is an intriguing smart politician, she was the soul of this new society in the interest of her paper, which became the organ of the Assoc., and is now transferred from Chicago to Boston. (Cited in Heinzen 1940, 216)

Midwestern feminism was thus affecting, and being affected by, events on the national level. By the end of 1869 the schism in the national movement was reproduced in the Midwest in the rivalry between Livermore and Anneke. Yet the most striking aspect of that rivalry was that as late as mid-August, there were few clues it would occur. Until then Livermore seemed willing to work with the Stanton/Anthony organization, and she counseled others including Stone to do the same. Livermore's commitment to Stone emerged only with Stone's firm declaration that she was going ahead with plans for another national organization. In addition, part of Livermore's commitment appears to have been an attempt to salvage her paper from further financial difficulties. The evidence suggests that, at least in the Midwest, the schism emerged largely for tactical, situational, and idiosyncratic reasons. While not denying the existence of ideological differences between, for example, Livermore and Anneke, it should be stressed that these differences did not produce a split in the midwestern movement until Stone intervened and Livermore conformed to her wishes. Thus, while a range of viewpoints had always existed in midwestern feminism, the intervention of national figures and rivalries was crucial in producing a corresponding schism in the Midwest.

THE EARLY MOVEMENT IN SOCIAL CONTEXT

This analytical section clarifies the scope of issues and concerns in the Illinois movement through 1869 and interprets the movement's orientation in its sociohistorical context. The conceptualization of movement breadth sketched above distinguished four dimensions. First, early movement breadth was in part a function of the sociohistorical context of mid-nineteenth century American society and its near total subordination of women. Second, early movement breadth derived from the movement's multiple legal demands which sought a major shift in the social status of women relative to men. A third component of breadth was the early movement's critical focus on the interlocking of domestic, marital, and economic realms and its criticisms of the sexual division of labor. The final dimension concerned the extent to which the movement allied with other dispossessed groups seeking greater justice and equality. From the evidence already presented, I will argue that the Illinois movement conformed to the first three dimensions of breadth, although its relation to the fourth dimension was more complex.

The Illinois movement conformed to the first dimension of movement breadth almost by definition; to raise the demand for the ballot anywhere in the United States in the mid-nineteenth century was to challenge the prevailing subordination of women to men. In addition to the arguments of Ellen DuBois (1978) outlined earlier,[20] the wide scope of the ballot demand also derived from its universalistic character. That is, if granted it would apply to all (otherwise eligible) women in a single stroke. By contrast, most other movement demands (e.g., easier divorce) were more particularistic in their application, thereby posing a less universal challenge to the subordinate status of women.

It is clear on more empirical grounds that the Illinois movement also conformed to the second dimension of movement breadth. The wide-ranging demands of the Illinois movement included changes in women's economic status (including the right to own and dispose of property, control wages, inherit estates as widows, etc.), changes in women's marital status (permitting the use of maiden names after divorce, restricting commitment of women to asylums by husbands, allowing women the right to sue for divorce and alimony in cases of bigamy, etc.), and changes in women's occupational status (the right to enter all occupations and employment without discrimination by sex). As in the national movement, these multiple demands for legal change constituted a wholistic challenge to women's legal subordination and thereby contributed to the movement's broad scope.

The same correspondence between the Illinois movement and the national movement was evident with respect to the third dimension of movement breadth, as could be seen in the *Agitator* as well as in the views of prominent leaders of the Illinois suffrage movement. This critical focus was best exemplified in the case of Mathilde Anneke. What was especially significant was not just Anneke's radicalism but her leadership role on both local and national levels. If her orientation had not resonated with the membership of the suffrage movement, it is unlikely Anneke could have achieved such positions. Myra Bradwell's and Mary Livermore's biographies demonstrate that feminists could travel rather different paths to reach at least some of the same conclusions. Bradwell and Livermore were no less adamant than Anneke on the need to change the sexual division of labor that structured women's subordination in both public and private spheres. In sum, the evidence warrants the conclusion that the Illinois movement conformed to the first three dimensions of movement breadth during this early period.

The same was not equally true of the fourth dimension, best exemplified by the Stanton/Anthony faction and its vision of a broad reform coalition that included blacks, women workers, labor in general, and other disadvantaged and dispossessed groups. While the Illinois movement did not cast its reform net as broadly, it did include blacks and working women in its vision of a reform coalition, and its arguments on behalf of working women were among the most powerful to be found anywhere in the suffrage movement. But what was decidedly lacking in the Illinois movement—or at least the sector of it that quickly prevailed—was even a ritual acknowledgment of the interests and position of labor. Thus the Illinois movement did not fully conform to this dimension because its vision and conception of the beneficiaries of reform were not as broad as in the Stanton/Anthony wing of the movement.

The above characterization must itself be amended by recognizing the multiple factions in the Illinois movement and the struggle between these groups. The Sorosis group headed by Cynthia Leonard and Delia Waterman espoused a view of multiconstituency reform much closer to that of Stanton and Anthony. But as we have seen, the Livermore group mobilized against the Sorosis group and established its hegemony over the Illinois movement in a relatively short time. The Sorosis group, its convention, and its short-lived Universal Suffrage Association indicate that this dimension of movement scope was not completely absent from Illinois, rather that it was overwhelmed by a different and at least somewhat more restricted orientation. A more complex and accurate picture of the Illinois movement must acknowledge these two different orientations, which themselves clashed and competed for leadership of the movement.

The analysis becomes more complex if we consider the relative priority these organizations gave to women's rights and how this related to movement orientation. The Livermore group was apprehensive that women's rights issues might get lost altogether in the crush of other causes. This posture is virtually identical to the stance that Stanton and Anthony took later in the year when they abandoned the hopelessly divided Equal Rights Association in favor of their own suffrage association. In other words, the strategical moves of the Livermore group in Illinois not only paralleled but foreshadowed the strategical moves of Stanton and Anthony on the national level: both groups perceived threats to the relative autonomy of feminist causes in relation to other issues, and both moved to establish and preserve this relative autonomy by forming suffrage organizations exclusively devoted to pursuing women's rights.

In purely organizational terms, it can be argued that the most important step for the women's rights movement in this particular historical conjuncture consisted precisely in preserving the autonomy of the women's rights agenda. This is consistent with a conception of feminism that connotes, first and foremost, a challenge to patriarchal power. This challenge could best be maintained in this historical moment by the strategy that both Livermore and Stanton/Anthony pursued. Thus, while the Livermore faction of the Illinois movement was demonstrably narrower in ideological terms than the Stanton/Anthony group, it nonetheless detected and pursued the crucial organizational step necessary in this context to preserve the autonomy of the women's rights movement.[21]

In sum, the Illinois movement conformed closely to the first three dimensions of breadth we have distinguished. With respect to the fourth the picture was more complex, but notable conformity to this dimension was evident in organizational strategy if not always in ideological scope.

A major premise of this study is that systematic connections exist between social structure and movement orientation and that as the former changes the latter will also undergo transformation. We are not yet in a position to analyze changes in the movement, but we can consider some important connections between social context and movement orientation for one point in time; this will provide a foundation for comparisons across time in later chapters.

The most important link between social structure and movement posture was social class. The accompanying table 3.1 summarizes available information about the social-class background of a number of prominent women connected with the Illinois movement. Several predictable patterns appear in the table. First, where data on education are available, it is clear that this group of women was significantly more educated than the general population. Second, the women's occupations were concentrated in areas that linked them to the broader public in some editorial, informational, educational, or political role: 9 of the 12 wrote for the public in some capacity or another, 5 of the 12 were educators, 7 of the 12 were engaged in reform activity above and beyond the women's movement, and 3 of the 12 could be classified as professionals.

TABLE 3.1

Social-Class Background of Midwestern Feminists Active from the 1840s through 1870

Name	Occupation	Education	Father's occupation	Husband's occupation
Mathilde Anneke	Author Educator Reformer	Private tutors	Prosperous mine owner	Prussian officer
Myra Bradwell	Lawyer Editor Publisher	Ladies seminary	Baptist minister	Lawyer Judge
Prudence Crandall	Teacher Abolitionist	Boarding school	Prosperous farmer	Baptist minister
Mary Davis	Reformer Journalist	—	—	Editor Publisher Printer
Octavia Grover	Editor Reformer	—	—	Editor Publisher Reformer
Jane Jones	Lecturer Editor Reformer	—	—	Quaker editor Antislavery lecturer
Cynthia Leonard	Philanthropist Author	—	—	Editor Publisher
Mary Livermore	Teacher Lecturer Editor	Female seminary	Laborer Unsuccessful farmer	Universalist minister
Elizabeth Packard	Teacher Reformer	Female seminary	Congregational minister	Congregational minister

Mary Safford	Nurse Physician	Boarding school	Farmer	(Never married)
Jane Swisshelm	Teacher Journalist Reformer	Local school	Merchant Speculator	Unsuccessful businessman
Catherine Waite	Lawyer Journalist	Knox College Oberlin College	Farmer	Lawyer

Notes: This format for presenting data on social-class background has been adapted from a similar table on suffragists' social background in Turbin 1978, 63–67.

I attempted to gather information on all women who played a prominent role in the midwestern movement at this time and who appear in this narrative. No such information was available for five women (Ann S. Bane, Kate Doggett, Sarah Mills, Mary L. Walker, and Delia Waterman). Lack of information on Waterman and Mills is particularly disappointing since they were members of the Sorosis organization that split with the Livermore group. The limited information on Cynthia Leonard (also of this group) suggests that if she deviated from the group as a whole, she was perhaps slightly more well placed in the class structure. The only biographical sketch I could find (Willard and Livermore 1893, 457–458) identified her as an early club-woman, a member of the Chicago Philosophical Society, and an accomplished musician and singer. However, the account also mentioned that she "was the first saleswoman to stand behind a counter," indicating she had some working, if not necessarily working-class experience. The table should not be taken to imply that all of these women were equally influential in the movement or that they participated simultaneously in the movement. With these cautions in mind, the information forms the basis for discussion of the social-class background of the majority of the acknowledged leaders of the Illinois movement in this early period.

While this list is impressive, these categories must be interpreted in historical context and in a manner consistent with the rhythm of these women's lives. Most important is that few of the occupations represented were life-long careers. Teaching, editing, and reform work in particular were episodic involvements that depended on circumstances and opportunities. Allowing for this, however, these occupational pursuits were significant departures from the norm and suggest the distinctiveness of this group of women. The occupations of the husbands and fathers of these women exhibited a wider range of variation, but one that stopped short of extreme wealth or poverty. Some indications of social mobility can be seen in the table,[22] but here too the extremes of such mobility are found within a middle-class range.

Given that almost none of these women, their fathers, or their husbands were either wage laborers or independently wealthy, they may accurately be characterized as old middle class. A strong strain of social, and sometimes economic, enterpreneurship is evident in this group. These were individuals who set their own goals, organized their own activities, and offered some good or service (ranging from knowledge, ideas, sermons, and reforms through agricultural products and professional services) to the larger community. This social-class background was typical for reformers in the third quarter of the nineteenth century and also corresponded with available data on suffragists involved in the national movement for women's rights.[23]

Identifying the class background of prominent suffragist leaders is important, but this background must be understood in a historicized manner. This can be done through the related concept of class situation, that is, by examining the immediate prospects, perceptions, and consciousness of this class at the historical moment under discussion. Important light is cast on this question by Robert Wiebe's description of "healthy" nineteenth-century communities:

The health of the nineteenth-century community depended upon two closely related conditions: its ability to manage the lives of its members, and the belief among its members that the community had such powers. Already by the 1870s the autonomy of the community was badly eroded. The illusion of authority, however, endured. Innumerable townsmen continued to assume that they could harness the forces of the world to the destiny of the community. That confidence, the system's final foundation, largely disappeared during the eighties and nineties. (1967, viii)

This general characterization is particularly apt as a description of the class situation of the old middle class in this historical period. By and large this group experienced relative comfort and moderate success, and in cases where this was not a current reality it certainly appeared an accessible future.

On the basis of these factors, this group often operated with a relatively "classless" view of the society around them. This does not mean they were unaware of distinctions of wealth, status, and power. Rather it means that such factors were not perceived as insuperable barriers to the aspirations and efforts of those seeking to change their social position. The consciousness of the old middle class in this period was clearly class conditioned, but simultaneously it denied the enduring significance of social-class factors. This amounted to a bourgeois form of class consciousness, but one mediated and filtered through the historically specific realities and visions of mid-nineteenth century, midwestern, community life.

These considerations suggest a further source of inspiration in the early women's rights movement—a source derived precisely from the contradiction and disjuncture between the vision of this class as a whole and the situation of women in this period. While the middle class as a whole may not have perceived insuperable barriers to its aspirations, middle-class women perceived them clearly when considering their own situation. A rather glaring contradiction existed between this form of class consciousness and the very real material, legal, cultural, and symbolic limitations on women's activity. Probably this contradiction encouraged a broad analysis of women's position and the relation of subordination and dependence that defined that position.

This focus on forms of old-middle-class consciousness and situation also explains some of the limitations in the orientation of the early movement. These limits were most apparent in the individualistic remedies and solutions the movement proposed. Essentially the movement sought to bring all women into the world of middle-class opportunity and mobility on the same terms as their middle-class male counterparts. While this accomplishment would have been considerable, the goal nevertheless reflected the situation and consciousness of the old-middle-class base of the movement. In this, the Illinois movement was hardly unique. Carole Turbin (1978) has forcefully demonstrated that in the northeast as well, the women's rights movement addressed women's needs largely as matters of individual opportunity and mobility rather than as collective problems that required collective solutions.

These considerations shed helpful light on the movement's claim to speak in the interests of "all women" in a relatively class-blind fashion. It is apparent that the demands of the women's rights movement would have brought the greatest benefits to the very middle-class women who were making those demands and leading the movement. To the extent this was true, there was a strain of disingenuousness in the claim to speak for all women and an element of ideology in projecting their middle-class concerns as universal interests. Thus there was a limit to the validity of the movement's claim to speak for all women; however, this limitation was relatively modest, both in the conditions of the times and in comparison to later stages of the movement. Most important, large numbers of women in fact shared a wide variety of cross-class similarities that contributed to their subordination. Many of these were indexed by the wide-ranging set of legal demands that the movement raised. Although these legal limitations were themselves mediated by social class and had a differential impact on women, the changes sought in these laws would have been of potential if uneven benefit to women in a wide variety of classes. Also, the very breadth of the movement program for change meant that it offered at least some significant benefits to women in a wide diversity of situations.

A visual image may clarify this argument. Let us envision a circle of beneficiaries in relation to the movement's program for change; the closer a group is to the center of the circle, the greater the benefits it receives. At the core of the circle are those women who led the movement for women's rights in this historical period. A solid majority of women fall somewhere inside this circle of beneficiaries, given the breadth, depth, and diversity of the movement's program for change. Working and working-class women would have to be placed within the circle given the movement's attentiveness to the conditions and situation of working women.[24] The only groups that clearly fall outside the circle are extremely wealthy women whose class advantages canceled out the bulk of their gender disadvantages and women whose situations were overwhelmingly defined by racial and ethnic considerations (black women, native American women, some recently arrived immigrant women, etc.).

In sum, the movement's claim to speak for all women cannot be accepted at face value; nor can it mean that the movement spoke to the situation of all women equally. However, the movement did offer some significant benefits to a large number and wide diversity of mid-nineteenth-century American women. This conclusion provides a baseline for judging this question at later points. It also grounds the argument that the movement's claim to speak for all women became less and less legitimate as it underwent transformation.

An adequate understanding of early movement orientation requires looking beyond class factors alone and considering the impact of organizational processes on the movement's posture. The Illinois movement involved considerable conflict over goals and priorities once the process of organization began.[25] Two factions vied for ascendancy during this process in a dispute over both principles and personalities. The Livermore faction won not just because of its ties with prominent national figures but also because it provided the most appealing organizational stance for individuals primarily interested in the cause of women's rights. If Livermore's description was at all correct, the Sorosis group in Chicago (like the ERA in New York) was simply too heterogeneous to be organizationally effective at pursuing any one goal. By specializing in women's rights, the Illinois Woman Suffrage Association became a more effective organizational form for pursuing the cause of women's rights at this historical moment.

A related issue involved the internal structure of the IWSA organization. The IWSA constitution, which was drafted and approved at the Library Hall convention, provided some insight into at least the formal aspect of this question. This constitution stated that membership in the organization was open to all persons favorable to woman suffrage and could be accomplished merely by signing the constitution. The organization was composed of five annually elected officers and an annually elected executive committee. Officers automatically served on the committee, but it was formally chartered "not to exceed 25 members" and hypothetically contained space for up to twenty nonofficer members elected at large. (At the founding convention, nine nonofficer members were elected, yielding a committee of fourteen.) The constitution explicitly identified this committee as the initiator and decision-making body for most organizational actions. In short, and on paper at least, this organizational structure was relatively open and democratic with casual membership requirements, no prohibitive dues, all positions open to any member, and the possibility that a member-dominated executive committee could override officers in the determination of organizational policy.

Such formal aspects of organizational structure are important but less crucial than actual organizational processes and functioning. Unfortu-

nately, virtually no data exist. The closest one can come is an impressionistic view of the IWSA founding convention culled from newspaper reports. Such reports convey the impression that the convention evoked
high levels of interest from members but relatively low levels of substantive
input to the proceedings. This was not surprising given the participation
of such famous figures as Stanton and Anthony and the relative lack of experience of most members in establishing reform organizations.[26] Even so,
members made their opinions known in direct ways for speeches were
often punctuated by applause, booing, bursts of laughter, and the like.
Thus the overriding impression was of an open organization, even if actual
participation rates were higher for prominent leaders than for ordinary
members. Finally it should be emphasized that this founding convention
was a one-time event, so strong inferences about the day-to-day functioning of the IWSA cannot be made. While these impressions remain incomplete and unsystematic, they provide some baseline for evaluating later
changes and continuities in the internal structure and process of Illinois's
major suffrage organization.

A third organizational issue concerns the national rivalry in the suffrage
movement and the relation of the Illinois group to this split. We have already suggested that Livermore's alliance with Stone was not inevitable
and was instead based on tactical, situational, and idiosyncratic factors. On
the basis of Livermore's writings, a parallel argument may be made regarding the split between Stanton/Anthony and Lucy Stone. Historians (e.g.,
Flexner 1975; Kraditor 1965; O'Neill 1969; and Sinclair 1965) have traditionally overdrawn the contrasts between these groups by simplistically la-
beling one group "radical" and the other "conservative." This caricature
needs to be balanced against the following points established within this
chapter: (1) most women felt the need for an independent women's rights
organization; (2) Livermore's vision of such an association closely paralleled the NWSA then being organized, though unbeknownst to her;
(3) the *Agitator* and the majority of women's rights advocates heartily
endorsed the formation of the NWSA once aware of its existence; and
(4) Livermore's major reservation—the seemingly exlusionary manner in
which the NWSA was organized—was about actions she conceded may
well have been unintended. Livermore's reactions make it at least plausible
to speculate that if the NWSA had been more diplomatic and inclusive in
its initial organization—and had Stanton and Anthony courted Stone in
particular—they might have preempted the chain of events that led to the
founding of a rival AWSA some months later.[27]

This is not to deny the subsequent emergence of important differences between the two suffrage organizations, but these differences were largely tactical. There were few differences in the overall analysis of women's position associated with each organization. Perhaps most instructive, there were no significant differences in the membership and following of the two national organizations (see DuBois 1978, 198ff.). In sum, the split on the national level is best understood as a situational and circumstantial outcome resulting from contingent conditions and some preexisting differences among a small minority of nationally prominent movement leaders.

Alongside class and organizational factors, movement analysis and ideology shed further light on the nature of the movement's orientation in this early period. Their most striking aspect was the sheer diversity of the arguments the movement made for the vote and other women's rights. The earlier survey of the *Agitator* columns revealed that natural rights and justice arguments prevailed in this period. These arguments presented powerful and clever proactive claims (Tilly 1978, 143ff.) by virtue of their reference to America's own revolutionary tradition and conception of popular sovereignty. However, these arguments by no means exhausted the ideological repertoire of the movement. Expediency arguments that portrayed the vote and women's rights as means to some further end were also put forward in this period. Corresponding to these diverse arguments were a heterogeneity of orientations among movement participants. In a word, the breadth of the early movement's program for social change accommodated a dazzling diversity of arguments and orientations related to women's issues.

This diversity requires a modification of Kraditor's (1965) image of changing movement ideology over time (see Leach 1980, 8ff., for related points). Her thesis, most simply, is that the early movement put forward rights and justice arguments for the vote while the later movement advanced expediency arguments. The explanatory problem posed by her analysis is thus why the early movement made one sort of argument while the later movement made another sort. My analysis of the early period suggests a different explanatory problem: why did the early movement make a wide variety of arguments (both justice and expediency) for the vote while the later movement concentrated on only one type of prosuffrage argument (expediency)? From this perspective, the movement narrowed and limited the types of arguments it made for the vote over the course of its history, ultimately relying heavily, if not exclusively, on expediency arguments.

This narrowing raises the further question of what caused some arguments to be eliminated from the movement's repertoire and others to be retained. Probably some causes were exogenous—factors beyond the movement's control made some arguments more appealing than others. However, endogenous causes were also at work; movement leaders made choices about the movement's direction, and different historical circumstances prompted different choices. These endogenous processes will be of particular interest in tracing patterns of movement transformation through the later nineteenth century.

FOUR

Patterns of Transformation, 1870–1890

The period from 1870 through the 1890s is a "black hole" in our knowledge of the suffrage movement. Virtually all accounts of the movement focus either on the pre-1870 period (e.g., DuBois 1978) or on the post-1890 period (e.g., Kraditor 1965). Works that include the 1870–1890 period tend to be broad and general social histories of women (e.g., O'Neill 1969 or Flexner 1975) and fail to provide a detailed and specific analysis of the suffrage movement. The reason for these omissions is not difficult to discover. This period was one of relative dormancy for the movement, and the narrative historian finds little to report. These decades contained neither the vibrant activism of the early period nor the sustained mobilization of the later period. As a result, our perspective on the movement as a whole is oddly bimodal: we see clearly both the Civil War period and the turn-of-the-century period, but in between we see nothing more than a flat and unremarkable landscape between two high points.

This bimodal vision is deceptive in several respects. For one, it blinds us to the fact that women continued to work hard for their political goals in this period, even though the balance of effort and gain shifted to their disadvantage. More important for our purposes, this bimodal vision obscures the fact that it was precisely during this period that major social changes rippled throughout the social structure and altered every facet of American life. More specifically, the position of the middle classes and the position of women changed in important and dramatic ways. It is not surprising that these changes affected the middle-class suffrage movement, but this impact has yet to be clearly identified and explained. This chapter attempts to do so. It will also show that while these decades are the least interesting from the perspective of narrative history, they are the most fascinating from the perspective of explaining movement change.

The major goals of this chapter are to document and explain the pattern and process of movement transformation undergone by the Illinois suffrage movement during these decades. My general argument is as follows: During this period, changes in the class structure and the social position of women combined to exert pressure toward a more conservative movement. One such pressure derived from the development of a new middle-class worldview and ideology that stressed ameliorationist reform, sought a harmonious social order, and denied the role of class conflict. As this perspective was transplanted into the suffrage movement via its middle-class leadership, it contributed to the transformation of that movement. Additional pressure derived from a series of changes that led to the greater social differentiation of women. As industrialization reduced gender commonalities among women and increased class differences between them, it became more difficult for the suffrage movement to maintain a broad orientation and political focus. By the 1890s these forces had produced a transformed movement which subsequently remobilized for an eventual suffrage victory after the turn of the century.

The first section of this chapter presents a brief chronological overview of major events in this period. The very brevity of this section testifies to its major theme: the suffrage movement experienced declining momentum from a peak of 1870 to a valley of 1890. The next section introduces the movement's main leader during this period—Elizabeth Boynton Harbert—and indicates the enormous influence she exercised over the movement. Of particular interest are the ways she redirected the movement's philosophy and goals into more moralistic and class-conscious directions. The third section examines the ties between the suffrage movement and related movements and organizations. These data suggest that although the suffrage cause survived through this period, it often did so at a disadvantage relative to other causes and organizations that attracted women's attention. These competing involvements presented the suffrage movement with a basic dilemma: it could maintain its distinctively political focus but remain small or it could dilute this focus in hope of recruiting larger numbers. At various points the Illinois movement tried both strategies, but never in a truly effective way. The fourth section describes the newspaper *New Era* edited by Harbert in the mid-1880s; it provides a convenient symbol of the transformed feminism of the time. The concluding section seeks to synthesize the theory and data that bear on the patterns of and reasons for movement transformation.

THE DECLINING MOMENTUM OF THE SUFFRAGE CAUSE

In 1870 the Illinois Woman Suffrage Association (IWSA) held its first annual convention in the state capital of Springfield to coincide with the state constitutional convention. The latter offered a good opportunity to secure female enfranchisement, and the movement came closer to doing so than it would for several decades. The issue arose within the constitutional convention when the minority report of the committee on elections and suffrage recommended that the issues of Negro suffrage and woman suffrage be submitted to the voters. In April 1870 the convention agreed, but before this could be done the convention reversed itself and withdrew the popular vote. In the end the convention wrote Negro suffrage into the constitution on its own initiative but declined to write in woman suffrage (ISHS, Journal of the Constitutional Convention of 1869–1870, 107–109).

These actions involved shifting patterns of pro- and antisuffrage sentiment to which the convention responded. From January to April the convention received only prosuffrage petitions totaling over 1,600 signatures. Under this pressure they decided to submit the issue to the voters. In April they received a massive antisuffrage petition of 1,381 signatures, followed by several smaller antisuffrage petitions. In May under the antisuffrage pressure the convention withdrew the issue from a popular vote and proceeded to write a constitution for Illinois that did not include female suffrage. Only a rapid and timely mobilization of antisuffrage forces prevented a popular vote on woman suffrage. It is of course impossible to say how voters might have responded to this issue (see ISHS, Debates and Proceedings of the Constitutional Convention of 1870, 129, 451, 479, 487, 510, 1077, 1277, 1377, 1502, 1842; Buechler 1982a, 264–270).

The defeat constituted a serious setback because another constitutional convention could not legally be called in Illinois for twenty years and did not actually occur for fifty years—ironically the same year as women were enfranchised at the federal level. The virtual elimination of this option for winning the vote had an important impact on the tactical choices the suffrage movement made after this point. On one hand, it made the state organization particularly interested in federal-level strategies that could bypass the machinery of state government; on the other hand, it promoted imaginative legal maneuvers on the part of the later movement that eventually enfranchised women on the state level.

While suffering a setback on suffrage, the movement registered other legal gains during this period (see Buechler 1982a, 262–264; Pierce 1937, 2:457–458; Spector 1975, 232, 238–239; Wheeler and Wortman 1977, 52–54; *HWS* 3:570–575). These included women's right to control their own earnings, to equal guardianship of children after divorce, and to share in a deceased husband's estate. What distinguished these victories from suffrage defeats was that the former all involved rights that had a somewhat particularistic application. That is, none of the reforms won at this time affected the status of all women simultaneously, as enfranchisement would have done. As a result, none of these rights carried the symbolic significance of the ballot, and none implied the equalization of sexual status that the vote would have connoted—surely part of the reason why some demands were achieved while the suffrage victory was delayed for so long.

By the mid-1870s this string of victories came to an end. As the possibilities for concrete gains evaporated, the movement returned to educating, proselytizing, and organizing as a long-term strategy of building a more effective foundation for pursuing the suffrage cause. As organization proceeded, it raised the inevitable issue of affiliation with the national suffrage associations.

In late 1869 and 1870 Mary Livermore sought to affiliate the IWSA with Lucy Stone's American Association. In 1871, however, the IWSA elected as president NWSA sympathizer Catherine Waite; she was followed in turn by Jane Graham Jones, whose preferences, if any, never became part of the historical record. Thus, from its founding in 1869 to the mid 1870s the IWSA vacillated on the question of affiliation, probably assigning the whole issue less importance than the rival national associations. With the election of Elizabeth Boynton Harbert to the IWSA presidency in 1876, the state organization became firmly allied with Stanton and Anthony's NWSA and remained so until the national organizations themselves merged in 1890.

Harbert had participated in the founding conventions of both the IWSA and the AWSA in 1869. Some months later, however, Harbert objected to the exclusionary character of the AWSA and its efforts to split the suffrage movement; her sympathies came to rest with Stanton and Anthony's NWSA. By the time Harbert assumed the IWSA presidency in 1876, Anthony regarded her as a trusted political confidante, and Harbert's allegiance never wavered after that point. These events indicate that on the state and local level the rivalry was both less important and less ideological than standard suffrage histories imply, and that alliances were formed more on the basis of perceptions of fair and equal treatment than on broad ideological differences (see HL, EBH Papers, Stone to Boynton, 5 and 19 April 1870; Livermore to Boynton, 9 May 1870; Livermore to Harbert, 20 April 1876; and Anthony to Harbert, 15 March 1875).

Soon after assuming the presidency of the IWSA in 1876, Harbert noted a shift in sentiment from woman suffrage to the temperance issue:

> About the close of the year 1876, a noticeable change in the direction of thought and effort was very apparent in the State of Illinois. . . . Women had tested their powers sufficiently to realize their strength, and were impatient for immediate results, hence many of the active friends of woman suffrage, believing that the temperance ballot could be more speedily secured than entire political equality, joined the home protection movement. (*HWS* 3:583)

The newly founded Illinois Social Science Association also drained members from the suffrage cause: "The enthusiasm in this society branching out in so many practical directions, absorbed for a time the energies of the Illinois women. Our membership reached 400. This may account for the apparent lethargy of the Suffrage Association during the years of 1877–78" (*HWS* 3:584). Over the next two years the suffrage movement consciously withdrew while the temperance movement tested its strategy for legislative reform: "For two years the advocates of woman suffrage in this State have held their claims and kept their work in abeyance, in order that the advocates of home protection might thoroughly test the power of petition" (SL, EBH Papers, newspaper fragment "The State Suffrage Association," n.d.). These events will be analyzed in more detail below; for now, it is worth noting not only the declining momentum of the suffrage cause but the self-conscious awareness of this decline (and some of the reasons for it) which was evident in the movement by 1880.

During the summer of 1880 a series of events stirred the embers of suffrage agitation without restarting the fire. These events were inspired by the NWSA's call for a mass meeting in Chicago to coincide with the Republican convention; NWSA hoped to pressure the Republican presidential nominee into supporting woman suffrage. These efforts were less than successful. The NWSA encountered opposition from Chicago suffragists in a relatively rare instance of rivalry on the local level. James Bradwell, for example, stridently refused a NWSA invitation to address the mass meeting and insisted that his name not be used in connection with the event (HL, EBH Papers, James Bradwell to Anthony et al., 28 May 1880). The NWSA also failed to extract any commitments from the Republican party to a more active role in the struggle to enfranchise women. Despite these failures, the meeting elicited hundreds of letters from women who could not attend. These letters provide a rare glimpse of the views of the followers and members of the suffrage movement at this time.

Overall, these letters suggest that the broad orientation of the NWSA was in tune with the perspective of women who responded to the convention call. Most of the letters described personal experiences that implicitly endorsed a broad approach to women's rights and equality between the sexes. The letters contained little that questioned the NWSA's orientation and much that validated the approach that the organization took toward women's rights (see CHS, NWSA 1880 Convention Correspondence).

The popularity of these sentiments is theoretically significant because it is sometimes argued that the suffrage movement was transformed because its followers were more conservative than its leaders, and thus the former eventually tamed the latter. These letters provide no support for such an interpretation, at least in this time and place. Of course these correspondents were not a random sample of movement followers; hence these conclusions must remain tentative. Nonetheless, it appears that the orientation of the NWSA was consistent with the views of many politically interested women and that it had a significant constituency for its broad orientation.

After the busy summer of 1880 the local movement fell back into its doldrums. Suffrage leaders expressed concern about why the movement was stuck and what it might take to get it moving again. Some pointed to competing associations that also sought the participation of women, including, by the 1880s, an increasingly powerful temperance movement as well as moral reform organizations and philanthropic groups. Also of concern were apolitical involvements that increasingly occupied women's time. Elizabeth Cady Stanton became especially incensed about women's preoccupation with seeming irrelevancies while they ignored the major political questions of their own day:

> I think American women better study the question of individual rights and fire their souls with the [one word illegible] of justice and liberty, than to form art clubs to read about the Coliseum at Rome, the leaning tower of Pisa, and Egyptian pyramids, while ignorant of

the significance of our great experiment of republican government, of our system of jurisprudence, and all the principles of political economy. (HL, EBH Papers, Stanton to Harbert, n. d.)

Throughout the 1880s movement leaders expressed concern over women's lack of involvement, or apolitical involvements, or misguided political involvements, and they tried (without much success) to find ways to combat these tendencies.

During this period the IWSA sought to organize statewide by trying to establish local suffrage organizations in every county and congressional district within the state. Convention reports from the 1880s (mostly from HL, EBH Papers) indicated that these efforts were only partially successful. By the mid 1880s the suffrage movement faced a dilemma that it never successfully overcame during this period: When the movement restricted its focus to political issues like the vote, it lost potential members to other reform organizations. When it expanded its focus to include such issues as moral reform, social purity, and temperance, it attracted more members but devoted less effort to political questions. As a result of these pressures, the suffrage movement was never able to exert a strong, persistent influence for the vote during these years.

In 1884 Harbert stepped down from the presidency of the IWSA to pursue other activities. The organization elected Mary Holmes as president, and she proved to be a weaker and more uncertain leader than Harbert had been. Anthony voiced misgivings to Harbert, expressing a hope that "your retiring will not stop the organization of your state" (HL, EBH Papers, Anthony to Harbert, 6 October 1884). Changes within the IWSA organization in the 1880s symbolized the declining momentum of the movement and illustrated its pattern of transformation. For one, the organization decided in 1884 to limit its efforts to municipal suffrage in various towns and villages throughout the state (HL, EBH Papers, "Report from Illinois," n. d.). For another, the organization changed its name and object at its 1885 meeting. The name change was from the Illinois *Woman* Suffrage Association to the Illinois *Equal* Suffrage Association; the object change was from seeking "political equality with men" to seeking the "political enfranchisement of women." Both changes symbolized the narrowing focus and the less explicitly feminist stance of the organization in this period.

The most poignant symbol of declining momentum occurred at the 1889 convention. As Harbert was reelected to head the organization, outgoing president Holmes "expressed disappointment that an active campaign had not been made last year for municipal suffrage [and] advocated as a specialty for this year, the distribution of suffrage literature" (SL, EBH Papers, *Woman's Tribune*, 7 December 1889). While the movement actually experienced a series of ups and downs throughout these two decades, nothing better symbolized the secular trend of declining momentum than the contrast between an 1870 movement that (arguably) had come close to enfranchisement and an 1890 movement that was reduced to the distribution of suffrage literature as its major activity for the upcoming year.

This sketch implies why this period in the history of the suffrage movement is so often neglected. On the level of events, there is very little to relate. The real significance of this period resides not in specific events (or the lack of them) but in the social changes and the politics of this period. The remaining sections in this chapter examine these topics.

ELIZABETH HARBERT AND THE REDIRECTION OF FEMINISM

No one was more instrumental in sustaining the suffrage movement throughout this period in Illinois than Elizabeth Boynton Harbert. In addition to her role as president of the IWSA, Harbert played an even more important role as the major ideologist and spokeswoman for the movement throughout this period. Harbert's distinctive version of feminism and its impact on the Illinois movement thereby warrant further analysis.

Harbert first became active in the movement in1869, in Crawfordsville, Indiana. Shortly thereafter, having moved to Iowa, she successfully lobbied the Republican party to include a woman's plank in its state platform (Willard and Livermore [1893] 1967, 357). She served as vice-president of the Indiana suffrage association and president of the Iowa association before assuming the presidency of the Illinois association for a total of twelve years that spanned a quarter of a century (1876–1884, 1889–1890, 1900–1901). Finally, she played an important role in the NWSA throughout this entire period; many of her contributions were chronicled in *History of Woman Suffrage* (1969).

Important as these contributions were, they represented only a fraction of the activities of this Renaissance woman. A sampling of Harbert's other commitments in the last quarter of the nineteenth century include the following: writer of a weekly column on women for a major Chicago paper during a five-year period around 1880; publication of a suffrage paper in the mid-1880s; founding member of the Illinois Social Science Association in the late 1870s and the Illinois Women's Press Association in 1884; member of the board of managers of the Girl's Industrial School in Evanston; affiliate of the national Woman's Congress; founder and first president of the Evanston Women's Club; and organizer of countless conferences on the relations between women, the home, industrial society, and the federal government. Harbert thus led a remarkably active life as a journalist, reformer, author, and activist, which transcended and shaped her contributions to the suffrage cause.

Harbert's multiple involvements in a rapidly changing society reflected and nurtured an equally broad ideology of social relations and a vision of how the emerging industrial society should be organized. Virtually all of Harbert's statements on feminism and suffrage reflected this larger ideology of social relations and, in a sense, were derived from it. This ideology stressed social harmony and equilibrium and underscored the special role that women could play in introducing these elements into social life. Harbert's career represented in microcosm the emergence of a historically specific and distinctly bourgeois reformist impulse in response to the dislocations engendered by rapid industrialization and urbanization.[1] Of particular interest is how Harbert came to envision the role of women given these premises and how that vision in turn influenced her conception of the suffrage movement.

One set of answers was provided by Harbert's second novel *Out of Her Sphere*, published in 1871. The novel told the story of two girlhood friends who grew up to experience very different lives. The heroine successfully resisted all attempts to confine her to "woman's sphere" and lived a joyous and fulfilling life. Her friend, who succumbed to societal pressure to conform to women's stereotyped role, suffered a disastrous marriage and a lifetime of dependence on others. Around this basic plot, developed in a highly sentimentalized and romantic style, Harbert constructed a feminist morality play about the damage done to women and society by the confining and limiting notion of woman's sphere.

The major theme of the novel was that conventional patterns of child-rearing, which were gender-specific and implied participation in distinct sex role spheres, were harmful to women and damaging to society. They harmed women by artificially restricting their activities to the narrow realm called woman's sphere; they damaged society because it lost the contributions women could make if they were not so restricted. The narrative traced these restrictions throughout a young girl's lifetime, noting her envy of boys' greater opportunities. Harbert used adult figures in the novel to develop these themes; through plot and narrative she criticized women who emulated the ideal of helpless femininity, slavishly followed fashion, selfishly used feminine wiles to win husbands, and married to pursue a life-time of idleness in a state of dependency on men.

Harbert's real criticisms were directed at sex role socialization and the separate spheres that produced these outcomes. Her objections were simultaneously economic and moral. Economic realities, she argued, made this a formula for disaster because it prevented women from becoming self-sufficient, thereby making them victims when men did not or could not fulfill their role of economic support. Harbert's moral objections were grounded in the Protestant ethic: women, like men, were obligated to lead productive lives, and failure to do so was a moral shortcoming. For Harbert, social customs and prejudices created these conditions; she particularly criticized those customs and prejudices that blandly accepted abusive relations within marriage while condemning the most noble pursuits of women outside marriage. Harbert's novel suggested that this problem could only be overcome when girls were provided with "something to do" that granted them the same dignity men derived from their labor. In more concrete terms, Harbert recommended equal education for women and urged them to strive for the same balance between family and work that was found among men.

While Harbert's novel contained a clear emancipatory theme, the theme's limits became evident in her defense of the women's rights movement within the novel. One of the novel's characters drew a distinction between "femininity" (a pejorative category) and "womanliness" (a positive category), which Harbert then used to reassure her readers about the suffrage movement. She informed readers that women's rights advocates represented the height of womanliness and the direct opposite of freeloveites; that women would retain their womanliness with the vote; that political involvement would not alter women's positive virtues; that women's rights did not rest on, encourage, or lead to conflict between the sexes; and that motherhood was completely consistent with the women's rights movement. In part, these messages were clearly intended to counter criticisms of the movement, but they also reflected a larger tension that was becoming increasingly evident in movement ideology.

This tension arose from two arguments, paraphrased in their most extreme form as follows: on the one hand, achieving women's rights would make an enormous difference in women's lives and solve all their problems; on the other hand, such victories would not change in the least those qualities that society defined as desirable in women. From this point on, Harbert's arguments for equality increasingly emphasized the sex-specific traits that constituted "womanliness." Harbert's own version of these traits was nicely summarized in the quote that appeared on the title page of her book: "The mission of woman on earth? To uplift, purify, and confirm, by her own gracious gift, the world, in despite of the world's dull endeavor to degrade and drag down and oppose it forever. The mission of woman? Born to soothe and to solace, to help and to heal the sick world that leans upon her" (Harbert 1871).

A quarter of a century later the same themes were evident in Harbert's feminism. In the intervening decades, however, the stress on womanliness overcame the search for equality:

> Convince woman that she is needed to help heal the sick world that leans on her, and convince man that in thus giving aid and comfort she will not lose the very womanliness he loves or her capacity for home-making and the battle for her enfranchisement is won. Our favorite thought has been ever since enlisting in this reform, "It is not the woman question but the human question." (HL, EBH Papers, "The Philosophy of Suffrage," n. d.)

By the late 1890s when this speech was delivered, Harbert had developed a distinct political worldview within which the suffrage cause found its appropriate place. In this worldview the struggle for woman's equality was minor in comparison to the benefits that society could reap from women's full participation. The rationale for demanding suffrage had thereby shifted from justice and equality to what would benefit society. The latter rationale, in turn, was consistently defined by Harbert in a manner that legitimized many of the very traits, stereotypes, and characteristics she had criticized in her 1871 novel about separate spheres. In a word, the thrust of Harbert's feminism became not what the country could do for women, but rather what women could do for the country.[2]

This speech on the philosophy of suffrage contained four major themes that became the cornerstones of all of Harbert's pronouncements on feminism and suffrage. The first was that although the question of rights was important, women's duties to family and society were even more important. The goal of the movement thereby became removing obstacles to the performance of these obligations rather than securing rights for a particular interest group. A related theme was that the movement was not really concerned with the "woman question" but rather with the "human question." A claim made throughout Harbert's career, this terminology depoliticized many feminist issues and goals by implying a fundamental, underlying commonality of interests between men and women. A third theme made the second even more explicit: Harbert consistently denied that any competing or conflicting interests existed between men and women as distinct gender groups. A fourth consistent theme involved Harbert's sanctioning of the role of motherhood. Her feminism accepted the role as primary for women (leading her to describe women as "mothers of the race"), rather than critically analyzing it and distinguishing its positive and oppressive aspects (see HL, EBH Papers, "The Philosophy of Suffrage," for specific examples of these themes).

These premises constituted a distinctive form of feminist thought—one that often diverged from the ideology of the early movement and even the posture of the NWSA with which Harbert remained affiliated. But these premises resonated well with the larger social ideology that Harbert had developed throughout the 1870s and 1880s. For instance, just as Harbert denied that there were any real conflicts of interest between men and women, she also denied that there were any real conflicts of interest between social classes in the emerging industrial order.[3] Thus she exemplified a trend in the suffrage movement whereby a new version of feminism—itself derived from a general middle-class social ideology emphasizing harmony—came to displace the emancipatory orientation of the Civil War period. One good place to examine the development and propagation of this ideology and its application to the women's movement is in a newspaper column Harbert wrote entitled "Woman's Kingdom."

This column appeared under Harbert's editorship in *Inter-Ocean* from 1877 through 1884. Since these were also years when she was presiding over the IWSA, the columns provide a good indication of the ideology of a major suffrage leader in a particular historical moment. The most striking aspect of these columns was a new and persistent middle-class consciousness evidenced in at least three ways. First, it appeared in frequent appeals to "solid, self-reliant, industrious" middle-class women to participate more fully in the movement. It was also evident in pejorative references to the "wives of capital" who made no productive contribution to society. Finally, it could be seen in references and appeals to the "laboring classes," which attempted to link the struggle of workers with the cause of woman suffrage. It was around these reference points that Harbert formulated a much more self-consciously middle-class approach to the reform of society in general and the cause of woman suffrage in particular.

Harbert's articles on labor typically criticized in strikingly populist terms the aggressiveness of capital. The solution she always advocated, however, was that enfranchising women was the best way to redress the grievances of labor because women would support legislative changes in labor's interest. Writing in 1878 under the title "Woman Suffrage—Why It Would Prove Advantageous," Harbert argued

women of today would restore the disturbed equilibrium by legislating in the interests of labor rather than of capital. . . . during the last quarter of a century scarcely a law has been enacted for the benefit of the laboring classes while 200,000,000 acres of land have been given to railroad corporations alone. Capital has bought votes, has thereby been elected to office, and, once in office has continued to legislate in the interests of capital. The laboring classes now asking for representation, redress and relief, can best secure it by giving the ballot to woman. Why? Because a large majority of the women of the country who would hasten to consecrate their energies, intellect, and "mother instinct for government" to the political interests of the country are women from that best grade of society, the great industrial, self-reliant middle class.

As the article continued, Harbert called for a reform effort that would be the moral equivalent of war and would be conducted through the voting power of women. By the end of the article, however, the focus had shifted from the grievances of labor to the need for social control: "With the sale of intoxicants prohibited, with the vagrant children educated and restrained, with the homes of the poor free from taxation, with the best thought, experience, patriotism, morality and statesmanship crystallized into law, the future of the government would seem more hopeful" (SL, EBH Papers, "Woman's Kingdom" scrapbook, vol. 2, 3 August 1878).

A second column, from 1883, revealed the same pattern. Harbert began by gesturing at some features of class conflict, but proceeded to suggest that a large proportion of "the wrongs, misery and poverty of the wage laborers of the world is directly due to intemperance, ignorance and war."

Of these three, intemperance loomed largest, for Harbert's argument linked labor's difficulties with the unconstrained flow of liquor:

> In regard to intemperance, the direct cause, statisticians tell us of three-fourths of the ignorance, crime and poverty, while who can estimate its blighting and weakening effect upon the physical, mental, and moral powers of its victims, to say nothing of the gigantic levy of taxes to keep up the penal institutions made necessary by the crime it engenders and directly causes? . . . the astounding amount of the drink bill of the United States, together with the enormous taxes levied in order to secure jails, police stations, asylums, and alms-houses for incapacitated victims of the liquor habit, is a tremendous factor in the inequalities of labor and capital. (SL, EBH Papers, "Woman's Kingdom" scrapbook, vol. 6, 17 November 1883)

For this analysis, temperance became the major solution to class conflict: "With three-fourths of the crime and poverty eliminated we begin to catch glimpses of a happy, industrious world." Through her focus on temperance, Harbert ignored and implicitly denied the depth and range of causes that produced labor's problems. The real appeal of this view was to middle-class reformers who increasingly believed they had to take class conflict into account, but sought to do so within their own worldview and program for reform. Just as the vote was becoming overburdened as a solution to problems, intemperance was becoming overburdened as a cause of problems.

A third example, from Harbert's speech "Wrongs of the Working Classes," provides a more general statement of the reformist themes of class conciliation, interdependence, symmetry, and equilibrium:

> The rich, the poor, the high, the low, should work together in "symmetrical diversity." . . . The correlation of opposing forces produces harmonious action. Freedom of natural development will produce the highest progress, and homogenous unity out of apparent contradictions. Let the desire for reciprocal good be the basis and the object, and the result is best attained by diversity of effort. . . . there is an interdependence of mankind calling for a mutual helpfulness, the reflex influence of which enobles and inspires. . . . So shall we find that in the right adaptation of affairs there is a perfect harmony between individual and national interests; that class legislation does not long benefit the class it is intended for, that truth, though often of lowly

and obscure birth, is above all sect, party, prejudice or traditional belief, and that the truth shall indeed make us free and tolerant as well.
That reciprocity is a religion of duty, which will eliminate man's in-
humanity to man, and make countless millions rejoice. (HL, EBH
Papers, "Wrongs of the Working Classes," n. d.)

The speech concluded that woman suffrage was a major means through
which such harmony could be achieved.

These arguments expressed a new awareness of and a new posture toward class antagonisms. Earlier references to labor within the suffrage
movement (i.e., in the late 1860s) had explicitly recognized the economic
and political nature of class conflict and had advocated economic and
political solutions. Harbert's perception—through an increasingly well-
focused middle-class lens—was that these problems were rooted in social
disorder (indexed by intemperance, vagrancy, unstable homes, etc.), that
they could be solved through social control, and that enfranchising women
was an important step in this direction. In this way, middle-class consciousness (and reformism) dialectically developed along with the crystallization of capital and labor as a major axis of conflict within the industrializing society.

Another aspect of this class consciousness was the critical posture Harbert adopted toward upper-class women. She vacillated between condemning them for their luxurious and wasteful life-styles and appealing to them
to become more productive by joining the movement. Mostly she viewed
this group as either neutral or harmful to the interests of the suffrage
movement:

> The women of capital, with rare exceptions are so enervated by luxu-
> rious habits that "they have no interest in politics." (SL, EBH Papers,
> "Woman's Kingdom" scrapbook, vol. 2, 3 August 1878)

> Where have the loudest complaints been heard in regard to the ne-
> glected children of our philanthropic women? From the idle, fash-
> ionable women who, for weeks and months at a time, desert husbands
> and children . . . careless of everything but their own comfort. (HL,
> EBH Papers, "Woman's Corner," n. d.)

> Read the history of the lobby at Washington today and you will dis-
> cover that the mistresses of capitalists play an influential part in the
> rings of monopolies. (SL, EBH Papers, "Woman's Kingdom" scrap-
> book, vol. 6, 17 November 1883)

The development of middle-class consciousness fostered a self-conscious distancing from upper-class women along with a reaffirmation of the middle-class values of productivity and industriousness.

Another middle-class value that preoccupied Harbert was respectability, and she devoted numerous columns to defending the respectability of the women's rights movement. While such defenses were understandable given the growth of antisuffrage sentiment, they often conceded too much to the critics. One column, "The Best Home-Makers, They Are The Advocates of Woman Suffrage," argued that "the noblest mothers, the best home-keepers, and what is of far more importance, the truest home-makers are found among our woman suffrage advocates," (SL, EBH Papers, "Woman's Kingdom" scrapbook, vol. 6, 19 July 1884). Another column pointed to the increasing fashionability of suffrage among cultivated and religious classes and approvingly cited Elizabeth Phelps's comment that

> We may prophecy that the first large class of women to insist upon the right of the ballot will be composed of gentle wives and mothers, who do not desire to be in Congress; who will stitch and ruffle at their sewing machines, who take care of their own babies, and who can make sweet bread; who believe in their ministers, receive the four gospels, and say their prayers. (SL, EBH Papers, "Woman's Kingdom" scrapbook, vol. 3, 18 September 1880)

The introduction of this class-conscious concern with respectability also contributed to the moderation of movement goals and rhetoric throughout the 1870s and 1880s.

A final noteworthy theme throughout these columns was Harbert's portrayal of movement goals as a matter of altruism, duty, and self-sacrifice. On several occasions, this was expressed through a critique of individualism and women who construed movement goals in individual terms:

> Let our watchword from henceforth be, not what can our country, our government do for us, but rather, what can we do for our country and for the perpetuity of our government?

> . . . Forever be silenced the selfish assertion, "all the rights I want . . ." the time has come when the patriot men of America must call in the reserves and summon women to the glorious service of aiding to save our country from the combinations of vice and selfishness . . . our hour for self-sacrificing service is here. (SL, EBH Papers, "Woman's Kingdom" scrapbook, vol. 5, 28 June 1883)

[Women] must recognize that a great part of this good will lie in the growing habit and continuous custom of deferring immediate and personal gratifications, whether of bodily ease and luxury or of self-love and ambition. (SL, EBH Papers, "Woman's Kingdom" scrapbook, vol. 2, 1879, quotation from Julia Ward Howe)

The significance of these recommendations was that the sanctioning of individualism led not to a call for a collectively oriented woman's movement as much as to a collective subordination of movement goals to other objectives ranging from patriotism to good government, from child welfare to stronger homes and families. This posture was both ascetically bourgeois and stereotypically feminine; deferred gratification and self-sacrificing service to others become intertwined in this distinctly moralistic view of the world and women's role within it.

These selections from Harbert's writings and speeches from the 1870s through the 1890s exemplify the development of a more conservative orientation within the suffrage movement. The example is all the more striking given that Harbert was a prominent movement leader and that her leadership in general and her columns in particular were closely followed and widely praised by publicly active women. Harbert, therefore, was able to exercise considerable influence on the redirection of feminism on the basis of a newly conscious middle-class perspective.

In 1884 Harbert resigned her position at the *Inter-Ocean* in a dispute over editorial policy. The disagreement involved the paper's unfavorable stands on labor, woman suffrage, and temperance. Harbert's resignation letter cited as the major cause for leaving her post an *Inter-Ocean* editorial that had criticized the National Women's Christian Temperance Union and its move to form a Prohibition party. Her resignation on these grounds provided one indication of the increasing interpenetration of the suffrage and temperance issues (see SL, EBH Papers, "Woman's Kingdom" scrapbook, vol. 2, "Blunder of the N.W.C.T.U.," n. d., and vol. 7, October 1884; also HL, EBH Papers, "Good Bye to the Readers of the Woman's Kingdom," 1884).

SUFFRAGISM, TEMPERANCE, AND WOMEN'S ORGANIZATIONS

The temperance issue had considerable impact on the suffrage cause in the late 1870s and 1880s in the Midwest. Three factors contributed to this drama. First, some suffrage organizations were split on the desirability of temperance and prohibition. Second, some temperance organizations were divided over the vote for women. Third, the Prohibition party entered party politics in the early 1880s under the leadership of temperance men, most of whom were opposed to woman suffrage but receptive to women's support for the temperance cause. In more dynamic terms, the suffrage movement was losing momentum and beginning to lose its political orientation while the temperance movement was gaining momentum and beginning to move from a purely moralistic condemnation of drink to more politicized attempts to introduce temperance legislation. The Prohibition party was the culmination of this trend: a single-issue political party seeking elective office. It was inevitable that the suffrage and temperance causes would influence one another during this period and perhaps inevitable that their relation would be a stormy one.

The major temperance organization in this period was the Women's Christian Temperance Union (WCTU). Throughout the 1870s the WCTU disavowed the suffrage movement and sought very limited voting rights for women. A prime example was a temperance convention held in 1878 that passed a resolution seeking votes for women on saloon openings:

> In taking this position we repudiate the insinuation that our unions thereby intend to affiliate with women suffragists; and we refute that absurd insinuation by pointing to the fact that at three successive annual conventions we have never asked the ballot on this single question, and yet have never made to the suffragists, nor received from them, the slightest intimation of a union of our efforts.

Harbert reprinted this resolution in "Woman's Kingdom" with the following rebuke:

> we must protest against the twelfth resolution, offered by Miss Frances Willard. In view of the eminent services in the cause of temperance by such "woman suffragists" as [a long list of suffragists involved in temperance followed], we think the last half of this resolution very unnecessary, and, in view of Miss Willard's occasional indorsement of woman suffrage, quite a conundrum. (SL, EBH Papers, "Woman's Kingdom" scrapbook, vol. 2, 19 October 1878)

As of 1878 no alliance between temperance and suffrage forces was evident in Illinois.

To whatever extent the suffrage and temperance causes competed for followers, it was a battle that the WCTU had temporarily won by 1878 in Illinois. Over the next two years the suffrage movement became dormant while the WCTU sought a "home protection" ballot for women. Despite a petition of one hundred and eighty thousand signatures, this campaign failed; its failure moved the WCTU into a more overtly political stance that eventually included advocacy of woman suffrage. The politicization of the WCTU had already begun with the election of Frances Willard to the presidency of that organization in 1879. Under her leadership the organization greatly increased its membership, adopted a departmental form of organization to implement Willard's "Do Everything" reform motto, began reform campaigns on several issues, sought alliances with other organizations, and eventually moved into party politics.

Indications of a rapprochement between suffrage and temperance were evident as early as 1879 when Willard wrote to Harbert: "And never is a word spoken in disloyalty to women who work for the general suffrage movement—only we make clear our single request as temperance women for the temperance ballot. We of Chicago WCTU today decided to join your social science com. in an appeal for scientific temperance teaching in the schools" (SL, EBH Papers, Willard to Harbert, 31 January 1879). Willard's qualified support foreshadowed future tensions between a temperance movement that conceived of the vote as an expedient tactic to achieve temperance goals and a suffrage movement that continued to see the vote as a right that should be extended to women on the basis of equality. The suffrage strategy of the WCTU was explicitly stated by Mary Willard: "Please say to your good women so earnestly working for woman's enfranchisement that the WCTU is working side by side in this endeavor, and believes that in so doing the end it seeks, viz—prohibition will be the more quickly and surely reached" (HL, EBH Papers, Willard to Harbert, n. d.). There was also pressure within the suffrage movement to join forces with the temperance movement (see e.g., HL, EBH Papers, Holmes to Harbert, 14 October 1878?), and in fact Harbert was generally receptive to the goals of the temperance movement. She nonetheless stopped short of a full endorsement of WCTU strategy, fearing that such an endorsement might subordinate the cause of suffrage to that of temperance.

Susan B. Anthony also remained skeptical about the organized temperance movement and the potential threat it represented to the autonomy of the suffrage movement. In 1880 she suggested that both movements would benefit by supporting suffrage, but saw this as unlikely given internal divisions within each (HL, EBH Papers, Anthony to Harbert, 5 August 1880). When the WCTU supported the Prohibition party and its instrumental manipulation of the suffrage cause, Anthony counseled suffrage women to maintain their independence from both temperance and prohibition (HL, EBH Papers, Anthony to Harbert, 19 March 1882).[4] By late 1883 Anthony dismissed the temperance forces as a potential ally, arguing that suffragists must "let them work out their suffrage salvation by themselves and in their own way" (HL, EBH Papers, Anthony to Harbert, 9 December 1883). Events vindicated Anthony's judgment in that the temperance movement suffered setbacks and lost much of its appeal after 1884, but in the interim it exercised considerable influence on the suffrage movement itself.

Harbert's own position was a complex product of all these pressures. In general, she maintained a cautious distance from the WCTU while supporting temperance as a general reform. On particular campaigns she always called for unity and harmony where there were common points of agreement, but she also urged that principles not be sacrificed to expediency. She continued to use "Woman's Kingdom" to gently criticize temperance forces for their hostility to suffrage, reminding them that it was the suffrage movement that broke the ground on which temperance women were able to espouse political reforms in the first place (for examples, see SL, EBH Papers, "Woman's Kingdom" scrapbook, vol. 4, 11 March 1882; vol. 5, 8 September 1881 and 15 November 1883). Finally, it is clear from Harbert's personal correspondence that many temperance leaders regarded her as a firm ally; that impression was supported by her resignation from *Inter-Ocean* in protest against its editorial policy on, among other things, temperance and prohibition.

Historians have given Willard credit for not only building up the WCTU but also for recruiting more conservative women into the suffrage movement by first involving them in the WCTU. Willard is typically portrayed as weaning these women away from narrow religious concerns and encouraging a more secular orientation to reform (see Flexner 1975; Wheeler and Wortman 1977; and Bordin 1981). Data from Illinois require a more complicated interpretation. While the standard interpretation that Willard and the WCTU politicized conservative women and mobilized them for suffrage may be true in the long run, in the period under analysis it was equally true that the temperance movement depoliticized the suffrage movement. It did so by providing a rapidly growing and seemingly powerful alternative movement espousing moralistic reform at the precise time when the suffrage movement was losing momentum. That leaders like Anthony devoted so much time to maintaining the distinctions between the movements testifies that, among many followers, the causes had become functional substitutes for one another.

From the perspective of those who sought to maintain an independent and relatively broad suffrage movement, the temperance movement's mobilization of larger numbers of women represented a double-edged sword at best. It promised to increase the ranks of the suffrage movement at the same time that it threatened to dilute its political orientation. Standard interpretations also exaggerate the relative ease with which Willard "converted" WCTU members to suffrage. Again, it was true that over several decades an increasingly prosuffrage majority materialized within the WCTU. But in the period under discussion, significant differences of opinion within each movement in regard to the other continued to be important. In short, antisuffrage temperance women and antitemperance suffrage women continued to be potent forces throughout this period, and the ultimately more powerful suffrage movement that emerged bore the imprint of these continuing disputes. The best single indicator was the increasing reliance on expediency arguments within the suffrage movement (Kraditor 1965).

The WCTU was one of the major forces pushing the suffrage movement in different directions, but it was not the only such force. The 1870s and 1880s saw a rapid increase in the number and variety of organizations, associations, and clubs that appealed to women and connected them to the public sphere in ever larger numbers. This phenomenon may be traced at virtually every class and status level, although the process was perhaps inevitably biased toward women who were relatively well situated in the economic order and had the time, education, and other resources to engage in such activities. As in the case of the WCTU, these organizations ultimately increased the number of women favorable toward suffrage, but this occurred in part because of changes in the way the vote was conceived.

Different types of women's organizations promoted differing types of feminism. Women's clubs promoted a "domestic feminism" whose goal was to extend women's traditional responsibilities, rights, and obligations to the society at large (Blair 1980). Reform organizations promoted a "moral feminism" whose purpose was to solve social problems by applying absolute moral principles. Professional associations promoted a "professional feminism" oriented to upward mobility, individual opportunity, and career advancement. The flowering of women's organizations thereby nurtured a variety of orientations to the woman question, all of which competed with the explicitly political feminism of the suffrage movement. Good examples of these tendencies may be found in the Illinois Social Science Association and the Chicago Woman's Club.

The Illinois Social Science Association (ISSA) was founded in October 1877. An affiliate of the American Social Science Association (ASSA), the Illinois group was the first such organization to be established on the state level. Its membership quickly expanded to four hundred, and it began publication of the *Illinois Social Science Journal* only two months after its founding.[5] The ISSA constitution described its purpose as follows: "The object shall be to suggest and develop plans for the advancement of industrial, intellectual, social, educational and philanthropic interests, to the end that we may help secure better homes, schools, churches, charities, and laws, and better service for humanity and God" (HL, EBH Papers, ISSA Constitution, 1877). Among the founding members of the ISSA were the familiar figures of Willard, Harbert, and Bradwell.

William Leach has described the ASSA as the queen of bourgeois reformist organizations (1980, 297–346). While the association was critical of particular practices in the emerging capitalist and industrial order, as a whole it reinforced existing social and economic relations. According to Leach, the leading themes of ASSA ideology were social equilibrium, symmetrical harmony, and interdependence. These notions were used by reformers to argue for the unification and integration of society into a healthy social body by subordinating both individuals and groups to the state. Taking organic metaphors literally, reformers reasoned that social problems were diseases that required universal, state-administered solutions or, better yet, preventative measures. Proceeding from this worldview, these reformers focused particular attention on such issues as sanitation, crime, and the need for better education.

Adopting an orientation simultaneously scientific and reformist, these social science organizations sought a bourgeois form of praxis that would unite knowledge and action toward perfecting the emerging industrial order. Frank Sanborn, a leading figure in the ASSA, described the work of social science as twofold: "to discover the principles upon which society is best organized, and to make a practical application of those principles in each particular country and place." Noting that "the two classes of men who carry social science forward . . . are too often at variance," Sanborn stated that "the function of associations like ours [is] to bring together the scientific research and the practical faculty—to reconcile them and set them both at work." In the same speech Sanborn endorsed Harbert's view of social science, stating that "she gives a definition of our common purpose which is perhaps as good as any: 'We understand the work of Social Science to be the devising of methods for setting good influences in motion and for counteracting the bad'" (HL, EBH Papers, "Social Science," 20 May 1878). Exemplary of the good influences to be set in motion were such things as middle-class culture; in the words of Laura Humphrey who spoke at an ISSA convention:

> As Americans we boast of authors, architects, and artists. What can be said of our musicians? Little is done toward establishing a musical taste in the lower classes of this country. Children must be taught it. For warlike purposes, the value of music is known. It rouses the timid, gives courage to the cowardly. . . . The moral tone of a whole village has undergone an entire change through the introduction of music, especially of the young, whom it will keep at home and away from dangerous amusements. Hearts, as well as intellects, must be cultivated, and no branch of education can accomplish this like music, which should be taught all children not as an amusement or pasttime, but as a study, and as much preparation for it exacted as for any other study. (SL, EBH Papers, "Woman's Kingdom" scrapbook, vol. 2, 4 October 1878)

Leach's book identifies Comtean positivism as a major underpinning of the worldview of social science reformers, and Harbert's address to the first annual meeting of the ISSA sounded a distinctly Comtean theme. Speaking on "The Relation of Social Science to Religion,"[6] she cited the Bible, commented on the "evident departure of many of our fashionable, luxurious, debt-dishonored churches from the teachings of their founder," and concluded by noting that

> Jesus had but three years of public ministry. How much of that time was devoted to the discussion of abstract doctrines, and how much to the practical work of healing the sick, feeding the hungry and preaching a plain, yet beautiful and practical morality to the poor?

> What relation has social science to religion? For answer, we refer you to the sermon on the Mount, and answer one question by asking

another, is not social science twin sister to religion—aye, is it not religion itself? (SL, EBH Papers, "Woman's Kingdom" scrapbook, vol. 2, 4 October 1878)

The ISSA came to conceive of female suffrage as a necessary tool for realizing its program of reform. In Illinois the mediating link between suffrage and reform was provided by the ubiquitous Elizabeth Harbert. Addressing the second annual ISSA convention on "Women as Related to the State," she claimed that women could not achieve their "full servicable value in social science without legislative enactment." She therefore broke her self-imposed rule about keeping her "radical views in abeyance at all social science meetings" and argued that it had become

an indispensable duty for women to unite in an endeavor to benefit the race. She advocated the incorporation of those principles which made home or parish virtuous and beautiful into the wider field of general government to improve the present perversion of the system of rights. The only means to the amelioration of the wrongs that spread ruin to right and proper government was the education and election of woman to her proper sphere of association. . . . Women in legislation was the ounce of preventive for the treatment of evils that swept the land in the train of crime. (SL, EBH Papers, "Woman's Kingdom" scrapbook, vol. 2, n.d., scrapbook page 103)

Two years later Harbert again linked the ineffectiveness of reform organizations to their lack of female suffrage:

Meanwhile many of the members of the Illinois Social Science Association were beginning to realize that its record was the same as that of every individual and association in these United States. Every measure proposed for progressive action, industrial, educational, political, philanthropic or moral was thwarted because of woman's inability to crystallize her opinions into law. Our earnest women were everywhere defeated in their efforts because of their disfranchisement. This has been our uniform experience in every department of reform, and sooner or later all thinking women see plainly that the direct influence secured by political power gives weight and dignity to their words and wishes. (SL, EBH Papers, "Woman's Kingdom" scrapbook, vol. 5, 15 July 1882)

Through organizations like the ISSA, the vote was reconceptualized as a tool for implementing an increasingly clear bourgeois program of social reform. This program was couched in gender-specific terms, the argument being that women's nature suited them particularly well for reform. Finally, the beneficiary of this reform was less often construed as women themselves (as a partially distinct interest group) and more often conceptualized as vague and abstract entities like society, the nation, the race, and civilization.

While the ISSA was articulating a vision of bourgeois reform and linking it with the suffrage cause on the state level, the Chicago Woman's Club (CWC) was functioning similarly on the city level. Established in 1876, the CWC grew out of the Fortnightly, an intellectual, literary, and artistic society founded in 1873. The impetus for the CWC has been described as follows: "it was originally organized to satisfy the desire of a group of women to be socially useful. Its founders, active in the Fortnightly, wanted to discuss current problems rather than the classic course of study the club had chosen" (Wheeler and Wortman 1977, 63). The CWC signified a turn away from purely intellectual pursuits and toward more practical involvement with social problems and humanitarian reform. The official historians of the club saw its origins in "the growth of leisure and the desire to use it well" and described its spirit as "a desire to enlarge our vision, to enable us to share in the wider interests of the community, to do our share of the world's work; we wished to prevent wrong and harm to those unable to help themselves, to bind up wounds, to create that which was lovely, to take the place of the unsightly" (Frank and Jerome 1916, 9).

The club originated the departmental form of organization which quickly spread to other women's clubs. The CWC initially consisted of four departments—home, education, philanthropy, and reform; it soon added departments of art/literature and philosophy/science. The rationale behind such organization was to match club tasks and individual temperament: "timid souls who feared that woman might get outside her sphere could surely not object to serving in the interests of the home, Mothers would all take a lively interest in education; all good church workers might lend a hand to philanthropy, and the unterrified would gravitate toward reform" (Frank and Jerome 1916, 16). Continually stressing that it was a task-oriented organization, the CWC insisted that every member be affiliated with one of its working departments, and the board calculated proportional formulas to insure each department was adequately staffed. The club attracted many trained and educated women, including teachers, lawyers, doctors, and journalists; it also attracted some who were "simply home-women, quite content to remain within the sphere of woman, then defined as limited to the fireside" (Frank and Jerome 1916, 9).

The reform ideology of the club bridged the gap between homemakers and professional women, legitimized the latter's public activities, and sanctioned conventional stereotypes of women's nature. This was accomplished by oft-repeated assertions that the city was nothing more than a greatly expanded home; just as the home required domestic labor to keep it running smoothly, so too the city required "municipal housekeeping" if it was to operate in a harmonious and cooperative manner. The stress on women's duty to the family thereby provided leverage for moving them into the public realm by equating home with community. In all of this, the CWC was not strikingly different from most other reform organizations of its day.

The distinguishing feature of the CWC was its decidedly wealthy social-class base, evidenced by the social-class backgrounds and self-perceptions of club members.[7] The club *Annals* described its membership as women of "leisure and culture" living in "the first of what could be called first-class apartments ever built in Chicago" (Frank and Jerome 1916, 16ff.). Overall, this was a reform group largely motivated by a sense of noblesse oblige toward less fortunate members of the society. This orientation contrasted sharply with the pragmatic, utilitarian, upwardly mobile orientation of reformers in organizations like the ISSA. Nevertheless, the CWC demonstrated a sincere and serious dedication to the difficult organizational work needed to implement the social changes it defined as desirable. If it was a group motivated by noblesse oblige, it was a group that took those obligations more seriously than most groups of high social rank. It was also a group that interpreted those obligations as particularly well suited to the situation of privileged women.

It is easy to document the prosperous backgrounds of CWC leaders; it is possible to make educated guesses about its membership as well. When first established, the membership fee was five dollars a year. This quickly increased to an entrance fee of fifteen dollars plus annual dues of ten dollars a year. While such fees did not guarantee an upper-class membership, they made it likely in an era when working women could not afford the fifty cents a month estimated as necessary to sustain a viable union (see Wheeler and Wortman 1977, 63, 76, for both sets of figures). Such fees and dues contrasted sharply with most reform and suffrage organizations whose dues were more nearly nominal (often one dollar a year).

The CWC exercised considerable organizational control over new membership as well. By the late 1880s the board established limitations on membership and urged a "more careful selection of new members" to insure "slower and sounder growth" of the club. These limitations took various forms: quotas were set restricting yearly growth, new positions were strictly allocated to departments on a proportional basis, members were allowed to nominate only one new member per year, new members had to wait two years before they could nominate anyone, and nominees had to be screened by a special committee and then meet the unanimous approval of the board (Frank and Jerome 1916, 64). In part, this centralized control over admissions stemmed from a desire to maintain the organization's working orientation, but such procedures also served to maintain the social base and social ideology of the club. Again, these procedures were in sharp contrast to virtually all other reform organizations, where membership simply involved signing the organizational constitution.

The CWC had little direct involvement with the suffrage cause during its first fifteen years,[8] although it supported the enfranchisement of women. A small meeting in 1885 went on record in support of woman suffrage, and the club declared its opposition to antisuffrage activity in 1887:

> October 21, 1885, Mrs. Tuley moved that all those who approved of the principle of suffrage should rise. The President asked all those to rise who desired suffrage now. Forty-five arose. The President called upon those opposed to suffrage to rise. Five rose. In November, 1887, it was stated that a member of the Home Committee desired to form inside that committee an Anti-Suffrage Society. The President declared such a society out of keeping with the character of the club. (Frank and Jerome 1916, 48)

During the 1890s the CWC attracted more women to the suffrage cause. At the same time, it contributed to the redirection of the suffrage cause toward the goals of bourgeois reform.

Most interpretations of the relation between women's organizations and the suffrage cause in this period subscribe to the "politicizing women" theme: these organizations drew out politically timid women and enlisted them in the suffrage cause. Among the processes this interpretation distorts and the Illinois data illustrate are the following: there was a simultaneous redirection of suffragism; these organizations relocated the vote in a larger reform program that was increasingly bourgeois and class conscious; this program was less politically feminist and emancipatory than that of the early suffrage movement; and the goals of these organizations had more to do with asserting their own view of the world (shaped by class affiliation, organizational position, and professional status) than they did with attracting more women to the suffrage cause per se.

These patterns describe the relations between the suffrage movement and middle- and upper-class women's organizations during the 1870s and 1880s. Analysis of working women and their organizations reveals two major points about their relation to these questions. The first is that working women, at least in Chicago, were part of the wave of women's organizing that occurred in the 1880s. The second is that unlike middle- and upper-class organizations, virtually no connections between working-class women and the suffrage movement existed in this period.

The organization of working-class women in Chicago began with the Working Women's Union founded in 1878 by socialist women including Lucy Parsons and Elizabeth Rodgers (Tax 1980). In 1881 this group affiliated with the Knights of Labor and participated in further organizing efforts. The union dissolved in the wake of the Haymarket tragedy of 1886, but was soon replaced by the Ladies Federal Labor Union established in 1888 as an AFL affiliate. This union played a prominent role in the Illinois Woman's Alliance which also formed in 1888. Tax describes the Alliance as follows:

> During the six years of its existence, the Illinois Woman's Alliance accomplished more in the way of practical reform and political education than many organizations that have lasted five times as long. . . . the Alliance drew in virtually every woman's organization in Chicago. . . . left and labor delegates led the coalition. . . . the Alliance is a key example of the merging of the labor movement and the broad women's movement under socialist leadership. . . . It deserves to be remembered because it shows what a united front can achieve. (Tax 1980, 66)

The Alliance undertook a wide range of reform work that was consistently informed by left, labor, socialist, and feminist perspectives. To summarize an interesting and complex story, it achieved numerous successes from 1888 through 1894 (including an eight-hour bill), thereby attracting powerful and wealthy opponents. Under attack from this newly mobilized opposition, the Alliance eventually splintered and dissolved in 1894, but it began an important tradition of working-class women's involvement in social reform in Chicago.

Tax's book substantiates that working-class women were active through-out the 1880s, forming organizations to defend and promote their interests. Substantiating that no significant ties existed between these working-women's organizations and the suffrage movement is more awkward because it requires documenting a nonevent. The strongest evidence is simply that in all documents examined from the suffrage movement and its leaders in this period—documents that contained literally hundreds of references to the WCTU and dozens of references to the ISSA and CWC—not a single mention of the women's unions or the Illinois Woman's Alliance was found. Judging from the records left by the organized suffrage movement, such working-class organizations did not exist.[9]

Meredith Tax mentions one thin link between the suffrage movement and the Illinois Woman's Alliance—the Cook County Suffrage Association under the leadership of Caroline Hurling. During the late 1880s this organization was part of the Alliance, and Hurling played a prominent role in Alliance activities. Hurling and the Cook County Association brought to the suffrage issue a working-class perspective that was much more attuned to the social disruptions of industrialization and urbanization than the IWSA's perspective. Perhaps for this reason the Cook County Suffrage Association was isolated from the IWSA and the rest of the organized suffrage movement in Illinois; virtually no references to this organization were found in standard suffrage documents. In sum, no evidence exists of any significant organizational connection between the suffrage movement and working-class women in this period.

The relation between the suffrage movement and many working women during the 1880s was symbolized by a telling incident that occurred during the 1880 NWSA convention in Chicago. In August of that year Harbert reprinted in "Woman's Kingdom" a letter from a Mrs. Bishop. The letter asked why no suffrage association existed in the state or city of Chicago and criticized the national convention proceedings because much time had been devoted to reading "hundreds of silly, non-sensical cards," but

when three delegates from the only woman's organization in this State presented their credentials from a body of sixty-eight intelligent women, they were denied the notice given to the postal cards. They did not go expecting to run the convention. They desired only to place on record the wage-working women of Chicago. They were denied recognition on the flimsy excuse that they were not members of the association. Imagine how easy it would be for a woman making shirts for 40 cents a dozen to spare a dollar, that sum being necessary to buy a membership. (SL, EBH Papers, "Woman's Kingdom" scrapbook, vol. 3, 16 August 1880, 24)

That same month Anthony wrote Harbert with another reference to the incident: "I have a most remarkable letter from Mrs. Chandler who tells me we snubbed the working women of Chicago—I sure heard nothing of any such—Then I find Mrs. Bishop's open letter in the *Inter-Ocean* to you" (HL, EBH Papers, Anthony to Harbert, 5 August 1880).

Both Harbert and Anthony responded that neither organization policy nor personal preference sanctioned such treatment. Harbert, writing for the public, said "somebody blundered because the sympathies and intense interest of every officer of the National Woman Suffrage Association center about our working women" (SL, EBH Papers, "Woman's Kingdom" scrapbook, vol. 3, 16 August 1880, 24). Anthony, writing in private to Harbert, said, "I surely would not have refused any representative sent by 76 more or less working women" (HL, EBH Papers, Anthony to Harbert, 5 August 1880). These statements gain further plausibility since the NWSA needed all the support it could get and would have welcomed such support on purely instrumental grounds.

The significance of this event resides in what it implied about the overall relation between the suffrage movement and working women. First, it implied that the organization's membership dues could function to exclude women who could not easily afford to join. Neither Harbert nor Anthony spoke to this issue in their responses. Second, that Bishop was unaware of the IWSA implied that the organization was not making any significant overtures toward a working-class constituency. Her ignorance could not simply be dismissed, as Anthony's letter did, by claiming that Bishop had not been "very wide awake." Finally, whatever really happened, the symbolic snub of working-class women must have contributed to their suspicions about the middle-class nature of the suffrage movement—suspicions that could not be overcome merely by statements of good intentions and formal resolutions sending "cordial greetings to the brave working-women."

As women became more differentiated by social class throughout this period and as they began to organize around their class interests, the suffrage movement became more closely associated with the middle and upper classes and even more distant from working women and the perspective of the working class. In the mid 1880s these trends crystallized with the publication of a new women's paper.

THE *NEW ERA* AND THE NEW FEMINISM

In January 1885 Elizabeth Harbert published the first issue of a newspaper called *New Era*. Like many of its predecessors, the paper failed financially in less than two years. During its brief existence, however, it publicized the leading ideas of the suffrage movement; its columns enrich our sense of the movement in the mid-1880s in the same way that Livermore's *Agitator* characterized the movement in the late 1860s. The most prominent themes in *New Era* involved the relation of suffrage to temperance, the need for greater organization of the movement, the changing ideological orientation of the movement, the concern with social control, the appearance of female opposition to woman suffrage, the movement's lack of concern with economic and class issues, and the movement's attempts to link the suffrage cause with other class reforms.

The columns of *New Era* reinforced the notion that woman suffrage and temperance were complementary reforms. An article by Helen Gougar celebrated the rapid growth of prosuffrage sentiment within the WCTU. In 1881 a prosuffrage resolution did not even draw a second within the WCTU; in 1885 it passed with only one dissenting vote. According to Gougar, the change occurred when women realized that temperance goals were not likely to be achieved without the ballot. Gougar did not ponder— or consider important—the possible contradictions between the temperance cause and the suffrage movement's orientation to reform. For her, and presumably for others in the movement as well, there were no inconsistencies between granting a right to women and their use of that right to restrict the behavior of other groups. Instead, both were seen as part of a larger reform effort to change the society (ISHS, *New Era*, December 1885, 375).

New Era also underscored the need for better organization if suffrage was to be won. May Wright Sewall called for a truly national suffrage movement to overcome the perception that woman suffrage was "as much a form of Northern fanaticism as abolition was" (ISHS, *New Era*, January 1885, 18). Sewall recommended that a NWSA convention be held in New Orleans to demonstrate the truly national scope of the suffrage movement.[10] Harbert's proposals for greater organization were more global. In "Mothers to the Rescue" she called for a united front of women's organizations (ranging from the NWSA and AWSA to the WCTU and the American Association of Women) to elect candidates favorable to their political interests. Noting that men were divided into competing organizations and parties, Harbert implied that united and organized women could exercise a significant "power behind the throne" (ISHS, *New Era*, September 1885, 282–283).

New Era also promoted changes in suffragist ideology that reversed the orientation of the early suffrage movement. For example, the December 1885 issue reported on the IWSA convention and its reaffirmation of the 1848 Seneca Falls resolutions.[11] However, this endorsement of early movement ideology was at odds with the posture expressed in "The Ideal Home" by Harbert. This article expressed a highly sentimental view of relations between the sexes—a view that rested on notions of sex-specific traits and stereotypic sex roles. Harbert described woman as the queen of the home who was "uncrowned" by virtue of her disenfranchisement. As a result, the "law of the mother," based on her "Godgiven woman-nature," was not enforced anywhere, and society suffered from numerous social ills. Harbert's conclusion tied women's nature to the demand for political power: "We accept our woman's sphere, glorious almost infinite in its opportunities and responsibilities, but by all the sacred rights of motherhood we demand, that *the hand that rocks the cradle shall help to rule the world*" (ISHS, *New Era*, February 1885, 42; emphasis in original). Through such arguments the movement built a new foundation for demanding the vote—a foundation that was notably less critical of the social order than the earlier movement.

A fourth theme evident in *New Era* was a concern with social control. Typifying this tendency was "A Higher Order of Amusements": "Popular amusements are a fact because they are a necessity; but they should be controlled. Amusement is not an *end* but a means, for the refreshing and the strengthening of both mind and body. . . . when amusement is made the *principal* object of pursuit and not its effect, it should be checked, lest in this pursuit the mental and bodily power be overstrained and enfeebled" (ISHS, *New Era*, January 1885, 13). Particular condemnation was reserved for those amusements that interfered with "hours intended for sleep," that competed with work and the "business of life," that aroused unlawful passions and morbid appetites, and that weakened "respect for nobility of character or reverence of spiritual truths." A class component was evident in this concern with social control, and special attention was called to "a large class who have not money for the comforts of life, yet find means sufficient to secure admission to low amusement halls" (ISHS, *New Era*, January 1885, 13). The article concluded by calling for a more rationalized and controlled form of amusement that would be "uplifting" rather than "debilitating" and that would build a sound, moral, national character by reinforcing the work ethic. Such articles signified the origins of what would become an increasingly professional, class-conscious, middle-class response to social ills that permeated both lower and upper classes.[12] The solution to these ills was sought in more effective mechanisms of social control to preserve, protect, and extend the vision of social order that middle-class reformers cherished and that they saw as challenged by powerful social forces on all sides.

New Era also provided some of the earliest advice on the problem of female opposition to woman suffrage.[13] Commenting on the role of women in defeating a suffrage measure in New York State, Frances Trumbull redefined this event as progress from the standpoint of politicizing women: "Next in value to the woman who breaks out of her sphere to demand the ballot, is the woman who breaks out of her sphere to oppose it"(ISHS, *New Era*, August 1885, 227). Trumbull suggested that the most important goal of the movement at that point was to draw all women into the discussion. If that were done, she claimed, "I have no fear of the result." Expressing the same confidence, she commented on a *Nation* article proposing that woman suffrage required "taking the sense of women on it": "The editor did not notice that in that sentence he was conceding the principle of our claim. When women have the right to say at the ballot box whether women shall be allowed to vote or not, Woman's Suffrage is already won" (ISHS, *New Era*, August 1885, 229). From this point, the movement devoted increasing attention to the organized antisuffrage movement and to countering its arguments against the ballot for women.

The letters column of the paper provided an outlet for other voices. Two letters that were atypical of *New Era*'s orientation came from Lucinda Chandler (implicitly criticizing the movement's narrowed approach) and from Frances Kelley (explicitly criticizing the suffrage movement for its middle-class bias).

Chandler's letter was reminiscent of the early movement's focus on how women's multiple status contributed to their oppression:

What we call civilization has achieved its successes and blessings largely, and in numerous instances, by an appropriation of the products of woman's labor and vitality. . . . [Today woman is] compelled to choose between a life of treadmill toil that is slavery, or the abandonment of womanly honor and purity. In marriage, too, she holds a position outwardly honorable on no less humiliating terms. . . . If the clergy and church would denounce unrighteous employers, who steal the vitality of women by starvation wages, who drive many homeless and despairing girls into brothels, or marriages of convenience they would establish a most effective divorce prevention league. (ISHS, *New Era*, September 1885, 279)

This analysis of the interrelationship of these factors was an ideological refugee from the early movement. Its appearance demonstrated that such a perspective was not yet gone, but neither was it still typical of the movement's orientation.

The other interesting entry came from Florence Kelley (Wischnewetzky), who wrote from Heidelberg several years before her migration to Chicago and subsequent involvement in the settlement house movement. In two letters she criticized the movement in the United States for excessive concern with middle-class issues and for ignoring the needs of working women and the working class generally. She wrote:

I do not think that our movement, in its present phase, represents the mass of American working women in *practical work*. That is, our organs and conventions discuss higher education and the laws affecting married women's property and the need of property-holding women getting school suffrage. . . . When I want to learn anything about immediate practical work in the interests of working-women, I am obliged to lay aside my [suffrage papers] and turn—it was a great surprise to me to make the discovery—to the organ of the working-men—the N.Y. Volkszeitung. (ISHS, *New Era*, May 1885, 150)

Kelley described working-class opposition to a bill that would have led to greater exploitation of women workers in sweatshops, concluding:

For what can we expect but contempt from working-men, if while we take good care of laws for the benefit of property-holding women while working for the ballot, we leave the working women's protective laws to the working-men to care for? . . . The foregoing extract is only one of a dozen in the course of a month. . . . It makes me thoroughly uncomfortable. It seems to show such a one-sided activity on our part, such a want of sympathy with the hard-struggling thousands, who we, of all people, ought to represent, and defend, and protect. (ISHS, *New Era*, May 1885, 150)

A second letter from Kelley informed *New Era* readers of the English translation of August Bebel's *Woman in the Past, Present, and Future* and recommended it to American audiences in particular. Her characterization of the American movement merits lengthy quotation for the way she touched on questions of class and economics:

> The especial value of the book for American women, however, is the fact that it deals with the economic side of the woman question with a force and clearness which has hitherto been sadly wanting in our literature of the subject. The legal, educational and political ideas of the question have been effectually discussed and investigated in America; the economic side has received, in proportion, amazingly little attention. (ISHS, *New Era*, July 1885, 215–216)

After discussing starvation wages, pay differentials between men and women, the growing power of employers, and the growth of prostitution, Kelley drew the following contrast between the American and German movements:

> It is difficult in these days to realize that this is really reactionary Germany, the movement among women is so many sided, so spontaneous, so widely diffused geographically; and it has one feature which distinguishes it radically from the woman movements of England and America—it does not proceed from the pecuniarily comfortable class struggling for political, civil and educational equality. The German movement is primarily one of the workers striving for a chance to live and work—without starving and slaving. (ISHS, *New Era*, July 1885, 215–216)

While *New Era* expressed the dominant themes of the movement in the late 1880s, the letters from Chandler and Kelley struck different minor chords and indicated that less than complete consensus existed on the movement's new orientation.

A final theme of interest in *New Era* involves the connections it sought and expressed between woman suffrage and a class-conscious vision of reform and social change. An article entitled "Progressive Tendencies or Stagnation" claimed that the Western world had always been distinguished by progressive social development, but this progression was currently threatened by a variety of negative forces: "Proletarianism is on the increase and insanity is in proportion to the financial pressure, which robs the poor and enriches the rich. Political corruption and bribery are admitted as factors to success and the judiciary is venal and corrupt. . . . A new impulse must rule civilization to guide and save it" (ISHS, *New Era*, December 1885, 355). The author discovered the needed impulse in woman's character and virtues, but these had to be freed through the vote to achieve the desired effect. Cast in this light, "the question of Woman Suffrage . . . is not a question of reform but of evolutionary progress" (ISHS, *New Era*, December 1885, 353–356).

If, for some, woman suffrage was demanded by social evolution, for others woman suffrage was consistent with some of the principles of populism. William Harbert's "A Plea for the People" presented a utilitarian argument for including the greatest number in political processes if the maximum good was to be achieved. Harbert contrasted the common sense of the "intelligent masses" with the specialized knowledge of experts, arguing for the superiority of the former. He then proceeded to argue as follows:

> Away with all order of nobility not based on manhood and womanhood, on character, on personal and reciprocal duty! In this country a sham aristocracy exists, based on the tripod of education, wealth and family. The first of these we have considered; the second is too fickle and sordid to notice, while the true verdict of heraldry is based on this instruction, give the greatest honor to him who can trace his ancestral line most directly to the least civilized barbarian. The men who depend on their own ability, who think their own thoughts and go through the world without artificial aids and with no flourish of trumpets are, though not yet recognized, the men of real worth and the true heroes of the race. (ISHS, *New Era*, May 1885, 131)

Despite these populist premises, Harbert retreated from the seemingly egalitarian implications by literally borrowing a page from his wife's *Inter-Ocean* column cited above:

> The rich, the poor, the high and the low should work together in "symmetrical diversity." . . . The correlation of opposing forces produces harmonious action. Freedom of natural development will produce the highest progress, and a "homogenous unity out of apparent contradications." Let the desire for reciprocal good be the basis and object, and the result is best attained by diversity of labor. (ISHS, *New Era*, May 1885, 129–33)

William Harbert concluded by calling for the enfranchisement of women; but once again suffrage was advocated as part of a larger program for change on behalf of increasingly well-defined middle-class interests.

The themes discussed above describe the orientation of *New Era* under Harbert's editorship; they also convey many of the concerns of the suffrage movement itself during this period. In its growing connection with temperance, its greater stress on organization, its new forms of ideology, its concern with social control, its attentiveness to female opposition, its insensitivity to class and economic factors, and its increasingly class-conscious voice, the movement in the 1880s had became distinctly different from the movement of the 1860s. Understanding these differences requires an analysis of the broader social context within which these movement transformations occurred.

THE SOCIAL CONTEXT OF MOVEMENT TRANSFORMATION

The transformation of the suffrage movement is evident when one contrasts the scope of the movement's early and middle periods. Briefly reiterated, early movement breadth was evidenced by the ballot demand itself, the multiple legal demands, the critique of the sexual division of labor, and the attempted alliances with other dispossessed groups challenging wealth and power. The movement in the middle period was more ambiguous on each of these dimensions.

Considering the last dimension first, it is clear that during the 1870s and 1880s the suffrage movement continued to be part of a larger alliance, but it is equally clear that this alliance differed from that of the Civil War period. The shift in movement alliances involved the evaporation of ties with abolitionists, working women, and labor and the creation of ties with temperance, moral reform, and social purity groups.[14] This shift constituted one aspect of the transformation of the suffrage movement; it altered the movement's reform program from one that challenged prevailing institutions and practices to one that defended those institutions and practices. This was one reason why suffrage ideology and rhetoric became much more ameliorationist during this period. While the movement did not abandon calls for social change, the change it called for was consistent with the prevailing social order rather than resistant of it. Thus, movement transformation was evident from its changing alliances in the middle period.

The transformation of the third dimension was most apparent in the new acceptance of gender-specific traits that supposedly distinguished the sexes. A strong elective affinity exists between endorsing gender-specific traits and sanctioning the sexual division of labor. Harbert's orientation, which increasingly became the movement's as well, exemplified this affinity. While she continued to seek increased opportunities for women outside of their sphere, her general orientation accepted and promoted the division of the world into separate spheres and argued for women's superior and privileged position in the domestic sphere.[15] Harbert did not question the separate spheres notion and the sexual division of labor as much as she argued for the expansion of one of those spheres to encompass the larger social world outside the confines of the home.

The movement did not fully retreat on this question; another illustration conveys the complexity of its posture. One source of seeming continuity from the earlier period was the movement's ongoing criticism of economic and marital oppression. But notable changes occurred in these criticisms. The movement showed less awareness of economic and marital oppression as institutional sources of women's disadvantaged position; instead it tended to view these forms of oppression as individual and exceptional aberrations. While the early movement never launched a frontal attack on marriage, it had hinted that the marital form itself, and its connections to other institutions, was the root of women's difficulties. In the middle period the movement recognized that occasionally individual marriages might fail for largely idiosyncratic reasons, but generally it gave unqualified endorsement to the form itself.

A second difference from the early period was that less attention was paid to the mutually reinforcing character of economic and marital dependence. Traces of this earlier view could be found in Harbert's 1871 book, but even this statement was qualified. What disappeared was a wholistic analysis of women's position as shaped by multiple institutions. Once this was lost, it became easier for the movement to endorse relationships it had formerly criticized, easier to see problems as idiosyncratic rather than structural, and easier to defend institutions that it had formerly questioned. It would be misleading to overdraw these differences and imply that the early movement was uniformly critical on these issues and that the later movement was completely quiescent. But it is clear that the direction of change was from a more critical to a less critical posture toward the sexual division of labor and that this change constituted an important aspect of movement transformation in the middle period.

Changes in the movement's legal demands were equally complex, and they too were an important aspect of movement transformation. Most relevant were changes in the types of legislation the movement sought for implementing its programs. The legal changes sought by the early movement were emancipatory with respect to women as an interest group—that is, even where individual mobility and opportunity were stressed, the impact of demanded legal changes eliminated (or rendered illegal) restrictions that impinged on women's entrance into the public sphere or their legal defense of themselves in the private sphere. The legal changes the movement sought in the middle period included demands that would have imposed restrictions on various elements of society. These later demands were both less emancipatory and less directed to women as a politically constituted interest group.

Some of these restrictive statutes were consistent with the intent of the early movement to provide women with a legal defense against the exercise of social power by men.[16] On balance, however, such demands were a minority plank in the movement's program for legal change in the middle period. More typical were proposed statutes intended to control groups that violated middle-class reformers' conceptions of socially appropriate behavior. Much of the legislation proposed by the temperance, social purity, and moral reform movements—movements that continually intersected with the suffrage movement in this period—reflected this social control impulse.[17]

Hence, transformation did not involve a reduction in the number of legal changes the movement sought; rather it involved alteration of the types of changes sought and the purposes they would serve. The emancipatory thrust of the early movement did not completely disappear, but it acquired a lower priority than the social control interests of the movement. These interests, in turn, derived from the ambitions of middle-class reformers to shape society as a whole and to restrict the activities of certain groups in the process.

The last aspect of movement transformation concerned the ballot demand itself. The meaning of this demand changed partly because the movement won other victories; thus the ballot no longer connoted the same symbolic challenge to women's subordination. Of greater interest were changes in the perceived scope of the ballot and in its relation to the themes of independence, rights, and justice. Although the ballot remained the most important demand of the movement through the 1870s and 1880s, the demand itself connoted a more limited concept of social change than it had in the earlier period. In fact, it was in the middle period, and for the first time, that some movement members went out of their way to stress that the ballot for women did not portend a radical change. This view was evident in frequent reassurances that the family, "womanliness," and other cultural constructs would not only remain intact but would actually be strengthened with the granting of the ballot. To draw the sharpest contrast, where early leaders saw the ballot as delivering a single massive blow to women's subordination, later leaders were just as likely to present the ballot as a means of reinforcing prevailing institutions. In this sense, the movement in the middle period operated with a transformed perception of the ballot demand.[18]

A final way of construing transformation involved the movement's emerging preference for expediency arguments over justice arguments (Kraditor 1965). As long as the vote was firmly tied to independence and justice arguments, it retained an inherent challenge to prevailing forms of dependency and injustice. Detached from this foundation, the ballot demand became a kind of floating currency that could be attached to any number of reforms. The only common feature of these reforms, in turn, was that they minimized the politically feminist implications of the demand for female suffrage.[19]

Having considered each dimension of the movement's scope, it appears that, at the very least, the movement's challenge to patriarchal power became more ambiguous in the middle period. In many instances, as the movement adopted more conservative positions than it had formerly taken, these changes culminated in a narrower and less fundamental challenge to this power. Without denying the lingering persistence of diverse elements in the movement, it seems equally undeniable that the emergence of a narrower view of women's emancipation was the dominant trend in the suffrage movement during these decades.

This pattern of movement transformation can only be interpreted by locating the movement in its sociohistorical context and by examining changes occurring in that context. It seems plausible to hypothesize that as a social context changes in major ways over significant amounts of time, social movements that survive the changes will register their effects in demonstrable ways. A conceptual framework for studying these connections is summarized in table 4.1. The following discussion is organized around three mediating links between social change and movement transformation: social class, organizational form, and ideological stance.

The first question is whether the social-class base of the suffrage movement changed from the early to the middle period. This question is surprisingly difficult to answer for there is no reliable information on the membership and only sketchy information on the leadership. Based on available sources, it appears that the class base of the movement did not change significantly. This was clear in the case of the middle period's most prominent leader, Elizabeth Boynton Harbert, whose class/occupational profile closely resembles that of leaders from the early period.[20] If any noteworthy change occurred, it probably involved a greater role for professional women. Again, Harbert typified this shift from early leaders whose occupations were often intermittent to later figures whose occupations were more continuous, specialized, and careerlike. But through the 1880s this professionalization of movement leadership was a relatively moderate tendency.

While the class base of the suffrage movement did not change dramatically from the early to middle period, the class situation of its middle-class leadership changed significantly. During these decades the middle class underwent a process of formation that profoundly affected its class consciousness. E. P. Thompson has described the process of class formation in general: "class is a relationship, not a thing, . . . we cannot understand class unless we see it as a social and cultural formation, arising from processes which can only be studied as they work themselves out over a considerable historical period" (Thompson 1963, 11). This notion of "the

TABLE 4.1
Conceptual Framework for Analyzing Movement Transformation

Social change			Movement transformations
Background processes ———→	Key changes ————————→	Mediating links ———→	Indicators of movement transformation
	Class structure		
	Class consciousness		Conception of vote
Capitalism		Class	
	Middle-class formation		Diversity of demands
Industrialization		Organization	
	Differentiation of women		Sexual division of labor
Urbanization	Immigration	Ideology	
	New economic role for women		Reform alliances/coalitions

making" of a class is crucial to an understanding of the U.S. middle class in the 1870s and 1880s, for in this period the middle class carved out a new role in an industrializing and capitalist society—a role that included a particular stance toward class conflicts between capitalists and workers.

This new role can be appreciated by contrasting the meaning of a middle-class orientation in the early and middle periods. The worldview of middle-class suffragists was class conditioned in both periods; that is, it was shaped by their particular location in class structure. But whereas that worldview was "class blind" in the earlier period, it became strikingly class conscious in the middle period. The perspective of middle-class suffragists shifted from minimizing the enduring significance of class factors (and generalizing their own class prospects to all sectors of society) to acknowledging this enduring significance as well as their distinctive location within class structure.

This change culminated in a new posture toward the class system itself—a posture in which the middle class assumed the ideological task of reconciling the conflicts and mediating the tensions between conflicting social classes in the name of a "unified society." Middle-class spokespersons worked at this task by calling for a stabilization and rationalization of the social order and by underscoring the need for harmony, equilibrium, and symmetry. Applied to class conflict, this position amounted to a minimization of such conflict and a call for greater social unity across class lines. Elizabeth Harbert typified the impact of this process of class formation on the orientation of the suffrage movement, as evidenced by her general reform activities, her involvement in social science associations, and her journalistic work.

As suffragists adopted this posture and spoke for "society," their feminist views increasingly conflicted with this class-conscious vision of how society should be organized. Middle-class feminists found it necessary to engage in a dual negotiation: reconciling the contradictions of classes as well as the contradictions between their feminism and middle-class consciousness. In short, when their feminism led these women to question fundamental aspects of social organization, their class consciousness led them to proceed with caution since many of these fundamental aspects of social organization corresponded nicely with their class-conscious perception of the world. One reason for the diversity of "feminisms" that emerged in this period involved this new tension between gender and class. The "feminisms" were attempted resolutions of the often contradictory imperatives associated with being members of an advantaged class and an oppressed gender.

If "class blindness" contributed to the breadth of the early movement, so did the many sharply drawn legal and sociocultural differences between men and women. Some of these factors that made it plausible to see the world as fundamentally divided into two gender groups changed in the intervening period, in part because of the very successes of the movement. As it won gains by removing legal restrictions and cultural confinements on women, the movement made important contributions to their freedom. But these gains did not emancipate an abstraction called "Woman"; they lifted some gender restrictions from particular women who were also members of increasingly conscious and distinct social classes. In this sense, women became "free" to be "determined" by their class location and situation.

Thus, movement accomplishments in the areas of legal status and cultural practice contributed to the social differentiation of women—a process already underway as a result of industrialization and urbanization. As more women moved into the public sphere in response to these changes, they became more differentiated in terms of employment, occupation, education, organizational involvements, and the like. While these processes did not automatically undermine a view of the world as fundamentally divided into gender groups,[21] they made that view more complex and multifaceted. It thereby became increasingly difficult to maintain a broad, politically feminist ideology at the basis of the suffrage movement.

A final contrast can be drawn in terms of the circle of beneficiaries relative to movement goals. Compared to the earlier period, this circle changed in several ways through the 1880s. First, the core group of prime beneficiaries expanded as more middle-class women entered public roles on the basis of their education, employment, and other organizational involvements; these women stood to benefit most from the accomplishment of movement goals. At the same time, the outer boundary of this symbolic circle of beneficiaries contracted in two ways. As the movement narrowed its program to the vote alone, it cast off some earlier political goals that might have benefited a wider group of women (or benefited women in more ways). The circle also shrunk by no longer including working-class women to the same degree, as evidenced by the lack of any meaningful inclusion of working-class women's interests in the movement's program for change during these decades.

The symbolic meaning of falling outside the circle of beneficiaries also changed. Earlier, this had simply meant that a group was unaffected by the movement's program for change. Now it came to mean that a group might be negatively affected by the suffrage movement's program for social change. This applied, for instance, to those reforms more concerned with the social control of nonnative groups than with the emancipation of women. A final contrast that cannot be captured by the circle metaphor involves the definition of the movement's prime beneficiary as society at large. Perhaps this change was the most significant for it transcended specifically female beneficiaries altogether.

A second mediating link between social context and movement transformation involved organizational dynamics and processes. The decades of the 1870s and 1880s saw the persistence of rival suffrage organizations on the national level. Traces of the national rivalry between the NWSA and AWSA filtered down to the state level at various times during these two decades, particularly when the national organizations held major conventions and meetings in Chicago. On balance, however, the impact of this rivalry on the local suffrage movement was minor, partly because Harbert had aligned the IWSA with the NWSA and partly because the AWSA had little power in the Midwest. More important, however, this affiliation did little to constrain the Illinois movement. The organization remained free to develop its own orientation and define its own issues with little pressure from the national association. The standard image of a suffrage movement divided between two competing camps had little relevance in Illinois, and perhaps in other states as well.

On the local level, the 1870s and 1880s were distinctive as the only time when no organizational rivalry existed over the leadership of the suffrage movement in Illinois. The IWSA had no direct competitor for leadership of the movement; organizational pressures toward transformation therefore did not occur in this manner. Also little evidence suggests internal struggle and conflict within the IWSA over its orientation and program. Its major goal throughout this period was introducing greater coordination and tighter organization throughout the state, and its success in accomplishing this relatively modest goal was limited.

Having eliminated national rivalries, local schisms, and internal conflicts as possible causes of movement transformation, it becomes clear that the real organizational struggle of the Illinois suffrage movement in this period was to maintain its existence as an autonomous organization with a strong political voice at a time when numerous other women's organizations entered the market and competed for movement followers. The IWSA survived, but it periodically lost its political voice while attempting to survive amidst the rapid growth of other organizations. These other organizations reflected the growing social differentiation of women and the new public roles becoming available to them. Most of these organizations were less political than the suffrage movement, and their success in recruiting followers made it more difficult for the IWSA to simultaneously maintain its following and its original orientation.

This situation is best illustrated by (though hardly limited to) the relations between the suffrage and temperance movements. The Illinois data are in agreement with the standard wisdom that temperance recruited more women than suffrage and that temperance followers eventually supported the suffrage cause. There is considerable room for disagreement, however, in the further argument that temperance radicalized otherwise conservative women, thereby drawing them into the suffrage movement (see, e.g., Flexner 1975). The Illinois data suggest that the transformation of the suffrage cause was at least as important as the politicization of temperance women. The temperance movement contributed to the transformation of the suffrage cause by forging a strong link between the demand for the vote and the defense of the home. Once this occurred, even conservative women felt comfortable participating in the suffrage movement.

The impact of organizational factors on movement transformation may now be summarized. The background processes of capitalist industrialization and urbanization combined with several gains of the early movement to promote the social differentiation of women. One result was a rapid increase in the number and variety of women's organizations. Pressures toward transformation were then evident in a general and a specific way. In general, this plethora of women's organizations encouraged a corresponding multitude of possible stances toward the suffrage cause, most of which were decidedly less political than the orientation of the early suffrage movement. This general situation assumed a more particular form through the WCTU. On the basis of its popularity, its very existence forced concessions from the suffrage movement. These concessions transformed and depoliticized the suffrage movement; they thereby opened the door to women whose primary interest was temperance and moral reform and who reinforced the trend toward transformation.[22]

Parallel arguments may be made about the role of ideology—the third mediating link between social context and movement transformation. Seen through the lens of ideology, the same social differentiation of women produced a wide range of feminist ideologies. These orientations were earlier described as domestic feminism, moral feminism, professional feminism, and political feminism.[23] All of these ideological orientations were present in the early and broad phase of the suffrage movement. In the early period, however, these diverse orientations intersected and were focused through the political dimension; this was necessary given the restrictions on women's activities. In the middle period, by contrast, these diverse ideologies became relatively autonomous and competing ways of conceptualizing the meaning of a feminist orientation and movement. Once the political dimension of feminism lost its privileged status as the lens that focused all types of feminist thought—once it became simply one possible orientation among others—the stage was set for transformation.

An earlier discussion of movement ideology proposed the notion of "endogenous selective mechanisms" to refer to the choices that social actors make within a larger set of social constraints. At the precise moment the stage had been set for transformation, the lead role fell to Elizabeth Harbert, and she made choices that pushed the suffrage movement toward a different ideology. In her tendency to subordinate justice arguments to expediency arguments, in her sense that women's rights should be subordinated to women's duties, in her willingness to define the issue as human rights and not women's rights, in her belief in sex-specific traits and the overriding significance of motherhood, and in her broader social ideology of ameliorationist reform, Harbert pushed the Illinois suffrage movement in a new direction.[24] Through these transvaluations, a movement seeking justice and equality for women was replaced by one more concerned with bettering society through the expansion of womanly influence. At times these orientations could and did coexist in Harbert's ideology and the larger movement, and they could coexist because they were not mutually exclusive. But neither were they completely isomorphic. When these orientations pulled in opposing directions, Harbert and the movement increasingly opted for the latter.

The Illinois data suggest that a continuing theme in the suffrage movement was the danger of a political movement for women's emancipation becoming subordinated to other goals. In the earlier period this subordination occurred relative to other causes like abolitionism, until eventually the movement was forced to establish its autonomy in the events of 1869. Once won, this independence was not easily maintained. In the 1870s and 1880s other causes and organizations raised similar problems for the suffrage movement. Its organizations survived this challenge, but in the process they were forced to reconceptualize the beneficiary of the movement in all the ways we have documented. That this is more than a post facto judgment can be seen in the writings of Susan B. Anthony, who not only did much to achieve the independence of 1869 but who also remained deeply concerned about the ways a different kind of subordination threatened the movement throughout the 1870s and 1880s. Though she pointed eloquently to these dangers, she could not prevent them from affecting the suffrage movement.

FIVE

A Specialized Movement, 1890–1920

While the middle period of the suffrage movement was one of declining momentum, the final period saw a reversal of this trend. From 1890 to 1910 the movement in Illinois gradually gathered momentum and began to win some limited victories. From 1910 through 1913 the pace of movement activity quickened, culminating in the adoption of the Presidential Suffrage Bill. While this law did not completely enfranchise Illinois women, it provided all the voting rights that were practically possible at that time, and the Illinois victory contributed to the momentum of the national campaign which itself culminated in the federal amendment victory of 1919.

As the Illinois movement came closer to winning suffrage, it continued to change in response to various circumstances. At the most general level it remained a narrowed movement; it never returned to the broad agenda of the early period. However, the later movement was substantially different from the narrowed one that had survived the 1870s and 1880s, in part because it became more receptive to some groups it had shunned in the middle period. In many ways the concept of a specialized movement best fits this later period, for while the movement focused more exclusively than ever on the vote, it did so in a way that attracted the support of a large and diverse body of allies.

This chapter focuses on the distinctive features of movement transformation in the twentieth century. As in earlier chapters, explanations for the movement's posture will be sought in the larger social context in which it operated. Of particular importance in understanding the final period are changes in both the class base and class situation of the movement leadership. In Illinois, the twentieth century brought greater participation in the movement by upper-class women and professional women, who incorporated the suffrage cause into the agenda of the Progressive movement.

Alongside these changes in class structure were ongoing changes in the social differentiation of women—a process that, already begun in the middle period, continued to affect its orientation. As in earlier periods, these aspects of the movement's social context shaped its orientation and its program for change, and they provide the best explanation of the movement's transformed posture in the twentieth century.

This chapter is divided into several sections. The first presents a brief chronological overview of movement accomplishments from 1890 through 1910; these accomplishments were important both for the momentum and the strategies they provided for later battles. The next section describes the wide diversity of groups that were either recruited into the cause or came to support it for their own reasons. This broad base of support—including both upper-class and working-class women and their organizations—was essential to the eventual suffrage victory. The third section considers prevailing forms of suffrage ideology in the final period, including the manner in which antisuffrage sentiment shaped the arguments that suffragists made for the vote. The fourth section chronicles the key events leading up to the suffrage victory in Illinois in 1913 when the state legislature granted women all the voting rights it was constitutionally capable of providing. The final section analyzes the transformed posture of the movement in the twentieth century and explains that posture vis-à-vis the social context of the later movement.

BUILDING MOMENTUM

The suffrage movement won its first concrete victory in 1891 when the state legislature passed a school suffrage bill drafted by the WCTU, supported by the IESA, and sponsored by state Democrats.[1] Since the same legislature had previously rejected a larger suffrage measure, the school suffrage measure was probably a compromise intended to mollify suffragists and their supporters. In actual impact the bill was extremely limited—it enfranchised women to vote for elective school offices only. Even so, the bill's constitutionality was quickly challenged and a series of court decisions limited its power still more. In effect, the courts decided that voting was permissible for legislatively created school offices, but not for those offices established by the state constitution. Given these restrictions and the fact that most school offices were appointed rather than elected, the increase in women's political power as a result of these actions was minimal.

The real significance of the 1891 school suffrage bill was technical and symbolic rather than practical. Technically, the bill established the precedent that the legislature could regulate suffrage concerning all the offices it had created. This decision reversed a prior judicial opinion that all voting privileges could only be granted by amendments to the state constitution. Thus, the decision opened up a legal wedge which the movement later used to great advantage in pursuing other limited forms of suffrage in Illinois.[2] The decision was equally important in more symbolic ways. For the first time in four decades of women's rights and suffrage agitation the state legislature had acted favorably on a woman suffrage bill. The decision encouraged the movement by indicating that legal change, however humble, was in fact possible. The 1891 bill thereby affirmed the general goal of the suffrage movement and also endorsed the particular strategies and tactics associated with its passage.

The events of 1891 shaped the legislative strategy of the suffrage movement in 1893, when the IESA sponsored a township suffrage bill modeled on the school suffrage bill. Supported by a letter-writing campaign and a petition with twelve thousand signatures, the bill passed the Senate but was referred back to committee in the House, thereby failing to pass the legislature. An attempt was made to repeal the school suffrage bill of 1891 in this session, but the measure was defeated in the House and failed to come to a vote in the Senate. Thus, while 1893 did not bring new gains, it saw a successful defense of the suffragist gain of 1891 (see Beldon 1913, 34–35; and *HWS* 4:601).

While suffragists were failing to extract concessions from the legislature in 1893, the Columbian Exposition was succeeding in mobilizing individuals and organizations who would eventually play a major role in the suffrage campaign. The Women's Congress at the fair expressed and encouraged the tendency for middle- and upper-class women to form organizations and pursue causes. While most of these activities were nonfeminist and apolitical, Stone and Anthony jointly organized a World's Congress of Representative Women which raised political issues and provided important publicity to the cause of suffrage. The IESA canceled their annual convention and participated in the congress instead, contributing to the total attendance of over one hundred fifty thousand people at the week-long congress. Within the congress, "the meetings on women's rights to vote pulled the biggest crowds, with more than 10,000 attending" (Wheeler and Wortman 1977, 67).

Perhaps the most significant aspect of the fair was that it mobilized truly upper-class women for eventual participation in the suffrage movement.

Bertha Palmer and Ellen Henrotin were good examples of upper-class women who played prominent organizational roles in the Exposition, subsequently became involved in other women's causes, and ultimately lent their considerable support to the cause of woman suffrage. As upper-class women increasingly participated in the movement, the truism that suffrage was a middle-class movement began to break down. By 1910 the role of upper-class women and their impact on movement orientation had become an undeniable feature of the suffrage movement.

In 1895 the IESA held its annual convention in conjunction with legislative hearings, addressed the legislature with a slate of speakers from around the state, and submitted the township suffrage bill again. The measure was narrowly defeated in the Senate (where it had won in 1893); in the House it was buried in a subcommittee controled by "three notorious opponents" (*HWS* 4:601).[3] In 1897 the IESA introduced three distinct bills, all on the model of the school suffrage bill. These bills (for township suffrage, bond suffrage, and suffrage for selected city officials) all failed to pass the legislature. At a special session in 1898 called to deal exclusively with tax-related issues, the IESA managed to raise the suffrage issue by introduction of a bill exempting the property of women from taxation until they were allowed to vote. In the regular 1899 session, the 1897 bills were reintroduced and redefeated. By the end of the decade, then, it was possible to draw both optimistic and pessimistic conclusions on the legislative fate of suffrage bills. On the pessimistic side, the movement had failed to capitalize on its 1891 victory despite a clearly defined tactic for securing legislative gains. On the more optimistic side, suffrage bills had acquired a legislative legitimacy they had previously lacked. From this point on, such bills were regularly introduced with considerable support and strong sponsorship.

The years from 1900 through 1905 revealed a slightly different legislative story. The suffrage movement witnessed victories of several bills indirectly related to its interests, but suffered more defeats on woman suffrage. The legislation that succeeded in this period concerned child welfare, and it succeeded in large part because of the considerable backing of the women's club movement. This was also the pattern for the passage of a Joint Guardianship Bill in 1901, a child labor law in 1903, and a bill raising the legal age of consent in 1905. In contrast to the success of child welfare legislation, woman suffrage legislation (including township, municipal, and presidential suffrage bills) was still defeated. Another avenue that continued to be pursued involved bills related to taxation—that is, either granting suffrage to tax-paying women or exempting women's property from taxation. The preferred approach of the IESA continued to be a straightforward amendment to the state constitution that would automatically equalize voting rights between the sexes. While this constitutional amendment strategy was the most difficult to implement, the legislative routes to suffrage were no more successful in this period.

In 1905 a new opportunity presented itself to Chicago suffragists when a convention was called to establish a new charter for the city of Chicago. Like the state constitutional convention of 1870, this offered an opportunity to gain female enfranchisement as part of a larger process of political reorganization. In response to this opportunity, Chicago suffragists channeled their efforts toward the charter convention and the municipal forms of woman suffrage that the convention could grant. Their interest in this route was not diminished by a double setback in the 1905 convention (the convention tabled the suffrage plank, and the state legislature tabled the entire charter), and woman suffrage fared better in later charter conventions. In 1907 the proposal for municipal woman suffrage lost by only a single vote. This charter was passed by the legislature but rejected by the voters of Chicago. A third attempt at a new charter for Chicago was launched in 1908, and it brought the suffrage cause even closer to a victory.

In the 1908 charter convention, suffrage forces were led by Catharine McCulloch and Jane Addams with the active support of nearly one hundred Chicago women's organizations. The results were complex and ultimately unsuccessful, but the process illustrated the growing sentiment for woman suffrage. For the first time, the municipal suffrage plank passed the charter convention by a 20 to 12 vote. The same plank was then endorsed by the state legislature, also for the first time. However, these endorsements from the charter convention and the state legislature were rendered inoperative when the legislature rejected the charter as a whole. Hence, the new support translated into no real change, the charter never came up for a popular vote in Chicago, and conditions remained exactly as before (see SL, CWM Papers, various documents from 1908 and 1909; Beldon 1913, 44–48; and *HWS* 6:142–143).

Having exhausted the city charter route to municipal suffrage, in 1909 the IESA refocused its attention on the state legislature and sought a statewide municipal suffrage bill. Reflecting a new flair for publicity, Chicago suffragists chartered a Suffrage Special train from Chicago to Springfield for the legislative session. Twenty-five women presented three-minute prosuffrage speeches from different perspectives, indicating the increasingly wide constituency that had come to support the suffrage cause by this time. This hearing was also the first in which the organized anti-suffrage movement addressed the legislature; four speakers from the Illinois Association Opposed to the Extension of Suffrage to Women were heard during this session. Suffragists had to settle once again for tantalizing progress but no real gain: the suffrage bill failed by a single vote in the state Senate, and it failed to move out of committee in the House.

This record of legislative activity has a paradoxical quality to it. The only clear victory occurred at the very beginning, and in a very limited way, with the school suffrage bill of 1891. Over the next two decades no other changes occurred in the voting rights of Illinois women. However, much was accomplished by way of moving closer to eventual victory. Some of this change is reflected in the legislative history, for the movement suffered ever closer defeats while seeking more and more significant forms of suffrage. The more important part of the story cannot be captured in legislative history, however, because the essential steps occurred outside of the legislatures and in the social processes by which the suffrage movement sought and received the support of an ever increasing number of individuals, groups, and organizations. It was these ties that made female enfranchisement more and more likely after 1910.

FORGING A NEW ALLIANCE

The eventual success of the Illinois suffrage movement was made possible in large part by the new alliances it formed during the two-decade period around the turn of the century. In 1890 the suffrage cause had relatively few allies. By 1910, when the final push for the vote began, the suffrage cause had numerous and diverse supporters. When all these forces pushed together, the vote was won with relative ease and quickness. However, the same processes that helped to achieve the eventual victory also displaced the suffrage movement itself from center stage in the fight for the vote. Paradoxically, the movement's efforts to recruit allies contributed to its own fall from the position of leadership in the fight for the vote. As we shall see, by 1910 the state suffrage association which had led the (often lonely) fight for the vote for several decades was no longer the major organizational actor pursuing suffrage. As this multiconstituency alliance developed, each participant joined and sought the vote for its own set of reasons. As these organizations and reasons overshadowed the suffrage organizations per se, the political and feminist orientation that had initiated the movement was lost amidst other rationales for the vote. Hence, the very factors that contributed to a victory for the suffrage cause simultaneously undermined the suffrage movement as it had traditionally been constituted.

At least three different constituencies were recruited into the new alliance for suffrage in this period. One group was the traditional and conservative women's club movement. A second group involved working-class immigrant women who were primarily recruited by settlement house workers in Chicago. The third and probably most important group was the urban-based, upper-class club movement and its organizations in and around Chicago. Once these factions were incorporated into the new suffrage alliance, the cause was immeasurably strengthened. This section presents a brief characterization of each constituency, including how it became involved in the fight for woman suffrage.

By the 1890s the traditional women's club movement was beginning to change its orientation from individual self-improvement to community betterment, and such clubs were becoming increasingly interested in social reform in the public sphere. Like the temperance movement, the club movement provided a legitimate public role for middle-class women that did not depart too far from conventional notions of acceptable feminine behavior and sex role stereotypes. This was accomplished through an ideology of social order and social change that could be labeled "household determinism":

> Sociological problems outside of the home may be studied forever; they will never be remedied until the social problem within the home is settled. Humanitarians who confine their efforts to alleviating existing conditions outside of home, only, merely touch the surface of human misery. Without knowledge and the best conditions in the home for the development and birth of new human beings, how can we expect different results? This applies equally to those who live in stately mansions and to those who live in the crowded tenement districts. (HL, EBH Papers, Annual Address to the National Household Economics Association, n. d.)

With such a view, expressed here by Elizabeth Harbert, a bridge was formed between women's traditional activities within the home and their involvement in the larger public world of social reform. That involvement eventually included advocacy of the vote for women as a means of carrying out the imperatives of the club movement's program for social change.

The best organizational example of this branch of the club movement was the Illinois Federation of Women's Clubs (IFWC). Organized in Chicago in 1894, the IFWC included 77 women's clubs in its first year; by 1904 it represented 246 clubs with a total membership of twenty-four thousand women. The IFWC was modeled on the General Federation of Women's Clubs (GFWC); the following description of the General Federation applied equally well to the Illinois Federation:

> The movement's attraction for more conservative women was both its greatest asset and its most limiting factor. The clubs did not really compete with other social feminist organizations, most of which required a much higher level of commitment than clubs could expect. . . . The General Federation went to great lengths to avoid antagonizing its cautious rank and file. Although most federation leaders were suffragists, it did not endorse woman suffrage until the eve of victory. (O'Neill 1969, 86–87)

The cautious and conservative posture of the IFWC was overdetermined. Its constituency consisted of conservative middle-class women; as a federation, it tended to avoid stances that were objectionable to any of its constituent members; and it brought together women from big cities, small towns, and rural areas whose social conditions varied dramatically.[4] The net effect was to direct the organization to those areas of work that were completely unobjectionable and noncontroversial. In this sense the IFWC was apolitical. With this, however, came a certain elasticity. When reformers appealed to the IFWC in a way that resonated with the worldview of its membership, they always received a sympathetic hearing and often won a supportive resolution. Given the sheer size of the IFWC, its endorsements were eagerly sought by reformers, including the suffrage movement. Like the GFWC, however, the Illinois Federation endorsed causes very cautiously and typically only at the eleventh hour when a given reform was all but inevitable.

Throughout its first decade the IFWC limited its efforts to child-related issues and the domestic science movement. It passed resolutions on compulsory education, free school supplies, the establishment of truant schools, the professionalization of teacher training, and the establishment of women's

dormitories at the University of Illinois. It also endorsed legislation to protect child labor and to systematize care of dependent children (ISHS,
IFWC Board Meeting minutes, 11 October 1895, 8 October 1896, 21 October 1897, 20 October 1898, 18 November 1910). The organization filed
reports that underscored the need for scientific training as a prerequisite
for household labor, advocated the professionalization of homemaking,
and defined the housewife's role as including full responsibility for the
health of all family members. In these actions the IFWC expressed its commitment to the perspective of household determinism: "Let every woman
of this Federation stand for home establishment, and by so doing they will
correct many of the social and economic conditions that exist in the home
today, that health and harmony will prevail where now are disease, discontent and unhappiness" (ISHS, IFWC Board Meeting minutes, 16 October 1901).

Only after 1900 did the IFWC gradually become involved in more controversial issues. The earliest reference in the board minutes to suffrage was
in 1902 when the board passed a motion to support a bill granting voting
powers to tax-paying women (ISHS, IFWC Board Meeting minutes,
17 October 1902). In 1904 the federation endorsed both tax-paying suffrage and municipal suffrage, and its Legislative Committee began actively
working for suffrage by publishing suffrage pamphlets, publicizing suffrage gains elsewhere, and criticizing the Illinois legislature for its political
backwardness.[5] From this point on the IFWC's Legislative Committee
regularly worked with suffrage forces, although the board itself did not endorse another suffrage measure until 1913 (see ISHS, IFWC Board Meeting minutes, 2 May 1905, 17 October 1905, and 14 April 1913).

While the IFWC was somewhat hamstrung by its commitments to a diverse membership, its constituent clubs could and did go further toward
involvement in the cause of woman suffrage. Many clubs formed suffrage
departments to work on the issue, and in some cases these efforts outweighed the contributions of the suffrage organizations themselves. In
1899 and 1900 organizational reports from the state suffrage association
acknowledged the important role played by the clubs and also noted the
deterioration of the network of suffrage organizations:

There are only about seven associations which keep up their regular
meetings and pay dues though in four or five other places the former
Presidents do considerable work. In sixteen other towns dead associations could be revived, if organizers visited them.

The work done by suffrage clubs is really but a small portion of the suffrage work in Illinois. Some of the women's clubs have suffrage departments . . . through which much suffrage work is done.

Considerable work has been done with the 229 Federated Clubs. . . . More money was contributed by these clubs than came from suffrage dues. (see SL, CWM Papers, "Report of the IESA, 1899," and "Report of the Chairman of the Executive Committee, 1900"; HL, EBH Papers, "Suggestions from Illinois," n. d.)

These reports indicated that although suffrage was a sidelight for many women's clubs, their combined contribution to that cause frequently rivaled the efforts of the suffrage organizations themselves.

The suffrage movement's leaders perceived the club movement as both a threat and an ally. At times the leadership fretted that "the rapid multiplication of women's clubs through the country had had the effect of making it more difficult to interest the members in equal suffrage" (HL, EBH Papers, "Women Want a Home Portfolio," unidentified newspaper clipping, n.d.). At other times the movement welcomed the mobilization of large numbers of women for any purpose and sought to bring already organized club women into the suffrage cause. This was the intent of an 1899 IESA resolution: "Be it resolved, That all department clubs in Illinois be requested to form a Political Equality department and that all clubs having organized such a department shall be asked to join and send delegates to the Annual meeting of the Illinois Equal Suffrage Association" (SL, CWM Papers, Report of the IESA, 1899). The club movement represented the same ambivalent force in the suffrage movement's later period that the temperance movement had represented in the middle period, and suffrage leaders responded with the same approach-avoidance pattern in both eras.

Whereas the temperance movement's impact on suffrage faded, the club movement's influence increased after the turn of the century. By 1910 the club movement was a major part of the new alliance seeking the vote. While the club movement helped win the vote, it simultaneously reinforced the transformed nature of the suffrage movement by espousing an ideology of social control and rationalizing the ballot as a means of implementing that ideology.[6]

A rather different constituency for the suffrage cause was found among immigrant and working-class women. In the final period of the movement this group also joined the suffrage alliance and contributed in important ways to its ultimate victory. Understanding their recruitment and participation, however, requires a prior understanding of the settlement house movement and its role in the cause of social reform in Chicago.

Henry Steele Commanger has described Jane Addams's role at Hull House in the following way:

> Over the years Jane Addams built a bridge between the immigrants and the old-stock Americans, between the working classes and the immigrants, between the amateur reformers and the professional politicians, even between private philanthropy and government. She made Hull House a clearinghouse for every kind of social service, an experimental laboratory in social reform, in art and music and drama and education as well. (Addams [1910] 1960, xii)

Perhaps the most important bridge she constructed was between social classes. The "raw materials" for this bridge were women from various classes, and the act of bridge building was a very self-conscious one: "Hull House was soberly opened on the theory that the dependence of classes on each other is reciprocal; and that as the social relation is essentially a reciprocal relation, it gives a form of expression that has peculiar value" (Addams [1910] 1960, 76). Addams brought to her work another version of the growing middle-class "consciousness of classes," translating it into important, material changes in the neighborhoods the settlement houses served.

Settlement house workers were generally supportive of the suffrage cause, but their most important contribution was bringing together upper-middle-class reformers and working-class women around issues in which they had some common interest. The original issue was protective labor legislation. Settlement house workers continually stressed to middle-class reformers that their life-styles rested on a material foundation provided by working-class women: "It requires cultivation of the imagination to enable women thus fortuitously endowed with leisure to perceive an organic relation between their own possession of it and the productive activity of other women, . . . to make the connection between this free gift of the new industrial order to themselves and the struggle of the garment-workers" (Kelley [1905] 1969, 114–115). Such arguments consciously nurtured a sense of cross-class obligation among public-spirited club women, particularly when harmful effects on the home were stressed. By appealing to this central concern of the club movement, Florence Kelley and other reformers brought middle-class allies into the fight for protective labor legislation.

Such appeals were also made to the suffrage movement, and it too adopted protective labor legislation as one of its own goals. Suffragist support for this and other working-class goals derived from mixed motives. On strategic grounds, suffragists recognized that they needed a broader base of support and that the situation of working-class women provided them with another powerful prosuffrage argument. At the same time, many middle-class suffrage leaders felt a sense of obligation to settlement house reformers for their support of suffrage; they also suspected that working-class women stood in greatest need of the ballot as a means of protecting themselves. If this mix of motives was sometimes more instrumental than authentic, it was nonetheless sufficient to move both groups into a cautious dialogue over related concerns.

The cross-class alliance that settlement house workers had begun to build around the issue of protective labor legislation assumed a more concrete form with the establishment of the Women's Trade Union League (WTUL) in the early 1900s. Jane Addams participated in the formation of the national WTUL in Boston in 1903; two months later she chaired a Hull House meeting that led to the formation of the WTUL of Illinois. The state branch elected Mary McDowell as its first president, Jane Addams as vice-president, and Ellen Henrotin as treasurer. In 1907 McDowell was succeeded by Margaret Dreier Robins. Although independently wealthy, Robins came to be regarded as a legitimate and influential spokeswoman for the working women the WTUL represented. She strongly supported strike decisions, stressed union organization over protective legislation, and sought the promotion of working women into positions of leadership within the WTUL. In 1913 the Chicago WTUL elected its first working-class president Agnes Nestor to that post.

Discussions of the New York and national WTUL have stressed the League's emphasis on union organizing and cross-class cooperation among women (see Dye 1973; Wertheimer 1977). The Chicago WTUL fit this pattern as well. Under McDowell and Robins, the organization sought to recruit more privileged women into the cause, but only if and when they supported the League's emphasis on union organizing. The Chicago WTUL was explicit about these goals:

> The object of this organization shall be to investigate the conditions
> of working women, to promote the best type of trade unionism in

existing organizations and to assist in organizing trade unions among women. (CHS, WTUL Collection, "By-Laws of the WTUL of Illinois, 1906–7")

The greatest immediate opportunity and one within her reach is trade union organization. This is the strongest factor helping to bring about fair wages, shorter hours and decent working conditions. These three demands constitute what may be termed a "living wage." (CHS, WTUL Collection, "Why Working Women Must Organize")

The latter pamphlet underscored the particular importance of organization for unskilled working women by arguing that skilled workers "owe it to their fellow workers to make such conditions impossible" and suggesting that skilled workers who remained aloof from the trade union movement were as responsible for misery in the sweated trades as the "daughters of privilege."[7]

While the WTUL did not abandon these goals, a marked shift occurred in its orientation in 1908 when the U.S. Supreme Court in deciding an Oregon case legitimized protective labor legislation.[8] Within the year the Chicago WTUL presented an eight-hour bill to the Illinois legislature. The next year the WTUL won a partial victory in the form of a limited ten-hour bill. (The WTUL continued to fight until 1937 before a full eight-hour-day bill was eventually won from the Illinois legislature.) As of 1908, then, protective labor legislation was an issue that linked the WTUL, the settlement house reformers, and the suffrage movement.

The connections between these three groups have been described by Barbara Wertheimer as follows:

Through the urging of WTUL President Robins and "allies" like Jane Addams and Florence Kelley, the suffrage movement began to reach out to working women. These women not only saw in votes for working women the potential for gaining legislation that would protect women, but they believed that unless suffragists supported both the organization of working women into unions and the legislation these women needed, union women would never believe the suffrage movement relevant to their cause. Therefore they set about convincing leaders in the suffrage movement that it needed the support of working women to succeed. (Wertheimer 1977, 281)

Cross-class support for the ballot developed for class-specific reasons. For middle-class suffragists the vote had become an overriding aim and a key to all further social reform. For the WTUL and its working-class constituency the vote was an important but secondary goal in a larger program for improving the situation of working women. On this basis, links between the two movements began to grow, as evidenced by the WTUL's endorsement of full suffrage in 1907, its ongoing organizational ties with the NAWSA from 1909, and the support WTUL members provided for particular suffrage campaigns.

Even as these ties were established, the need for distinct suffrage organizations within the WTUL became evident.[9] Recognizing that there was not a perfect overlap of class interests, WTUL members began forming wage-earner suffrage leagues, affiliated with the WTUL, that provided an organizational vehicle for conducting a working-class woman suffrage campaign. Through such actions WTUL members and working women found a way to support the suffrage cause while maintaining class and gender allegiances. Such actions were necessitated by the inability of middle-class suffragists to overcome their own class interests:

> Thus, despite the increased commitment to suffrage on the part of working class women in the early twentieth century, it cannot be said that the last phase of the woman suffrage movement represents an instance of the genuine achievement of sisterhood on a cross-class basis. . . . Ironically, it was the middle class feminists whose conscious and unconscious sense of class precluded the possibility of cross-class feminist solidarity. (Jacoby 1975, 135, 138)

In short, the WTUL was receptive to the suffrage cause but cautious toward the organized suffrage movement because the WTUL's stance on suffrage emerged from an overall political orientation that recognized both class and gender. Such a stance led them to criticize the narrowed suffrage movement, as when Mary McDowell reminded suffrage leaders that the pioneer suffragists "held that emancipation meant not only political but economic freedom," and when she directly criticized professional women and "extreme feminists" for their opposition to protective labor legislation (McDowell 1937, 52–54).

The growing receptiveness of the organized suffrage movement to the WTUL position was evident in the report of the 1907 NAWSA convention which met in Chicago. Again, settlement house activists provided the link, with Anna Nicholes, Jane Addams, Florence Kelley, and Ellen Henrotin all addressing some aspect of working women's relation to the ballot. The convention also heard reformer Graham Taylor describe the

WTUL as "most effective of all in bettering the condition of working women" (*HWS* 5 : 209). The earliest reference to suffrage in WTUL pamphlets was in 1908, where the ballot was described as "one of the most decisive methods by which she can command a hearing," although trade union organization was still described as the greatest, most immediate, and most important tactic for working women (CHS, WTUL Collection, "The WTUL of Illinois, 1907–08").

Ties between the two groups were substantial from 1910 on, when Agnes Nestor joined a group of suffragists on the Suffrage Special train to Springfield to speak in favor of a state suffrage bill. In 1912 Margaret Robins described the WTUL as strongly committed to the suffrage battle but depicted the vote as one working women's strategy among others, including unionization, self-government, and strikes (CHS, WTUL Collection, "Self-Government in the Workshop"). In 1913, on the eve of the major suffrage victory in Illinois, the WTUL formed a wage-earners suffrage league whose major task became organizing and educating women to utilize the ballot they had so recently won.

In short, the WTUL and suffrage movement gradually acknowledged some common ground while maintaining class and organizationally distinct ideologies. It was the suffrage movement that originally reached out to the WTUL (with the prodding of settlement house workers); it did so as part of an effort to reach every conceivable constituency that could aid the suffrage cause. These diverse constituencies reinforced the dominant suffrage ideology which saw the vote as the most important political goal for all women. The WTUL did not agree with this priority, and it maintained its own priorities as it moved into tactical alliances with the suffrage movement around particular suffrage campaigns. As on the national level, cross-class tensions prevented a true feminist alliance, but tensions were not so great as to prevent a strategic coordination between the two groups for class-specific reasons.[10]

The final and most important constituency that entered the suffragist alliance after 1900 consisted of upper-class club women. The social background of this group was markedly different from the middle-class roots of the suffrage movement and the traditional club movement. It was this third group of upper-class club women that completed the recasting of the suffrage demand as a civic necessity rather than a woman's right, thereby subsuming the suffrage cause under the broader program of Progressive reform. From the perspective of a politically feminist movement, this recasting perpetuated transformation and depoliticization because it altered the ideological basis for demanding the vote. At the same time, it permitted larger numbers of more powerful individuals to support the demand, thereby contributing to the victory of the suffrage movement in relatively few years.

The Chicago Woman's Club (CWC) was established in 1876 to play an active, practical role in improving the conditions of urban life. It perceived its role as one of translating domestic and feminine qualities into a kind of public utilitarianism that would serve the larger community of the urban world; the club "sought to give expression to all the directions of women's energy, translating the power that makes home attractive, that rears the children of the family into men and women ready to take up the burden of life, that works in charities and philanthropies, into a united striving towards the greatest good to the greatest number, besides the benefit accruing to the individual from association with others" (Frank and Jerome 1916, 12). One of the distinguishing features of the club was the tight control it maintained over recruitment and the deliberately slow pace at which it grew. Through a quota system and complex nomination procedures,[11] the club held its membership to only 750 women after its first twenty years. The club's rationale was that this policy maintained its practical focus by screening out idlers, but such procedures allowed for careful screening for social class as well. The club grew slowly by adding only the most energetic and socially concerned women with appropriate upper-class credentials.

Despite its limited membership but because of its exclusive character, the CWC became a major power, exercising considerable influence on the social, cultural, and political life of Chicago. A summary list of work that was initiated and supported by the club reads like an exhaustive checklist of Progressive Era reforms.[12] What further distinguished the CWC was the financial resources it commanded. From 1876 to 1916 the club collected and contributed almost half a million dollars to the causes, issues, groups, and institutions that furthered its goals (Frank and Jerome 1916, 368–378).

The stance of the CWC toward the suffrage cause was passively positive. The club *Annals* contain nine specific references to woman suffrage from 1885 through 1916; these typically express support for pending legislation of one type or another (Frank and Jerome 1916, 48, 127, 204, 242, 270, 308–309, 316–318). Writing in 1916 the club's historians summarized the trend of suffrage attitudes:

Who would have thought, when Susan B. Anthony was tendered a reception by this Club on June 27, 1888, the first formal recognition extended to her by a woman's club, that the upholders of woman's suffrage would ever form an overwhelming majority in our organization, and suffrage would become fashionable. In the early years, no one ever spoke of religion or suffrage or politics, for fear of stirring up strife and forgetting the amenities. We have changed all that. (Frank and Jerome 1916, 345–346)

The CWC itself did not take a more activist role in the suffrage campaign because in 1894 it established an entirely separate organization to work for woman suffrage as part of its Progressive Era program for social change. A true appreciation of the role of upper-class clubwomen in the suffrage cause in Chicago requires closer consideration of this organization.

At a CWC meeting on 23 May 1894—shortly after the Columbian Exposition—the club passed a resolution to establish a separate organization to promote political equality. The founding committee included only two recognizable suffragists (Catharine McCulloch and Ellen Henrotin) among twenty-one other clubwomen who had not been prominent in the suffrage cause until that time. The organization was officially established in October of 1894 under a board of directors from the CWC. As an additional safeguard, the CWC ruled that for the first year of the Chicago Political Equality League (CPEL), all officers must be members of the Chicago Women's Club.

Membership in the CPEL grew slowly, in a pattern reminiscent of its parent organization and for similar reasons. The membership clause was designed to insure tight control over who would be admitted into the organization.[13] After the first decade these restrictions were modified, and membership grew more rapidly; but screening of applicants remained a major preoccupation of the CPEL leadership. Thus, the CPEL embodied the same exclusivity and upper-class character as the CWC, and its status as an independent organization must be qualified by a recognition of the organic ties between it and the CWC which were built into its membership clause. The latter virtually insured an upper-class membership; it also insured that new members brought an orientation and worldview consistent with the class base of both organizations.

The extent of CWC control over the CPEL during the crucial years of the suffrage battle is suggested by table 5.1. The data reveal a gradually declining percentage of CWC members among active CPEL members—

from 33 percent in 1908 to 21 percent in 1912. However, 67 percent of the CPEL officers were CWC members throughout this period, with the exception of one year (1910–1911) when the proportion dropped to 50 percent. Throughout the four-year period the CPEL president was always a member of the CWC; from 1908 to 1910 the post was held by Lillian D. Duncanson, and from 1910 to 1912 it was held by Grace Wilbur Trout. Clearly the CWC constituted the dominant group within the CPEL. Given the upper-class base of the CWC and its control over the CPEL, the latter really signified the entrance of upper-class women (and men) into the Chicago suffrage campaign. By 1905 the CPEL had become a major organizational actor in the suffrage campaign; by 1910 most observers and participants recognized it as the leading suffrage organization in Chicago (see, e.g., Trout in CHS, CPEL Collection, CPEL Yearbook 1911–1912, who identified the organization as "the largest suffrage league in Illinois").

TABLE 5.1

CWC Representation in the CPEL, 1908–1912

	# in CPEL	# in CWC	% of CWC in CPEL
1908–1909			
Active members	189	62	33%
Officers	6	4	67%
Directors	21	11	52%
Honorary members	10	6	60%
1909–1910			
Active members	235	67	29%
Officers	6	4	67%
Directors	21	13	62%
Honorary members	9	5	56%
1910–1911			
Active members	391	97	25%
Officers	6	3	50%
Directors	20	6	30%
Honorary members	9	5	56%
1911–1912			
Active members	612	126	21%
Officers	6	4	67%
Directors	21	3	14%
Honorary members	8	4	50%

Source: CHS, CPEL Collection, CPEL Yearbooks, 1908–1912.

CPEL activity centered around woman suffrage campaigns, but its conception of suffrage must be understood in the context of the organization's larger goals and objectives. In 1895 the League defined its object as twofold: "to promote the study of political science and government, and foster and extend the political rights and privileges of women" (CHS, CPEL Collection, CPEL Yearbook, 1895–1896). The League divided itself into three sections devoted to propaganda, study, and legislation. By the early twentieth century, when the League became most active, its work included the entire spectrum of Progressive reform, and woman suffrage was conceptualized as a major tool for implementing this broader program of reform. Alongside suffrage, the League directed its efforts toward patriotism, citizenship, constructive education, industrial unity, crime, municipal amusements, compulsory education, national unity, delinquency, eugenics, and international unity. The League established dozens of special committees to address particular topics in the Progressive program; random examples include public utilities, dance halls, vocational training, ventilation, street temptations, white slavery, general vice, city waste and garbage, freedom of speech, birth registration, and many others. These programs were coordinated through the more general Bureau of Civic Efficiency (see CHS, CPEL Collection, CPEL Yearbooks for further examples).

Through organizations like the CPEL, the cause of woman suffrage was again wedded to a larger program of social reform. But this program in the early twentieth century made woman suffrage part of an effort to preserve basic social institutions and structures. As the suffrage cause became more and more the province of the professional and managerial sectors of the middle class and the more progressive members of the upper class, the purely feminist dimension of the vote was subordinated to other class goals and reforms once again. In some respects this process was similar to the blending of suffrage and temperance in the 1880s, but this blending was with more upper-class interests, and it led to greater success in winning the vote for women.

Another urban-based, upper-class women's club that was part of this alliance was the Woman's City Club (WCC). Explicitly founded on the metaphor of "municipal housekeeping," the WCC insisted that the city was really a large household that required caretaking and housekeeping through an extension of womanly and maternal roles. The most prominent figure associated with this organization was Louise deKoven Bowen, and her autobiography *Growing Up with a City* provided concrete illustrations of the involvement of upper-class women in the suffrage cause. Bowen self-consciously defined her role as bridging social classes in an attempt to replace "difficulties" with "sympathy." She described Hull House in this way:

> Miss Addams in these early days was really an interpreter between working men and women and the people who lived in luxury on the other side of the city and she also gave the people of her own neighborhood quite a different idea about the men and women who were ordinarily called "capitalists." To come in contact constantly with the people of that neighborhood certainly gave one a new impression of life in a great city, and I began to feel that what was needed more than anything was an acquaintance between the well-to-do and those less well off. Until an acquaintance of this kind can be effected, there will always be difficulties and there never will be that sympathy which should exist. (Bowen 1926, 93)

Bowen was equally aware of the larger political functions served by Hull House. In contrast to Bertha Palmer, who criticized Hull House for permitting anarchist and socialist speakers, Bowen's analysis was more sophisticated: "Talking out things is certainly a great safety valve. Miss Addams realized this at Hull House and has sometimes been criticized for allowing associations, whose ideas were most radical, to meet there and express their opinions. Miss Addams felt, however, that if the people who belonged to the organizations were allowed to talk freely, they would not be apt to do anything more" (Bowen 1926, 118). As exemplified by Bowen, the upper-class club movement was involved in many different tasks, including the mediation and resolution of class conflict.[14] Advocacy of the suffrage cause meshed with these larger imperatives and provided a means of advancing those interests. Through such individuals and organizations the suffrage movement acquired powerful and influential allies from the very top of the class structure.

By 1910 the suffrage movement had succeeded in forging a new multiclass alliance to push for the right to vote. This alliance included the traditionally conservative club movement, working-class and immigrant women, and the urban-based, upper-class club movement. Echoing this diverse support were equally diverse rationales for seeking the vote: every group in the alliance had its own reasons for wanting suffrage. Thus, as the suffrage cause became more popular, its transformation was perpetuated by the emergence of various new rationales for demanding the vote for women.

SUFFRAGE IDEOLOGY AND ANTISUFFRAGISM

The changes in the social base of the suffrage movement brought corresponding ideological changes. At least four major ideological changes can be identified in the final period. In addition, for the first time the movement had to confront an organized antisuffrage movement headed by conservative women. This section briefly describes these changes in movement ideology and discusses the significance of the organized antisuffrage movement in these changes.

Aileen Kraditor has suggested that the suffrage movement began to shift from justice to expediency arguments in the twentieth century (1965). While largely correct, this interpretation obscures another shift in movement ideology that, over time, had even greater implications for the movement's orientation. This second shift involved a change from arguments that challenged conventional notions of woman's role to arguments that endorsed those conceptions. We have already seen that in the movement's middle period its ideology began to endorse rather than challenge these roles; this tendency became even more pronounced in the twentieth century. Two examples from a NAWSA pamphlet series that began appearing in the 1890s illustrate the process.

The first, written by Elizabeth Harbert, was titled "Our Motherless Government." In it she argued

> the State is but an aggregation of individuals and homes. . . . What is the condition of our national home today? The opinions of mothers, wives, sisters and daughters . . . are not counted, and pitiable conditions ensue. We are organizing for action. This glorious opportunity for patriotic service is ours. We accept our woman's sphere, boundless as a mother's love, limitless as a mother's duty. . . . We march forward with the enthusiasm of a firm belief in the final triumph of the pure, the true and the good, and the banner over us is love, our watchword—Service. (SL, ESS Papers, August 1896)

Harbert had been making this argument for some time, but by the 1890s its popularity was increasing. One letter to Harbert indicates that of all the prosuffrage pamphlets published in the NAWSA series, demand was greatest for Harbert's article (HL, EBH Papers, Avery to Harbert, 9 October 1896).

Another leaflet in the series, "Mrs. Livermore on Suffrage," exemplified the tendency to develop prosuffrage arguments from sex-specific traits:

"Women are filled with a divine passion for being helpful. . . . they are doing everything in their power to put a lever under the lowest stratum of society and to raise it" (SL, ESS Papers, "Mrs. Livermore on Suffrage," January 1897). The common thread running through most expediency arguments for the vote was a tendency to divorce suffrage from emancipation and to link it with presumably feminine traits and attributes. Thus, the ballot became a floating currency that could be attached to any cause, and the transformation of the movement continued.

A second change in suffragist ideology involved a more specific instance of the first with a distinctively modern twist. Municipal housekeeping arguments explicitly endorsed women's domestic sphere and its duties and argued for the vote on this basis:

> For many generations it has been believed that woman's place is within the walls of her own home, and it is indeed impossible to imagine the time when her duty there shall be ended or to forecast any social change which shall release her from that paramount obligation. (UICC/JAHH: "Why Women Should Vote," 1910)

> The old division of labor, which defined man's work as that lying outside the home and woman's inside, had much to recommend it. (UICC/JAHH: "The Working Woman and the Ballot," 1908)

From this premise, the need for the vote followed:

> The trouble with us is that we have enlarged the boundaries of the home and have not enlarged the homemakers' power with it. (UICC/JAHH: "The Working Woman and the Ballot," 1908)

> many women today are failing to discharge their duties to their own households properly simply because they do not perceive that as society grows more complicated it is necessary that woman shall extend her sense of responsibility to many things outside of her own home if she would continue to preserve the home in its entirety. (UICC/JAHH: "Why Women Should Vote," 1910)

From this logic flowed more specific arguments about women's need for municipal suffrage in urban areas if they were to execute their household duties. Whereas earlier arguments were grounded on claims about "natural" traits, this argument was based on a more sociological understanding of women's contemporary role (Rosenberg 1982).

The municipal housekeeping argument was a tactically powerful one because it suggested that even conservative women had an interest in the vote. But its blend of realistic recognition and normative endorsement of women's traditional role represented a retreat from earlier forms of suffrage ideology that had challenged that role. By shifting the grounds for demanding the vote from political equality to traditional duties, the argument sanctioned the prevailing sexual division of labor. It also reinforced a piecemeal approach to winning the vote, for no equally strong argument could be made from these premises for full (as opposed to municipal) suffrage. In the end, these arguments denied women's interest in intruding on male spheres of power and action: "Public-spirited women who wish to use the ballot, as I know them, do not wish to do the work of men nor to take over men's affairs. They simply want an opportunity to do their own work and to take care of those affairs which naturally and historically belong to women" (UICC/JAHH: "Why Women Should Vote," 1910).

An intriguing consequence of this argument was its presentation of the vote as a technocratic cog in the rationalized machinery of government. Connecting the themes of the domestic science movement, the Progressive movement, and the suffrage movement, Sophonisba Breckinridge linked the vote and greater efficiency when she claimed that "the ballot was a labor-saving device, like the biscuit-machine" (UICC/JAHH: *Women's Journal*, 17 June 1911). With the ballot reforms could be achieved more efficiently; hence the fight for the vote was technically rational as well as socially desirable. Jane Addams reflected this technocratic perspective as well; in an apparent call for an "end to ideology," Addams wrote: "What would the result have been could women have regarded the suffrage, not as a right or a privilege, but as a mere piece of government machinery, without which they could not perform their traditional functions under the changed conditions of city life? Could we view the whole situation as a matter of obligation and normal development, it would be much simplified" (UICC/JAHH: "The Modern City and the Municipal Franchise for Women," 1917). Thus, while the feminist content of the ballot demand was already undergoing change, the vote itself was depoliticized by arguments that it was a technocratic imperative necessary to rationalize the administrative machinery of government.

The third ideological change evident in this period was the sheer diversity of the arguments made in support of the vote for women. This diversity reflected a growing sophistication within the movement about the differing groups it needed to recruit and the most effective means of doing so.

This change was physically embodied in the rapid growth of pamphlet literature targeting certain audiences with particular messages. Different arguments were made to rural women, religious women, property-owning women, and so forth, but all were urged to support the movement (see SL, ESS and CWM Papers for examples). By 1914 the literature department of the IESA offered more than two hundred titles which it promised to send "to any part of the world by mail or express upon request" for a modest fee (see LC, NAWSA: Illinois Collection, "IESA Catalogue and Price List of Suffrage Literature and Supplies," 1914).

On a tactical level, these arguments were instrumental in expanding the mass base of the suffrage movement. At the same time they reflected and furthered the process of goal transformation which created a one-issue movement for the vote. By recognizing, emphasizing, and appealing to the differences that separated women, suffrage became the only common thread that tied together these diverse interests and goals. And in this way the vote was detached from a larger feminist program, as a result of the felt need and strategy chosen, to develop a broader base for the movement.

A fourth change in suffrage ideology in this period concerned the growing appreciation, among some sectors of the organized suffrage movement, of the situation of working women. This concern was evidenced in a more historically informed understanding of how the work of women had been transformed by the processes of industrialization, urbanization, and proletarianization. In an essay "The Earnings of Women," Chicago suffragist Lucy Tilden discussed women's preindustrial roles and concluded:

> But now it is thought that she is unable to go on with these different forms of labor that she has developed. Thus it is the conditions under which work is done rather than the work itself with which we find fault. Weaving was domestic work when done at home, but ceased to be so when done in a factory. Extremes meet, and the organization of industry must be settled by giving back to woman what it began by taking from her: a place in the varied work of the world. (UICC, Lucy Tilden Stewart Papers, "The Earnings of Women," 1890)

A decade later Catharine McCulloch traced the same changes and rejected the "economically parasitic" roles they produced for women, argued for better economic opportunities, and discussed the inequities of unpaid domestic labor (SL, CWM Papers, "Talks of Woman," 1899 newspaper fragment).

These perspectives were not widespread, but they represented a new ideological trend within the movement. Even when suffragists agreed on this broad perspective, they still disagreed over the centrality of the vote for redressing working women's grievances. For some the vote was central; for others it was a secondary goal in a larger strategy, such as that outlined by the WTUL. But in either case the situation of working women received more recognition from the organized suffrage movement in the final period than it had for several decades.

As the suffrage movement entered the twentieth century, its ideology became more conservative as well as more differentiated. In many ways these changes allowed the movement to broaden its popular base by reaching out to previously uninvolved or indifferent groups. In the process it periodically bumped into an opposing force also seeking a larger base of support. The central figures in the organized Illinois antisuffrage movement were Caroline Corbin and the organization she founded in 1897 to oppose suffrage. This organization's relatively late start implies that antisuffrage activity had been mobilized on an ad hoc basis prior to this time. The need for a formal organization to oppose suffrage (Illinois Association Opposed to the Extension of Suffrage to Women) paralleled the gains of the suffrage movement in the 1890s and the possibility that the suffrage movement might succeed. Corbin's antisuffrage association fought against suffrage until the last minute of the suffrage campaign.

The association reiterated the standard antisuffrage arguments that had been voiced for decades.[15] What distinguished the Illinois antisuffrage association from the more diffuse world of antisuffrage sentiment was its conception of woman suffrage as merely one element in a political movement that threatened the entire fabric of middle-class life.[16] In Corbin's eyes, this threat was the allegedly indissoluble connection between woman suffrage and socialism. Corbin formed her political ideology in response to an 1886 encounter with Eleanor Marx and Edward Aveling, who spoke on the tenets of socialism in regard to marriage. Corbin left this encounter viewing socialism as the major threat to the family, and she developed a career commitment to opposing the threat. (See the interesting account in Corbin's "One Woman's Experience of Emancipation," ISHS, Cornell University Collection of Woman's Rights Pamphlets, microfilm.) Corbin's resistance to woman suffrage thus derived from a larger, profamily, antisocialist stance, and when the suffrage movement gained momentum in the 1890s, opposing suffrage became her major activity. Her perceptions were only reinforced when, as she continually reminded her audiences, the Socialist party proved to be the most long-standing and consistent political party to support full and equal suffrage for women.

The suffrage movement devoted considerable energy to justifying and legitimizing its position in the face of such opposition. At first glance, it appears that the organized antisuffrage movement extracted considerable ideological concessions from the suffrage forces. Consider newspaper coverage of a Harbert-Corbin debate:

> Mrs. Corbin was afraid that woman suffrage would endanger motherhood and the home. If she believed that, Mrs. Harbert said, all female suffragists would thank her for her opposition, because the object of the movement is to benefit mothers and children. . . . [Quoting Harbert:] "The suffrage movement sprang simply from the desire of motherhood to better the condition of children." (HL, EBH Papers, "Harbert and Corbin," newspaper fragment, n.d.)

The seeming concession here by Harbert in reality represented a restatement of what had become the dominant movement ideology during the 1880s. Thus, organized opposition did not so much change the ideology of the suffrage movement as it reinforced and helped to consolidate changes that had already occurred. A parallel argument could be made that Corbin's rhetoric prevented any meaningful alliance between suffragists and socialists, but suffragists already had serious reservations about allying with the socialist movement before Corbin appeared on the scene.

Thus, while the organized antisuffrage movement added its voice to the chorus of social control singers, it joined the group too late to have a major impact in changing movement orientation and moderating the movement's stance. At the same time, it indisputably reinforced the changes that had already taken place and helped make it more difficult for the suffrage movement either to return to its earlier breadth or to cultivate a new relationship with the growing socialist movement after the turn of the century (Buhle 1983).

By 1910, the suffrage movement had undergone considerable change. It had seen twenty years of increasing momentum on the legislative front, it had built a new alliance that created cross-class pressures for woman suffrage, and it had undergone corresponding ideological changes. In short, the stage was set for the final push for suffrage; once this push began, the vote was won relatively quickly in Illinois.

WINNING SUFFRAGE

The pace and style of suffrage activity changed dramatically in 1910—the year the Chicago Political Equality League became a major force in the suffrage cause. From 1894 to 1909 that organization had grown to only 143 members. Under its newly elected president Grace Wilbur Trout, it reached a membership of 400 in 1910 and over 1,000 by 1912. With an active president, a rapidly expanding membership, and a considerable financial base, the CPEL became a major force in the suffrage campaign.

Trout also helped introduce a tactical change when she arranged for a suffrage float in the Sane Fourth Parade in Chicago. While preparations were being made for the float, the IESA approached the CPEL with a proposal to organize a state auto tour to further publicize the cause. The CPEL agreed, and auto tours were soon a common suffragist tactic. Combining public relations and modern technology, auto tours, parade floats, and suffrage trains were all attempts to cultivate the more broad-based support that legislators always required of suffragists who appeared before them. The tours were especially effective, for they led to open air meetings that reached people who would not ordinarily attend suffrage meetings. Such practices reflected a new tactical sophistication among suffragists and a new appreciation of the public relations aspect of politics in the modern world.

Early in 1911 suffragists attempted to translate growing momentum into effective power at the state legislative session. Their full suffrage bill received its usual hospitable reception in the Senate (where it won by a vote of 31 to 10) but fell short in the House and thereby failed to pass. The veteran Catharine McCulloch was buoyed by the incremental progress evident in these results, but the newcomer Grace Trout was dismayed by the insensitive treatment the suffragist cause received in the legislature (Trout 1920, 96).

After the session McCulloch wrote selected legislators asking them to analyze the reasons for the defeat. The most incisive response was provided by Homer Tice, who sponsored the 1911 bill. Tice identified three "formidable lines of opposition:"

There was a very large foreign element, more than ordinary, in the last House. I think practically every one of them opposed the measure. I do not now recall your getting a single "wet" vote in the house and you lost some "drys." If I am correctly informed the Catholic vote was practically solid against you.

. . . your work was not systematic that is it did not carry with it the force of cohesion. Your analysis of the situation did not convince that you really had power behind the effort. Men laughed behind your backs at your optimism. . . . Now it seems to me that the object must be gained by reaching the heart and conscience of men. (SL, CWM Papers, Tice to McCulloch, 6 October 1911)

Other legislators recommended taking popular votes, organizing lobbies, converting legislators, electing legislators, and recruiting more women. Over the next two years suffragists utilized all these tactics in their attempts to win the vote.

Early in 1912 the movement successfully petitioned for a popular vote on woman suffrage in Chicago. This campaign united settlement house activists, club women, the WTUL, and the IESA, although some suffragists voiced reservations over the wisdom of a popular vote. The form of the vote presented several potential drawbacks. First, since it was an advisory ballot only, nothing could be definitively won but much could be symbolically lost. Second, the vote was part of an April preferential primary between Democrats and Republicans—precisely the parties where suffrage support was weakest, compared to smaller parties. Finally, the vote involved a separate ballot and ballot box, which would further reduce the number of votes cast on the measure.

Suffragists energetically confronted these difficulties. The WCC distributed leaflets and lobbied suburban women who might not otherwise participate in the election. Settlement house workers solicited support among male voters in the Hull House neighborhood. The Cook County Suffrage Alliance organized the campaign on a ward and district basis. The WTUL distributed prosuffrage literature to every labor union in the city and tried to persuade male unionists to vote and vote favorably on the issue. In short, the 1912 vote provided one of the earliest opportunities to mobilize the cross-class, multiconstituency, prosuffrage alliance that had been so carefully constructed during the preceding two decades.

Despite these efforts, the popular vote failed by almost a two-to-one margin (135,410 to 71,354), and every ward in the city returned an adverse majority. Many interpreted this result as a confirmation of long-standing reservations about popular votes, where general indifference and organized opposition were potent forces to overcome. Alongside this drawback of popular voting, several particulars of the campaign contributed to the defeat. For instance, it proved impossible to secure workers in all the wards and districts suffragists hoped to reach (Beldon 1913, 54). The advisory nature of the ballot and its linkage with a preferential primary also hurt the cause; the latter virtually eliminated small parties and independents from voting. Finally, it was suggested that in some districts ballots were either not available or not counted. Although the ever-optimistic McCulloch described the result as "something of a victory," the general perception was that suffrage had been given a fair test and failed to pass. If there was a counterbalancing positive aspect, it was that this diverse alliance of interests had coordinated their efforts and found that they could work together—at least on a specific and finite campaign. This lesson proved exceptionally valuable in a different campaign in the state legislature the following year.

The summer of 1912 was a busy one for suffragists. Settlement house workers sought a woman suffrage plank from the Republican party. Margaret Haley and Margaret Robins secured a prosuffrage resolution from the National Education Association. Jane Addams's role in the Progressive party brought publicity and support and presumably won Roosevelt's support for woman suffrage (see Abbott 1950, 2:8). Press coverage of the suffrage campaign also increased, stimulated by the formation of a press bureau within the IESA. Finally, the IESA refined its legislative strategy by welcoming party support from socialists, progressives, and prohibitionists but urging individual scrutiny of all candidates: "During the 30 days preceding election every legislative candidate must be pledged to our cause or relinquish hope of our help. No party label is enough. We must know that the man himself is a suffragist" (SL, CWM Papers, "Report of the Legislative Superintendent," 1 October 1912). In another important change, the IESA elected Grace Wilbur Trout as its new president, a post she held for the next three years. Trout had presided over the CPEL since 1910 when she initiated its rapid growth. With her election to the presidency of the IESA in 1912 (along with Louise deKoven Bowen's election to the vice-presidency), the same upper-class interests that predominated in the CPEL came to predominate in the IESA as well. On the eve of its victory, the suffrage movement in Illinois had become an upper-class movement, at least as measured by the social-class background of the movement leadership.

Early in 1913 the IESA established a permanent headquarters in Springfield to monitor the progress of suffrage bills. As of that year it had organized twenty-nine of the thirty-two senatorial districts outside of Chicago—a goal long proclaimed but rarely fulfilled. The organization also called on civic clubs to support the next major push for suffrage. By May 1913 the IESA claimed over a hundred affiliated suffrage clubs throughout the state of Illinois, each pressuring the state legislature. Finally, Trout began to professionalize and bureaucratize the IESA by instituting a staff of paid workers, thereby creating a more effective legislative pressure group out of the state suffrage association (see Beldon 1913, 55ff.).

While the IESA worked on the state level, the WTUL mobilized in Chicago. Throughout April, WTUL members wearing Votes for Women banners sold copies of *Life and Labor* on streetcorners and recruited suffrage support: "Whenever a male pedestrian stopped to buy a copy he was detained as long as possible by the ardent workers who hurled at him innumerable reasons why he should become an equal suffrage advocate" (UICC, WTUL clippings, 4 April 1913). In the important Seventeenth Ward, the WTUL conducted a house-to-house canvass and printed a daily newspaper in five languages to recruit suffrage support among immigrant populations. In June the WTUL formed its own Wage-Earners Suffrage League, aiming for a membership of ten thousand working women (see UICC, WTUL clippings from 1913; CHS, WTUL bulletins).

With this foundation, the chances for a suffrage victory were better than ever. Nonetheless, their legislative strategy proved to be less than elegant. Before the legislature met, the Progressive party had drafted a suffrage bill that it intended to submit as a party measure. However, Trout and the IESA suggested that the bill be submitted with bipartisan support by the IESA itself, and the Progressives agreed to withdraw sponsorship of the bill. When the session opened, however, Catharine McCulloch insisted on submitting her version of the bill, and the IESA deferred to her. At this point, the Progressives submitted their original bill because the IESA had violated the agreement.[17] After considerable confusion, the Progressives were persuaded to withdraw their bill and debate focused on the McCulloch bill.

In the meantime, Trout had secured Governor Dunne's support for a nonconstitutional suffrage bill.[18] However, in April a constitutional amendment was introduced, apparently by McCulloch.[19] Most suffragists regarded this tactic as further jeopardizing their chances, but they could not persuade the sponsor (presumably McCulloch) to withdraw it. The amendment bill was killed in committee, and having survived this clumsiness, the original McCulloch bill once again became the focus of legislative debate.

Suffragists had good reason to be optimistic in the Senate where they had won in 1911. They repeated the victory on 7 May 1913 by a vote of 29 to 15 (three votes over the required majority). The House presented the real difficulty; in 1911 the bill had fallen ten votes short in this body. With Senate passage, all eyes focused on the House and a frenetic month of lobbying ensued. These lobbying efforts were the major factor behind a favorable vote in the House. Suffragists converted an uncertain House Speaker, secured cosponsorship by a "wet" and a "dry" legislator, deluged the legislature with supportive telegrams, hounded representatives identified as "doubtful," organized a telephone brigade, shadowed favorable legislators to insure their presence at important votes, and much more. Their considerable efforts were rewarded on 11 June 1913 when the House passed the measure by a vote of 83 to 58 (six votes over the required majority). Governor Dunne solidified the victory and fulfilled a promise by ratifying the measure on 26 June. (For detailed accounts of the campaign see Trout 1920; Abbott 1950, 2; *HWS* 6 : 150–165; Wheeler and Wortman 1977, 107–108; and McCulloch records in SL, CWM Papers, 1913.)

Considerable opposition to the bill was voiced during deliberations in the House, and Trout claimed that close to a million dollars was spent on the antisuffrage cause (1920, 106). There was also pressure on the governor not to ratify as well as subsequent constitutionality challenges, but the bill survived all opposition and challenges. McCulloch's records of the movement (SL, CWM Papers, 1913) attributed the success to the election of twenty-five Progressive legislators in 1912. While not all of them voted for the suffrage bill, enough did to tip the balance.

The bill came to be known as the "Illinois Law" and the Presidential Suffrage Bill. It was modeled on previous Illinois suffrage bills that had granted the vote for offices not designated by the state constitution, but it was broader than the earlier bills on school suffrage, township suffrage, etc. It permitted women to vote for all national offices and virtually all municipal, county, town, and village offices. Given the unusual difficulties of amending the state constitution, this was the only plausible strategy within Illinois at the time. Thus Illinois became the first state east of the Mississippi to pass and maintain a suffrage bill of this scope. For all practical purposes, Illinois was added to the ranks of suffrage states.

The suffrage victory was made possible in Illinois because a cross-class, multiconstituency alliance agreed on the need for the vote. They did not agree, however, on why the vote was needed. The thread that connected all prosuffrage women proved strong enough to win the vote, but it unraveled shortly thereafter. A striking example of this unraveling occurred within two months of winning the vote in Illinois.

Shortly after the House victory, William Randolph Hearst approached the IESA and the CPEL, offering to print a special suffrage edition of the *Chicago Examiner* with the proceeds going into the suffrage treasury. Suffrage leaders agreed. However, the Hearst papers had been placed on organized labor's list of employers engaged in unfair labor practices. The Chicago Federation of Labor (CFL) accordingly sent the suffrage organizations a series of resolutions condemning Hearst, his influence over Chicago, his nonunion pressrooms, and his attempt "to gain control of the women's vote for his political gain" (SL, ESS Papers, CFL resolution, n.d.). Since the CFL had endorsed woman suffrage for almost two decades, they had good reason to expect reciprocal support.

The WTUL, as a CFL affiliate, made its position abundantly clear:

> The Equal Suffrage League will have to get along . . . without the aid of the workingwomen members of the Women's Trade Union League . . . [who] will have nothing to do with the suffrage edition of the Examiner. . . . Representatives of the labor unions have called on Mrs. Grace Trout and Mrs. Antoinette Funk of the Equal Suffrage League and asked them not to start the woman's movement off by playing Hearst's political game. (UICC, WTUL clippings, 10 July 1913)

The WTUL proposed a meeting with the suffrage organizations to air grievances. After agreeing to meet, the IESA and CPEL skipped the meeting, ignored the protest, and proceeded with the special edition. The entire venture was then condemned by the WTUL, and the movement split into two factions: WTUL members and settlement house activists (including McDowell, Haley, and Robins) who opposed the edition, and leaders of the major suffrage organizations (including McCulloch, Stewart, and Trout) who supported the edition. The WTUL charged that the IESA had become a "very exclusive club indeed" and accused suffragists of acting exactly like the corrupt male politicians the movement had traditionally condemned. Mary McDowell described the situation succinctly when she wrote: "Our sisters of the suffrage movement who worked so splendidly for us BECAUSE WE ARE WOMEN failed to understand the struggle we must make BECAUSE WE ARE WORKERS" (UICC, WTUL clippings, The Day Book, 12 August 1913; emphasis in original).

Suffrage organization records do not acknowledge the WTUL protest over the Hearst suffrage edition, but they note that the venture was a financial success, raising a total of $15,000 (*HWS* 4:158). The records also reveal that suffragists disputed at considerable length the appropriateness of placing a liquor ad in the suffrage special edition. They eventually rejected the ad, viewing it as a ploy to counteract temperance forces (see SL, CWM Papers, Stewart to McCulloch, 6 August 1913, and Willard Hall Speech, 23 June 1913). This attention to detail while ignoring the larger issues raised by the Hearst edition—the long-standing CFL endorsement of suffrage and the role of the WTUL in the suffrage campaign—reveal the strength of class and organizational interests among middle-class suffragists and demonstrate the fragility of the cross-class alliance that so recently had succeeded in winning the vote for women in Illinois.

The suffrage victory and the peculiar form it took changed the dynamics of suffrage work in Illinois. One new task involved defending the bill from challenges to its constitutionality until the Illinois Supreme Court upheld it the next year. Another task involved registration drives and educational efforts to persuade women to use their newly won power. A third issue involved the best way to win full suffrage throughout the state. As the IESA confronted this agenda, the NAWSA entered one of its most contentious periods, and national disputes began to affect the Illinois movement as well.

Faced with these conditions, the suffrage movement experienced an identity crisis in the interim period until national enfranchisement. The coalition that had won in 1913 fell apart not only across class lines but within the middle-class leadership as well. The latter group split into differing factions over appropriate state strategy, differing orientations to the NAWSA and national disputes, and personality differences. This split helped ensure that no additional suffrage gains were registered in Illinois from 1913 to 1920 (when national enfranchisement was won), but it is unclear whether even a well-coordinated effort could have achieved further success in Illinois.

What is clear is that the Illinois movement did not mount a well-coordinated effort. Schisms in Illinois were inspired by splits in the national movement. When the NAWSA hesitated over the Shafroth-Palmer Resolution, dissident suffragists in the Congressional Union broke with NAWSA and established the Congressional Union as an independent organization to work for suffrage on the federal level. This split was reproduced in Illinois, with Catharine McCulloch first supporting Shafroth-Palmer and later reversing her position (see SL, CWM Papers, McCulloch to Shaw, 27 March 1914; Shaw to McCulloch, 14 April 1914; and "New Amendment Not Workable," 9 May 1914). Like other supporters of the resolution, McCulloch criticized the Congressional Union for breaking with the NAWSA and introducing factionalism into the movement. Ella Stewart, on the other hand, defended the CU against attacks by Illinois suffragists, including her traditional ally McCulloch.

Grace Wilbur Trout also criticized Shafroth-Palmer and openly supported the CU policy of federal enfranchisement. In 1914 she blocked IESA approval of the amendment, and she also blocked a resolution the NAWSA had requested of its affiliates criticizing the Congressional Union. These actions made Illinois the only state organization not to approve the NAWSA resolution, and from this point on Trout became an increasingly controversial figure in the Illinois movement. When a suffragist parade was held in Chicago, many suffragists refused to march behind Trout. In the ensuing months she solidified control of the IESA, and disgruntled suffragists abandoned hope of recapturing the organization.

By 1915 the suffrage situation in Illinois was chaotic. In February Anna Howard Shaw scolded McCulloch for losing control of the IESA and urged her to form a new suffrage organization within the state (see SL, CWM Papers, Shaw to McCulloch, 15 February 1915, and Funk to McCulloch, 17 March 1915). The final straw came when Trout refused to support a campaign for a constitutional amendment, claiming that all IESA resources were needed to defend the existing suffrage law. Given this intransigence, McCulloch "sounded a call to revolt against the IESA" and established a new organization called the Suffrage Amendment Alliance. The sole purpose of this group was to seek passage of an amendment to the Illinois state constitution enfranchising women throughout the state on a par with men. In 1916 Trout's IESA declared its preference for a state constitutional convention and a new constitution as the best method of completing the enfranchisement of women in Illinois.

From this point on, the IESA and the Suffrage Amendment Alliance pursued the same goal through drastically different means with no mutual cooperation. Neither tactic brought any success, and in 1919 both groups were relieved of the need for further work when the federal amendment passed Congress.

In many respects the Illinois suffrage movement might best be regarded as having ended in 1913 with its major, though still limited, victory. From the 1890s until its victory in 1913 the movement had carefully knit together a web of support that finally led to a major suffrage gain. Extending movement history beyond that point implies that the movement ended not with a bang but a whimper. The manner in which the movement split indicates how fragile the alliance had been all along. The cross-class division that emerged was not surprising; more remarkable was the way the upper-middle-class core of the movement also splintered into differing factions. Once the common concern that held this alliance together was granted, the alliance quickly unraveled. Before victory this alliance was a testimony to the ability of the movement to overcome class differences, to find ways of working together, to reach at least minimal strategical agreement, and to keep forces sufficiently in line so that the vote could be won.

The Illinois movement was honored in 1920 when the NAWSA held its victory convention in Chicago. Suffragists came from all over the country for a week-long celebration. With full parliamentary flourish, the NAWSA disbanded and the League of Women Voters was created. Six months later the IESA also convened in Chicago and disbanded. The last sentence of the last document the IESA printed proudly proclaimed: "The political liberty of the women of the United States is forever established—WE ARE CITIZENS!"

MOVEMENT TRANSFORMATION IN SOCIAL CONTEXT

The suffrage movement's process of transformation continued as it entered the twentieth century. The result was a movement that differed from the broad scope of the early period as well as from the narrow conservatism of the middle period. In the twentieth century social forces coalesced to produce a specialized movement for suffrage. This section analyzes that movement in its social context.

The first dimension of the movement's scope involved the symbolic breadth of the ballot demand itself. Two processes underway since the 1880s continued in the final period. First, partial gains for women in other areas defused some of the symbolic power of the ballot demand because gradual progress seemed possible. Second, the detachment of the ballot demand from an organic program of emancipatory feminist change meant that the ballot demand could be, and often was, linked to quite different and sometimes conservative goals. These forms of transformation continued into the twentieth century.

What changed in the final period was the perceived radicalism of the ballot demand. In schematic terms, the early movement proclaimed and embraced the radicalism of demanding the ballot whereas the movement in the middle period was concerned about and sometimes disavowed the radicalism of the ballot demand. In the final period, the question of radicalism did not even arise. None of the primary sources from this period expressed any concern with this question. This normalization was surely due, in part, to simple observation of those states where women voted. By 1896 women voted in four western states, and after 1910 they acquired the right in other states as well. It was obvious to clear-sighted observers that the enfranchisement of women did not bring the radical changes that some suffragists envisioned. With this evidence, whatever lingering associations the ballot demand may have had with radicalism dissipated, and it was perceived as one reform among others.

The second dimension of the movement's scope involved the nature and extent of demands for legal change. The early movement was judged broad by virtue of the number and diversity of emancipatory legal demands it raised; the middle movement became transformed when it shifted much of its legislative program toward social control measures vis-à-vis other groups. The final period presented a third posture that was not as broad as the early movement, but neither was it as coercive as the middle movement.

The later movement's program for legal change was distinctive because of its diversity of demands—a diversity that reflected the multiconstituency alliance that constituted the movement. At least four separate types of demands were raised by the suffrage movement in this period. First, there was a partial revival of the early stress on legal changes that would increase women's political freedom and achieve parity between their legal status and that of men.[20] A second set of demands continued to center around social control, including prohibiting the sale of liquor in dance halls, censoring of moving pictures, and increasing the age of consent. Thus emancipatory demands reminiscent of the early period came to coexist with social control legislation derived from the middle period, and they constituted one part of the movement's program for change in the later period.

Two distinctive new categories of movement demands concerned legislation to solve problems associated with industrialization and urbanization. Good examples of the former include legislation that would limit the length of the working day for women and provide a minimum wage for both women and children (see, e.g., Kelley [1905] 1969).[21] With respect to urbanization, the suffrage movement became involved in legislation to provide city services, including garbage collection, meat inspection, and sanitation laws. These concerns were articulated into movement ideology through municipal housekeeping arguments (see, e.g., McDowell 1937).

In sum, the movement's program for legal change was more diverse than in either of the two earlier periods. While it did not have the emancipatory character of the early movement, neither did it reduce itself to the predominantly social control impulse of the middle movement. Thus the continuing transformation of the later movement resulted in a more progressive movement posture than had been evident in the movement's middle period.

The third dimension of the movement's scope concerned the movement's challenge to the sexual division of labor. During the middle period the movement came to endorse many aspects of the sexual division of labor—aspects it had questioned in its earlier broad phase. The endorsement occurred through the movement's promotion of women as mothers and nurturers who possessed a distinctive nature that set them apart from men. However, this worldview was also a basis for opposition and a source of resistance to an industrializing world that many reformers perceived as manipulative, instrumental, and overly rational. Thus, although their shift in worldview constituted a type of depoliticization, a romanticized basis for resisting an industrializing world nonetheless endured throughout the middle movement.

In the twentieth century the movement continued to endorse the sexual division of labor, but in a way that eliminated the basis for even a romanticized resistance to the industrial world. The endorsement shifted from an idealized view of gender differences to a rationalized sense of gender obligations, along with a more technological perception of the social world and the roles of men and women within it. Reflected in the domestic science and household economics movements as well as in the ideology of municipal housekeeping, these tendencies culminated in a new version of the separate spheres argument. Men and women were seen as playing complementary economic roles in the public and private spheres, and each sphere was seen as subject to the same processes of rationalization and industrialization.

Later movement ideology thereby involved a much closer fit between the movement's ideal conception of women's position and their actual position in the early twentieth century (among the middle class). In the early period the movement openly challenged the sexual division of labor. In the middle period it endorsed sex differences but nonetheless maintained a romanticized vision of an alternative world. In the final period an almost total rapprochement occurred between the movement's vision and the new social order of the twentieth century. Put differently, the movement's analysis of these issues became increasingly one dimensional, and that dimension was isomorphic with the actual position of at least those middle-class women to whom the movement was most attuned.[22]

Although the movement's normative ideal for women closely reflected the realities of middle-class life, movement spokeswomen were aware of deviations from that ideal and took them into account. For instance, the movement became more vocal with respect to women's occupational opportunities and the position of working women. At the same time, it became almost completely silent on women's marital status and domestic subordination. Hence, the movement offered new support to women who worked out of necessity or choice, but it no longer balanced this support with a corresponding focus on the domestic realm. In this sense, the movement had a less wholistic vision of women's position than it had had in the early period.

The fourth dimension of the movement's scope concerned the types of alliances the movement formed. A pattern of transformation occurred from the early to the middle period in which the suffrage movement shifted its alliances from dispossessed groups (blacks, women workers, etc.) to more advantaged groups seeking reform in the name of social control (temperance, moral reform, social purity, etc.). In the later period the movement shifted its alliances again. Temperance-like coalitions became less prominent and ties to working women were reestablished. On the surface, then, the later movement resembled the early movement in its inclusion of working women in the suffrage coalition.

Beneath this surface there resided an important difference. The earlier alliance reflected a broad-based emancipatory ideology in which the vote was one demand among others. The later alliance had a more instrumental character. In the twentieth century the suffrage movement reached out to dispossessed groups not out of an emancipatory ideology but out of a tactical necessity to broaden the suffrage ranks. In its final days the movement included working women, immigrant women, and some black women, but the major motivation for inclusion was the perception that such groups were needed if the vote was to be won.

Further support for this interpretation may be seen in the even greater enthusiasm with which the movement recruited upper-class allies in the final period. If the movement had been proceeding from a broad ideological stance against entrenched interests, these allies would have been odd indeed. However, they were perfectly sensible (and desirable) allies for a movement seeking the widest possible alliance around a single-issue demand. In short, the movement in the final period recruited new allies out of an instrumental sense of what was necessary to win the vote. Once again, this made it a less emancipatory movement than it had been in the early period but a somewhat more progressive movement than in the middle period.

The transformations described here were not part of a unilinear and mechanical process that started in 1870 and found each decade proportionally narrower than the former decade. The major break between broad and narrow phases of the suffrage movement can be located around 1870; before then the movement was broadly oriented, and afterward it narrowed its scope in various ways. It does not follow that the later period was necessarily narrower than the middle period, and there are too many counterexamples to support such a claim. It does follow that the later period was different from the middle period. The interesting question then becomes how the differences in movement transformation from the middle to the later period can be explained. The logical place to look for answers is once again in the changing social context of the movement over these decades.

If movements reflect their social context, then differing patterns of transformation must be analyzed by reference to differing social contexts. In the twentieth century, social class, organizational form, and ideological stance all continued to be important mediating links between American society and the suffrage movement. Considering social-class factors first, it was evident that in the movement's final period, the class background of its leaders, the social base of its following, and the class situation of its core all changed notably from the middle period. Each of these factors merits brief discussion.

The stereotyped view of the suffrage movement as a middle-class movement falters in the final period in Illinois because it obscures the major role played by upper-class women in the suffrage movement. The most prominent leaders in this period were Jane Addams, Louise deKoven Bowen, Ellen Henrotin, Catharine McCulloch, Margaret Robins, Ella Stewart, and Grace Wilbur Trout.[23] Of these, only McCulloch and Stewart fit the traditional mold of suffragists from middle-class and professional backgrounds. Four of the other five fit even the most restrictive definitions of upper-class standing, with Addams (whose father was a successful miller, banker, and state senator) being a borderline case. The conservative conclusion is that at least half of the leadership of the Illinois suffrage movement in the twentieth century consisted of upper-class women. This figure has been ignored in standard accounts of the suffrage movement, underscoring the need for research on other regional branches of the movement to determine whether the Illinois pattern was exceptional or typical.[24]

This pattern of involvement on the part of upper-class women in Illinois must be interpreted with some care. While these women represented amounts of wealth and property that had never before been associated with the suffrage movement, they did not bring an entirely different worldview to the suffrage effort when compared with their middle-class counterparts. In this regard upper-class involvement in the U.S. suffrage movement was not as dramatic as it would have been in numerous European countries where upper-class background signified truly aristocratic connections and concerns. In the United States, upper-class women tended to support the suffrage cause (if at all) for many of the same reasons as middle-class women; perhaps the major difference was that some upper-class women brought to their involvement a nascent sense of noblesse oblige which was lacking in their middle-class allies. Hence, the increasing participation of upper-class women did not cause the transformation of the suffrage movement as much as it testified to the already transformed nature of that movement. At the same time, the involvement of upper-class women on a large scale surely reinforced the new direction of the movement by making it less likely than ever that the movement would return to its earlier, more generalized attacks on all forms of wealth, power, and privilege.

Turning to the social base of the movement, the middle-class truism describes the majority of the movement but again obscures the extent to which women from virtually all class levels found some degree of representation in the suffrage movement. While all classes were not proportionately represented, the number of working-class women who worked for the movement in the final period was considerably greater than in the middle period. When working-class women did join suffrage organizations, their status in the organization tended to mirror their position in the class structure generally. More typically, they worked through their own organizations (often affiliated with trade unions) and participated in united fronts and coalitions around particular suffrage campaigns. Hence, both the broad movement and the suffrage organizations included more working-class women (as well as upper-class women) than they had in the middle period.

Perhaps most important, the class situation of the upper-middle-class core of the suffrage movement changed in this period. Again, the middle-class truism requires two important specifications. The first is that it was the professional-managerial sector of the middle class that came to dominate the movement in this period. The second is that this sector brought with it a distinctive set of interests in a rationalized social order which informed their approach to social reform. These specifications are best illustrated through comparisons between the middle and final period.

One informative contrast involves the type of middle-class woman that predominated in each period. The logical candidates for such a contrast are Elizabeth Harbert and Catharine McCulloch. Harbert was a transitional figure between the earlier period of episodic professional involvements for women and the later period of full-time careers. Reflecting this transitional status, Harbert was more consistently involved in occupational pursuits than women before her, but she still managed to be a Renaissance woman with numerous interests and involvements. McCulloch's career as a lawyer, by contrast, involved greater professional training, a narrower set of occupational involvements, and a more definite career line. In short, McCulloch followed the pattern of a modern career much more closely. As a result, she was more firmly located in a relatively privileged niche of the class and occupational order than Harbert and other figures from the middle period. The nature and strength of this class location had an important bearing on the ideological worldview of women like McCulloch, shaping their perceptions of and participation in reform movements.

These claims may be developed further by a second contrast—between the meaning of middle-class status in these two periods and the social ideologies that were associated with this status at different times. During the middle movement we observed the development of a middle-class ideology that stressed social harmony and equilibrium and sought a unified, symmetrical, and industrious society. In class terms, this ideology amounted to an appeal for reconciliation and accommodation by minimizing class differences and emphasizing common interests. In feminist terms, this ideology appealed to feminine qualities and the role women might play in realizing these visions. For all the vagueness of this ideology, it nonetheless contained oppositional elements that allowed women to formulate an alternative view of a world free of what they considered to be negative features of an industrializing society.

The ideological vision of the professional-managerial sector in the twentieth century was distinguished from this vision by the erosion of oppositional elements and alternative visions. These were replaced by an essentially technical interest in rationalizing, administering, and managing the new social order through a program of progressive reform. Evident in the domestic science movement, the professionalization of social work, the calls for trained parenthood, and Breckinridge's equation of ballots and biscuit machines, this orientation became widespread among middle-class reformers. It was within this broader vision that woman suffrage found its appropriate place. In sum, the class location, interests, and situation of professional-managerial, upper-middle-class suffragists in the early twentieth century oriented them to "fine-tuning" a social order that they found quite advantageous on class grounds. The fine-tuning was to be accomplished through the enfranchisement of women, who then would use this newly gained power to implement the reform program of this sector of the upper middle class.

To summarize this contrast: whereas the middle period saw the "making" of a broad middle class that supported a general ideology of social harmony, the later period witnessed the "making" of a professional-managerial sector of this class which promoted specific reforms designed to strengthen basic features of the existing society. The stances of these groups were class conditioned and class conscious in both periods, with variations that may be traced to differing class sectors and situations in each period.

These changes in class background, social base, and class situation render more understandable the pattern of movement transformation that occurred. The new leadership group and movement core were not interested in promoting the ballot demand as a radical one portending major shifts in power relations. Those women with the greatest interest in such a change— working-class women—were relegated to the least powerful positions within movement organizations. While the movement broadened its program for legal change in this period and became somewhat more progressive, most of these changes may be construed as part of the strategy of fine-tuning the social order which was so central to the reform ambitions of the movement's leadership and core in this period.[25]

An appreciation of the class orientation of the movement also renders more understandable its specific endorsements of the sexual division of labor and women's traditional roles. These derived in large part from the scientific, industrial, and technical imperatives that informed the movement's approach to reform. When these imperatives combined with women's emergent role in the household as promoted by the domestic science and household economics movements, the movement again assumed a position of affirming existing social arrangements.[26] Finally, the tactical and instrumental nature of the movement's alliances in the final period was consistent with the class character of the movement. This leadership had no reason to form substantive alliances with dispossessed groups and every reason to seek tactical coalitions around the single issue they deemed important. These connections illustrate how particular dimensions of transformation in the early twentieth century may be traced to specific changes in class-related variables within the same historical period.

The importance of class factors is also suggested by the social differentiation of women that accompanied these processes. This increasing differentiation was reflected in the movement's articulated perception of social-class differences in each period. In the early period women's rights activists spoke as if class differences were a relatively minor matter when set aside the commonalities of gender. In the middle period class differences were acknowledged as more important, but still as something that could be overcome on the basis of common social interests and the pursuit of social harmony. In the final period movement leaders consciously recognized the class structure as a major, permanent, and fundamental feature of their society, and as one that necessitated carefully calculated, self-conscious appeals across class lines to recruit the broader base the suffrage leaders needed.

As this process of differentiation proceeded (mediated primarily by social-class differences, but also by ethnic, racial, and urban-rural differences) and as it became more evident to suffrage leaders, pressures toward transformation increased. To whatever extent a broad feminist movement can only be built and sustained on numerous gender commonalities shared by large numbers of women, this sharing of commonalities became increasingly difficult as the movement entered the twentieth century. One of the few remaining commonalities shared by all women and distinguishing them from all men was precisely the formal lack of voting rights. In large measure, this accounts for why the movement became a single-issue one as it entered the twentieth century.

This analysis of the relation between social class and the suffrage movement has challenged from several angles the often-cited truism that the movement was middle class. Nothing said here has disproved that description, but the Illinois data demonstrate its limitations for analyzing selected transformations of the movement. Explanations become possible when that deceptive concept is decomposed into its constituent elements and the analysis is sensitized to variations in historical contexts. One can then begin to explain patterns of transformation in what remained—at the highest level of abstraction—a middle-class movement from beginning to end.

These changes also clarify how the circle of potential beneficiaries changed over time. Compared to the middle period, this circle expanded in the twentieth century to include more groups of women. It came to include urban women who might be able to use the vote to deal with undeniable problems associated with urbanization and industrialization. It also came to include working women in a more substantial way than earlier; for them the ballot acquired a more concrete value in an era when labor was turning to legislation for partial redress of grievances over wages, working conditions, and length of the working day. In this sense, the circle of potential beneficiaries expanded as a function of the practical value the vote acquired for implementing legislative change.

At the same time, this circle "flattened out" because the only benefits the movement offered were related to the vote. In becoming a single-issue movement, the potential benefits became isomorphic with the possibilities of electoral politics. These possibilities were limited in important ways. When women actually did vote, their vote fragmented along the predictable lines of class, ethnicity, and party politics. Even before winning the vote it was clear that women perceived its benefits in class-differentiated ways. Hence, it was not surprising that it proved impossible to mobilize a "female vote" in the way that many suffragists had hoped. This did not mean there were no benefits to be promised or won with the vote, but it meant that the bulk of those benefits occurred in class-specific ways.

A final change continued a trend from the middle period by identifying a movement beneficiary that transcended women altogether. In the 1880s middle-class reformers had sought the vote as a means of reforming and benefiting society in general. In the twentieth century Progressive reformers usurped the suffrage issue as a means of implementing the reform interests of the professional-managerial sector of the middle class. For this group, the beneficiary of woman suffrage would not be women, but rather the classes, occupations, and interests most closely connected with Progressivism after the turn of the century. From beginning to end, therefore, the woman suffrage movement faced the danger of having its major demand subordinated to the interests of other groups and classes.

A second mediating link between social context and social movements involves organizational factors. In the final period of the suffrage movement the existence and continuity of the IESA was more secure as a result of its 1891 victory and a new generation of stronger leaders. Though more secure, it remained difficult to substantially increase the membership of the suffrage organization. Thus a conscious decision was made by the leadership in the 1890s to promote suffrage work by nonsuffrage organizations and associations.

A striking parallel here to the earlier temperance movement can be seen, although in the twentieth century the role was played primarily by the club movement. Just as the alliance with temperance had diluted the more political aspects of the ballot demand, the coalition with the club movement also diluted this content. When and where the club movement supported the vote, it did so not out of a commitment to women's emancipation or equality but rather for reasons of expediency. The parallel was even more pronounced because the temperance movement and the club movement brought a similar orientation to suffrage in these two periods. The common theme was that the vote was required to protect the home and defend the family (and particularly children) from a hostile world. In both periods the temperance and club movements respectively introduced this rationale into the suffrage movement; in both periods it fragmented a politically feminist ideology into a range of more specific and occasionally opposing concerns. This further encouraged the tendency for the ballot to become a floating currency that could be linked to all sorts of expediency causes.

A distinct contrast with the middle period was the emergence of multiple and ultimately rival suffrage associations in Illinois. Organized around clubs, neighborhoods, colleges, professions, and trades, such associations reflected the multiconstituency base that the suffrage movement was developing. The most interesting case of parallel organizations involved the CPEL and the IESA. Our analysis has already suggested the extent to which these organizations pursued different goals. The IESA became the only organization in the state espousing a politically feminist ideology (alongside other orientations) that demanded the vote on the basis of justice and equality (alongside other arguments). The ideology of the CPEL was more class bound and less politically feminist. It absorbed the suffrage demand into a larger program of reform whose focus was the preservation of basic social institutions and practices. For the CPEL, female suffrage was one useful tool for eliminating corruption, extending social control, and rationalizing the social order, and the League promoted woman suffrage for these reasons. When the CPEL became the dominant suffrage organization after 1910, another facet of movement transformation materialized: the CPEL redirected even the single-issue suffrage demand of the IESA to nonfeminist ends.

During the last decade of the movement, this redirection was symbolized by the election of Grace Trout (a member of the CWC and past president of the CPEL) to head the IESA. With Trout dominating the IESA, there was no longer any suffrage organization that spoke to the political interests of women as women in ways that the suffrage movement traditionally had done. Upon winning the 1913 bill, Trout contributed heavily to the schism that divided the remnants of the movement and prevented any further effective work. As we have seen, the suffrage movement thereby spent its last five years in Illinois in organizational disarray.

A final mediating link between social context and social movements involves a movement's own analysis and ideology. The most striking feature of the twentieth-century movement was its new flexibility in tailoring prosuffrage arguments to the particularistic concerns of the audience they were addressing. This was one of the ways the movement implemented its strategical commitment to broadening the base of the suffrage movement. With this increasing flexibility, the movement abandoned its traditional conversion strategy (proselytizing small numbers in an intense way) and began seeking minimal commitments from large numbers of people. In general, these changes in movement ideology accentuated its endorsement of women's traditional roles because this was the logical place to build particularistic appeals to differentiated audiences. Put differently, movement ideology followed an instrumental principle whose goal was to maximize the number supporting suffrage for whatever reason rather than to promote a consistent and coherent ideology of female emancipation.

This summary implies a final refinement of Kraditor's thesis about the movement's shift from justice to expediency arguments (1965). While the direction of the change is indisputable, it is also true that expediency arguments were found at the beginning of the movement and justice arguments at the end. A slightly different formulation captures the nature of these changes more precisely. What distinguished the later period in Illinois was not that it made only expediency arguments but that all of its arguments for the vote were motivated by an expediency principle whose intent was to maximize support for the cause. Thus, justice arguments were made when they were expedient vis-à-vis the goal of maximizing support. Put differently, the instrumental orientation of movement ideology in this period led speakers to make justice/equality arguments to those audiences that would be most moved by such appeals and would therefore support the movement. The same instrumental orientation led the same speakers to make expediency arguments to other audiences, with the same goal of recruiting movement support. Thus, while expediency arguments predominated over justice arguments in the later movement à la Kraditor, justice arguments lingered in the movement repertoire because of their instrumental utility for mobilizing some audiences.

This orientation also bears on the question of endogenous selective mechanisms within the movement. The instrumental orientation characterized traditional suffragists like McCulloch and Stewart as well as the more traditional IESA. These leaders and this organization favored whatever arguments would maximize pressure on the state legislature. The other major choice was exercised by the CPEL, which subsumed the suffrage demand into a larger program for rationalizing the social order. For the CPEL, maximizing suffrage support was not as important as directing that support to the Progressive reform program. In both cases, however, these endogenous choices were consistent with the trend of movement transformation.

This analysis of endogenous selective mechanisms makes sense only if it is reasonable to think that other choices were possible. If public opinion or class background were overwhelming pressures, these would be patterns of determination rather than issues of volition. It can be demonstrated that other choices were possible, though they were not adopted within the suffrage movement. This availability of choices was evident in the bifurcation among middle-class women over class interests and reform goals. One group, truer to their class position, did not challenge the basic social order but rather sought to strengthen it. The other group defected from their class background to ally with working women and speak for and from their interests, and thereby raised more basic challenges to the social order. The first group constituted the suffrage movement proper; the second was found in explicitly cross-class associations such as the Women's Trade Union League.

In the Chicago case, this bifurcation correlated perfectly with one crucial factor in the biographies of the women who made up the two groups. The crucial factor, shared by virtually all who adopted a working-class perspective and absent from those who did not, was involvement in the settlement house movement. Women from relatively privileged backgrounds who participated in the settlement houses came to conceptualize political questions from the perspective of working women rather than Woman in the abstract. Examples include Margaret Robins, Mary McDowell, Anna Nicholes, Jane Addams, and to a lesser extent Louise deKoven Bowen. Women from similar backgrounds without settlement house experience (including McCulloch, Trout, and Stewart) were notably less interested and less informed about the needs of these women and remained more firmly anchored by their class, occupational, and organizational interests. It was this latter group that made choices about the orientation of the suffrage movement. Because such choices were possible, it follows that endogenous selective mechanisms really did operate in influencing the orientation of the movement. Because not closely involved with the settlement houses, leaders of the organized suffrage movement remained consistent to their class position and advocated suffrage ideologies that best fit that position.

In all these ways the mediating links of social class, organizational form, and ideological stance clarify the connections between social context and movement posture. By focusing on these links, the particular shape of movement transformation in the twentieth century becomes more understandable; by focusing on them throughout the history of the suffrage movement, the general contours of movement transformation have emerged.

The above analysis has stressed how much the suffrage movement changed over time relative to its origins. In one sense, this is the story of a movement that gradually shifted toward a more "winnable" agenda. However, the adoption of this more winnable agenda by no means guaranteed the success of the movement. The notion of a direct correspondence between transformation and "winnability" is belied by the movement coming close to enfranchisement on national and local levels at its broadest point in 1870. It was also belied by the fact that movement prospects for success did not improve throughout the nineteenth century after distinct patterns of transformation had already occurred. In short, the struggle to win the vote even in a transformed agenda as a single issue remained a difficult one. Hence, it is reasonable to ask which factors made the difference in producing the victory of 1913.

This question can be divided into two subquestions; one concerns how the movement contributed to its own victory while the other involves the larger historical circumstances in which the victory occurred. An answer to the first question must underscore the manner in which the suffrage movement broadened its base in the early twentieth century by successfully soliciting support from many sectors of society. Only in the last decade could the movement plausibly claim widespread support, and it is difficult to envision a victory without this factor.

There were several reasons why broad support was a necessary (but not sufficient) condition for winning the vote. For one, the goal the movement sought could be achieved only through legislative channels, and there was no obvious reason why legislators should have been favorable without substantial pressure. For another, one major method of influencing legislatures is precisely through voting, so the movement was in the paradoxical position of being denied a major method for seeking legislative change. Finally, the relative exclusion of women from the public realm and existing structures of power meant that women had little institutional power to bring to their movement. All of these factors put a premium on mobilizing the broadest possible base of support to win the vote.[27]

Put differently, the movement's major contribution to its own success was its ability to develop a cross-class, multiconstituency alliance bringing effective pressure to bear on existing power structures. This alliance resembled what Meredith Tax (1980) has called a "united front of women" in that women from different locations in the social structure, with disparate long-term interests, nonetheless acted together to win woman suffrage. They acted together for differing reasons, but the alliance itself became feasible when its participants came to see their common goal as more important—at least for the moment—than their differing reasons for seeking it.

The most important feature of this united front was its cross-class character. Just as it is difficult to envision the movement succeeding without expanding its support in general, it is also difficult to envision it succeeding without support from both working-class women and upper-class women. The former group provided some of the most cogent and persuasive arguments on why the vote was needed (as well as some of the most energetic workers), while the latter group provided influential spokeswomen whose social credentials added great legitimacy to the movement. When the contributions of these groups were added to the ongoing efforts of the movement's middle-class core, movement effectiveness reached its greatest level. The movement contributed to its own victory in these ways, but another "contribution" was made in the form of new historical circumstances.

This second question may be posed through a minor revision of the Marxist dictum on men and history: movements make their own history, but they do not make it just as they please; they do not make it under circumstances chosen by themselves but under circumstances directly encountered, given, and transmitted from the past (Marx [1852] 1963, 15). For much of the suffrage movement's history, its inherited circumstances were not favorable. In the last decade of the movement, circumstances became more favorable when many sectors of American society articulated an interest in social and political reform of various sorts. There was no more common agreement throughout the society on which reforms were needed than there was among women on why the vote was needed. But just as the ballot had become more important than the differing reasons for it, so too agreement on the need for some kind of reform became the dominant political tone of the Progressive Era.

The manner in which Progressivism created more conducive circumstances for winning woman suffrage in Illinois may be described at three different levels of abstraction. Most generally, the overall climate of reform added legitimacy to the cause of woman suffrage and contributed to a more serious consideration of the issue than it had previously received. A more important and specific connection involved the manner in which the vote was wedded to the Progressive agenda. In the last decade of the movement the vote became a crucial link in the chain of social change sought by progressive reformers. The partial merger of these causes was a natural one because both rested on a similar social-class base of upper- and middle-class reformers in general and professional-managerial interests in particular. This alliance perpetuated movement transformation by minimizing the feminist content of the ballot demand. In this sense, the Progressive Era was the final chapter in a long history of feminist orientation becoming subordinated to other issues, ranging from abolitionism and black enfranchisement through temperance and social control to absorption into the Progressive agenda. The obvious difference in this final subordination was that it won the vote for women.

The final and most specific way in which the Progressive Era contributed to the suffrage victory was the Progressive party's endorsement of suffrage and the role of party legislators in the 1913 vote. Though the party was too small to guarantee victory, it made the critical difference. When the votes of Progressive party members in the Illinois legislature were added to the partial support from other parties, the total reached the majority required to pass the bill. It is also difficult to imagine the Illinois victory occurring when it did without the reform context provided by the Progressive Era.

On the level of inherited circumstances, then, the Progressive Era was the major factor that contributed to the Illinois victory of 1913. As such, Progressivism in Illinois was roughly analogous to the role of World War I in contributing to the national suffrage victory. But just as the war did not "give" women the vote independent of their own mobilizing efforts to achieve it, neither did the Progressive Era "give" women the vote. What produced the victory was a combination of elements in which the movement made its own history by broadening its base and establishing a cross-class, multiconstituency alliance, while simultaneously inheriting circumstances that at last were more favorable to achieving its goal. Only when all these factors came together did women in Illinois win the right to vote.

A New View of Woman Suffrage and Social Movements

The suffrage movement that won the vote in the early twentieth century was profoundly different from the movement that initiated the fight in the middle of the nineteenth century. This study of the movement in Illinois has attempted to describe and explain these differences for at least one regional sector of the suffrage movement. In the process, a new view of the woman suffrage movement has emerged alongside a different approach to the analysis of social movements. These concluding remarks summarize this new view and this different approach and discuss their implications for further research in the area of woman suffrage and social movements.

ON THE WOMAN SUFFRAGE MOVEMENT

The history of the woman suffrage movement in the United States is increasingly well known. This study has built on that knowledge and sought to advance it in several different directions. Four sets of concluding comments are in order regarding the woman suffrage movement. The first involves the existence of regional variations within the movement, which heretofore have been overlooked. The second concerns the explanation of movement transformation that has emerged from this analysis of the Illinois movement. The third addresses the question of generalizing from the Illinois movement to the U.S. suffrage movement as a whole. The fourth identifies some distinctive features of women's movements of all sorts which are suggested by this analysis of the suffrage movement. These concluding remarks begin with the most specific and detailed aspects of the study and move toward greater generalization and speculation about the national suffrage movement and about women's movements in general.

Existing knowledge about the U.S. suffrage movement is derived almost exclusively from the suffrage movement in the Northeast, probably because the movement originated there and continued to be centered around New York and Boston throughout much of the nineteenth century. However, our knowledge is skewed too far toward the Northeast; virtually no attention has been paid to the suffrage movement in the South, the Midwest, or the Far West (a notable exception is Grimes 1967). This one-dimensional and reductionist view of the suffrage movement has made us inattentive to the movement in other areas and to variations between different regional branches of the movement. The data from Illinois demonstrate the existence and the extent of such variations between the Northeast and the Midwest.

The major variation of theoretical interest concerns patterns of movement transformation in each locale and historical period. Briefly summarized (see the appendix for a more detailed, comparative analysis of the suffrage movement in the Northeast and the Midwest), the suffrage movement in the Midwest started later and lagged behind the movement in the Northeast throughout the antebellum period. By 1870 the movements had become more synchronized around common goals and interests, although the midwestern movement had a less extensive network of alliances with other disadvantaged groups. More striking contrasts emerged in the middle period, when the midwestern movement underwent a relatively thorough process of transformation whereas the northeastern movement (at least the NWSA) remained relatively broad. In the final period both movements became specialized efforts to win the vote, but the midwestern movement was less elitist, racist, and nativist than the northeastern movement (at least the NAWSA). At the most detailed level, then, notable movement variations occurred in these different regions of the country.

An awareness of the nature of the suffrage movement in the Midwest provides a more well-rounded view of a major social movement than has traditionally been available. The Illinois data challenge some aspects of the traditional view and call for certain revisions in how the movement has typically been described. These findings imply that the suffrage movement cannot be reduced either to the national suffrage organizations or to the northeastern region without considerable distortion. Since this pattern has prevailed to date, a focus on regional variations would seem especially timely in future research on the woman suffrage movement.

This study has also proposed a distinctive explanation and interpretation of the woman suffrage movement as it unfolded in Illinois. Since this interpretation differs from prevailing ones, it may be useful to briefly reiterate the essence of previous interpretations by Kraditor (1965) and O'Neill (1969) and to indicate how the present interpretation differs from these standard accounts.

Kraditor's major thesis concerned the ideological shift in the woman suffrage movement from justice to expediency arguments around 1900. The data from Illinois sustain this thesis if it is construed as meaning shifting emphases rather than mutually exclusive alternatives. However, three modifications to this thesis have emerged on the basis of this analysis. First, a closer examination of the early movement reveals that it advanced all manner of prosuffrage arguments;[1] in the twentieth century the movement narrowed its focus to rely heavily, if not quite exclusively, on expediency arguments. This narrowed focus was motivated both by external social pressures and by internal movement choices. Second, what distinguished the later movement was not that it relied exclusively on expediency arguments for the vote, but rather that all of its prosuffrage argumentation was motivated by an expediency principle and an instrumental orientation whose goal was to maximize support for the cause. The argument varied with the audience; this usually led to expediency arguments, but occasionally it led to justice arguments for some audiences. Finally, it was suggested that for comprehending movement transformation, a more important change in movement ideology occurred than the justice-expediency shift. The more profound change from my perspective involved the shift from early prosuffrage arguments that challenged conventional notions of women's social position to later prosuffrage arguments that endorsed those conventional notions. Over time, the ballot demand was reconciled with the existing sexual order rather than being part of a larger challenge to that order, and this reconciliation was an important aspect of the transformation process.

The present study has also looked more closely at the role of what Kraditor called "socially conscious women" and their impact on the movement's changing orientation over time. Three themes in my analysis bear on this issue. First, an investigation into both the changing class background and fluid class situation of movement leaders is essential to interpreting the participation of these "socially conscious women" and their impact on the movement. To a considerable extent their social consciousness was shaped by a class consciousness which informed their participation in the movement. Second, while numerous external pressures pushed toward a narrowed movement, socially conscious women made choices that contributed to the pattern of movement transformation as well. This is evident in that other directions were possible for the movement, and some of these directions are illustrated by the participation of some middle-class women in organizations like the Women's Trade Union League. Finally, this account has sought to demonstrate that the changing orientation of the movement involved not just a tactical change in rhetorical style to appease opponents, but more fundamentally reflected differing worldviews and alternative visions of feminism that distinguished early and later leaders.

O'Neill's broad-ranging study of the woman movement proposed two major explanations for the transformation of the woman suffrage movement. First, he suggested that social control exercised by society at large contributed to the narrowing focus of the movement over the course of its history. Second, he argued that the movement's own analysis of women's position was ultimately inadequate and incomplete and thus contained the seeds of its own dissolution. Taken together, these explanations seem to preclude the possibility of success, for the movement is alternately portrayed as too radical to be tolerated but not radical enough to succeed.

This study has explored some of the complications involved in O'Neill's social control explanation. For one, social control efforts were evident from the very beginning of the movement, but they did not succeed in taming the movement until considerably later in the nineteenth century. This is best explained by pointing to the multifarious ways in which social control became more pronounced toward the end of the nineteenth century; the key question then involves the timing of these events. In the Illinois case, the data reveal that major patterns of movement transformation either preceded or accompanied increasing social control rather than following it in an unambiguous causal relation. In this instance Illinois may be somewhat atypical, for its process of transformation seems to have occurred earlier than in some sectors of the national movement. In light of these considerations, my interpretation may be seen as complementing O'Neill's "external social control" account with an "internal social class" account of how the movement was transformed by its own leaders and participants as their larger social interests and consciousness changed throughout the movement's duration.

This study has proposed an alternate way to conceptualize changes in the movement's analysis of women's social position. The Illinois data suggest that the early movement's analysis did not simply become diluted over time and thus dissolve from within. The data rather suggest that different historical conjunctures gave rise to fundamentally different analyses of women's position and needs. These different analyses were rooted in the equally different social interests of earlier and later leaders and participants. Hence, the later movement's analysis of women's situation was both more and less than a pale copy of the early movement's analysis. It was more because it fundamentally changed some of the premises of the early movement; it was less because these changes failed to preserve the broad scope of the early movement's stance.

A third set of issues raised by this study concerns whether this interpretation can be generalized to include the whole suffrage movement. On a descriptive level I have already stressed the importance of regional variations in the movement. On an interpretive level, however, the explanation developed for the Illinois movement is generalizable to the suffrage movement as a whole at an appropriate level of abstraction. The generalization is possible because both the Illinois movement and the national movement underwent similar processes of transformation over the course of their history. With variations noted above, both started as broad movements and both ended as specialized movements. While the precise timing and exact details of transformation differed, the overall direction of change was the same, meaning that the interpretation developed here can be generalized to the suffrage movement as a whole.

By arguing that the interpretation is generalizable at a suitable level of abstraction, I mean that the same conceptual framework that explains the Illinois movement can be used to explain the national movement. It survived alongside the same set of major changes in social structure examined for Illinois, and the effect of these changes on the national movement was broadly similar. While this conceptual framework contains common features that make for a generalizable argument, it also accounts for the variations in different regions noted above. This is accomplished by recognizing the differential operation of mediating links between social change and movement transformation in different regions and on different levels of the movement.

Two brief examples will illustrate my meaning. One variation noted above was the more thorough transformation of the Illinois movement in the middle period when compared to the NWSA. The factor that best explains this variation involves organizational processes. In Illinois the movement was unable to maintain organizational independence, strong leadership, and a distinctly political focus, which contributed heavily to its transformation. In the NWSA, Stanton and Anthony maintained these qualities until 1890 when the NWSA and AWSA merged; thus the broad scope of the national movement was maintained throughout the middle period. Organizational processes also account for variations in the final period, when the Illinois movement remained less racist, nativist, and elitist than the national movement. In this case a key factor was the NAWSA's attempt to accommodate southern suffragists within a national organization, and the subsequent pressure exerted by southerners led to a very conservative organizational posture. The Illinois movement faced no such imperative, thereby escaping such pressure to a much greater extent than was true in the national movement.

In short, the conceptual framework developed for explaining transformation in the Illinois movement may be used to explain similar changes in the national movement as a whole. In broad strokes, the explanations do not differ markedly because the processes were largely similar. Where they were different—at a more detailed and descriptive level—the same framework may still be used although in this case the goal is to discover how the differential operation of mediating factors led to differential outcomes in the two movements.

While the theoretical explanation of movement transformation may be generalized to the suffrage movement in this way, other features of the suffrage movement may be generalized to women's movements of all sorts. These suggestions are much more speculative, but the suffrage movement provides vivid examples of two intriguing patterns. Both derive from women's unique location in the social structure and involve the way this location puts a distinctive stamp on the nature of women's movements.

The first unique feature of women's location in the social structure is their proportional distribution (relative to men) throughout all levels of the class system. There are few other minority groups for whom this is the case. To a greater or lesser extent, most other minority groups that generate social movements are disproportionately located at lower levels of the class system. Hence, the potential constituency of a women's movement is dispersed throughout the class structure in a way that the potential constituencies for racial, ethnic, religious, nationalist, or labor movements are not. This feature of women's social location provides at least an indirect clue to why women's movements have historically tended to be middle-class movements in composition and orientation.

Judging from the suffrage movement, it appears that the class location of upper-class and working-class women weighs more heavily (or at least differently) in their orientation to the social world and their propensity to adopt purely feminist perspectives than is the case for middle-class women. That is, while women at all levels mobilize and organize as women, such actions among upper-class and working-class women are simultaneously permeated by a strong sense of their class location which precludes an exclusive focus on gender and a purely feminist stance. The latter emerge—when they emerge at all—precisely among middle-class women and the movements they organize, mobilize, and lead.

In essence, this is a thesis for the sociology of knowledge: a middle-class location encourages a view of the world as primarily structured around gender relations; other class locations promote different conceptualizations. In earlier chapters this view was characterized as a class-conditioned but class-blind view that typified the orientation of many middle-class suffragists. Thus it appears that the social identity of middle-class women—as members of a class, a gender group, or both—is historically variable in a way that is not true for women from other class locations. Posed this way, the present study has been an investigation into how these different social identities vied for ascendancy throughout the course of the suffrage movement and how successive stages of the movement involved different combinations of these class and gender identities.

Historical evidence and theoretical speculation thus combine to illuminate why women's movements tend to be middle-class movements as well. When women from other classes mobilize for some goal, feminism may emerge as one dimension of that mobilization but it is typically not the dominant one. When women from the middle class mobilize for some goal, it is much more likely that feminism will be the dominant or exclusive principle of mobilization. This may be why the leadership, social base, and political orientation of many women's movements are so often focused through a historically specific middle-class lens.

The second unique feature of women's location in social structure which puts a distinctive stamp on the nature of women's movements involves their actual or normative restriction to the private realm. In this feature both parallels and differences with other minority groups can be identified. All minority groups have been victims of restricted access to the public realm in some fashion or another, and minority movements typically address this as one issue in the movement's program for change. But alongside women's exclusion from the public realm has been a much more specific and distinctive restriction—as empirical fact or normative ideal—to a private, domestic realm with distinctive role obligations rooted in the sexual division of labor. This distinction between public and private spheres, and the normative assignment of men and women to each sphere, was especially pronounced in the nineteenth century under the impetus of industrialization and related social changes.[2] While these spheres have since become somewhat reintegrated, this duality in the structure of social relations has persisted throughout the twentieth century.

This unique aspect of women's location in social structure has fostered a second distinctive feature of women's movements: an ongoing, systematic attempt to reconceptualize the connections between public and private as they affect the social position of women. The stances taken toward this issue by women's movements have varied enormously—from direct challenges to their assigned sphere, to attempts to dignify and legitimize the domestic role, to efforts to move into the public realm through an expansion of the private realm, to proposals to fundamentally alter the relation between the two realms. But underlying this diversity of stances has been a common, consistent concern with the duality itself, and it is this universal concern that distinguishes women's movements from other types of social movements.

The structural location of women in the private realm and the elaboration of the public-private distinction over the last two centuries are, in a sense, inherently feminist issues. Other groups and movements may or may not address these issues; women's movements can hardly avoid doing so. Women's movements thereby occupy a privileged position for understanding and conceptualizing these questions. To conclude with a second thesis for the sociology of knowledge: the location of women in the private realm gives them a distinctive perspective on these issues—a perspective that is more developed and more self-conscious than that of other social groups and political movements.[3]

ON THE SOCIOLOGY OF SOCIAL MOVEMENTS

This study also has implications for more general approaches to the study of social movements. The first concerns the type of structural explanation that has been developed for understanding movement transformation. The second involves the role of mediating links such as class factors, organizational processes, and movement ideology for understanding changes in the orientation of social movements. The third considers generalizable features of this study which speak to questions of interest and concern within the study of social movements generally.

The underlying premise guiding this study is that social movements are conditioned by the social structure and social context from which they emerge. It follows that different structures and contexts will promote different orientations within social movements and that changes in structures and contexts should produce correlative changes within social movements. In this highly abstract form, the premise predicts nothing about the direction or the nature of the changes on each level of analysis, but merely asserts that meaningful connections between the two allow explanations of what happens to the orientations of movements over time on the basis of what happens to their social context. In bringing this premise to bear on the transformation of the woman suffrage movement, social change was divided into background processes and key changes while movement transformation was divided into mediating links and indicators of movement transformation. These relations are summarized in table 4.1 on p. 141.

This framework guided the analysis of movement orientation in each of the three historical periods. In the earliest period the broad scope of the movement derived in part from a type of class consciousness (or "class unconsciousness") as well as the relatively undifferentiated status of preindustrial women. In the middle period the considerable transformation evident in the Illinois movement was promoted by changes in class structure and class consciousness, processes of middle-class formation, and the social differentiation of women. In the final period these factors continued to be important, while the emergence of a new economic role for women also contributed to the transformation of the movement.[4] In no period was the orientation of the movement understandable apart from these features of its social context and changes within them over time.

The key changes included in this analysis of movement transformation have indirect relevance for a more basic question about whether class relations or gender relations are the more "fundamental" aspect of social structure. This question may be unanswerable in this form, but one promising way of approaching such questions is to examine the interaction of class and gender factors over some significant amount of historical time. Having done so for this study, it appears that the relative weight of class and gender factors is itself historically variable. At different moments in the history of the suffrage movement, class and gender factors had a differential weight and importance in defining the course of the movement. Whether the same can be said for social structure in general remains an important theoretical question.

The key changes identified in this framework are crucial for understanding the transformation of the suffrage movement, but their impact was mediated by more specific factors. This analysis paid particular attention to the mediating links of class factors, organizational processes, and movement ideology. In explanatory terms, it now appears that class and organization were crucial mediating links between social structure and movement transformation, while the role of movement ideology was less central in explaining transformation.

Movement ideology was by and large a reflection (though often a complex one) of class factors. While it was an effective way to document movement change, ideology did not add greatly to the explanation of such transformation. In cases where ideology was relevant to explaining movement transformation—for example, instances where developing forms of middle-class consciousness led the movement to alter its analysis of women's situation—a class factor stood behind the ideology factor and was responsible for the change.

The role of organizational processes was more complicated and more important as a mediating link and an explanatory factor. This issue may be subdivided into two questions about internal and external organizational effects. Internally, the issue involved changing organizational structures, within the movement, that may have affected its orientation. While some changes in internal organization were evident by the final period of the movement, such changes tended to appear after the major patterns of movement transformation had already occurred. Hence, internal organizational change does not take us very far toward an explanation of movement transformation.

Externally, the issue involved varying relations, with other organizations and movements, that may have altered the movement's course. Here, the movement in Illinois is richly suggestive, for such external organizational relations were important in every period of the movement. In 1869 a major organizational battle was fought for movement leadership as different groups sought a legitimate claim on organizational leadership of the broad women's rights movement. During the middle period the state suffrage organization continually struggled to maintain an independent organizational identity as women mobilized for numerous causes and goals. In the final period multiple suffrage organizations pursuing a variety of different objectives were an important part of the reform landscape. From beginning to end, then, the movement for suffrage in Illinois involved a tussle of organizations that, by active intervention or exemplary presence, influenced the course of the movement and altered the scope of its program for change. Understanding transformations in the suffrage movement is impossible without an appreciation of the role played by these external organizational relations throughout the movement's history.

Beyond specific alliances and rivalries, it is worth noting that social movement organizations frequently exist in a field or network of other such organizations and that the size of the field and the location in the network can be a major influence on movement orientation (Rosenthal et al., forthcoming). When the early movement put forth its broad agenda, there were relatively few organizational vehicles for expressing women's grievances. It was also a time when a high level of social movement activity was occurring throughout the society and when the potential for progressive change was great. When this potential failed to materialize, suffrage organizations found it necessary to regroup for a longer fight that included some very lean years. During this very time, however, other women's organizations flourished and enjoyed rapidly growing membership. Hence, just as the prospects for enfranchisement worsened, the network of movement organizations relevant to the suffrage cause became much more dense and complex. In response to these circumstances (as well as others), the Illinois movement narrowed its agenda and fought to strengthen and extend its organization for more fruitful efforts at a later time.

By the turn of the century, that time had arrived as the potential for progressive change increased once again. But now the major suffrage organizations were part of a dense network of women's organizations, most of which were sympathetic to the suffrage cause (or at least not actively opposed). These circumstances allowed the suffrage organizations to become a specialized movement for the vote and to invite the support of a large constituency with diverse reasons for wanting the vote. The later movement succeeded in this role, for it attracted the mass support and broad base it needed to win the vote. As a specialized movement pursuing a normalized demand at an optimal moment in the ebb and flow of social movement activity, the suffrage movement finally achieved the success that had eluded it for so long.

External organizational relations—both specific organizational ties and the generalized network of women's groups—thereby exerted an important influence on movement orientation and transformation. At the same time, many of these organizational processes were themselves related to social-class factors. In the middle period, for instance, competing women's organizations were often associated with different sectors of the middle and upper classes and their ideological perspective. In the final period, organizational processes involving both internal structure and external relations rested in part on class-related factors and in particular on the movement of upper-class women into the suffrage movement. In some instances the effects of both ideological shifts and organizational processes may themselves be explained by reference to class-related factors.

Finally, this investigation reveals that social-class factors are essential links between social structure and movement transformation. While class factors are crucial, it should be stressed that this concept is complex and multifaceted. The starting point of a class analysis of the suffrage movement and its transformation obviously involves an investigation of the class background of its leadership and following over time. This investigation reveals some important shifts over time, but taken alone such shifts in class background are clearly inadequate for understanding transformations in the movement.

The explanation is considerably strengthened by analyzing two further aspects of the class factor. First, class situation is crucial in accounting for how and why individuals from similar backgrounds act in different ways over the course of the movement. Focusing on changes in class situation—the manner in which opportunities and access to social resources shift over time—reveals how changing class prospects influenced the nature and extent of the feminist perspective that informed the suffrage movement. Without this sensitivity to changing class situation, the class factor does not succeed in explaining movement transformation.

Distinguishing class sectors adds further explanatory power to the account. These distinctions are especially important for analyzing the middle class since that term so often serves as a residual category for those who fail to meet the defining characteristics of other classes. Sensitizing the analysis to different sectors within the middle class, to their partially distinct interests, and to their different patterns of ascendancy and decline refines the account of movement transformation. Without this element, the account would be less complete. By taking class background, class situation, and class sector into account and by supplementing them with further attention to organizational processes and ideological shifts, a plausible and consistent explanation of the transformation process emerges.

The plausibility of this explanation of movement transformation is indirectly supported by the failings of other possible explanations of the same phenomenon. The underlying logic of two such possibilities discussed earlier will be briefly reiterated here. First, one might explain transformation through an internalist argument about the bureaucratization of movement organizations and the conservatizing influence this often has on social movements (Michels [1915] 1962; Buhle and Buhle 1978). The problem with applying this explanation to the Illinois suffrage movement is that transformation occurred before significant trends toward bureaucratization and hence cannot be explained in this way. Second, one might explain transformation through an externalist argument about social opposition to the movement and the moderating influence this often has on social movements (McCarthy and Zald 1977; O'Neill 1969). The problem with applying this explanation to the Illinois suffrage movement is that significant movement change occurred both before and alongside any noteworthy increases in opposition to the movement, and hence it is difficult to see how opposition can explain these early changes.

An additional reason exists for questioning the social opposition argument. The evidence that most strongly supports this argument indicates that the public face of the movement became tactically transformed in response to opposition while the private face remained committed to its original feminist goals. Having examined sources ranging from public statements to organizational records to private correspondence, it is clear that substantial changes occurred on both levels. Hence, while the opposition argument is well suited for explaining tactical shifts on the public level, it is less persuasive in explaining the changing desires and worldviews of leading suffragists.

Thus neither internalist/bureaucratization arguments nor externalist/ opposition arguments exhaust the range of factors at the root of movement transformation. This warrants the search for an alternative explanation, and in particular the search for an explanation more tailored to the longevity of the suffrage movement and the myriad of social changes that occurred over its duration. The conceptual framework developed herein suggests that the most important mediating links between social structure and movement transformation were class factors and organizational processes.

The Illinois data thereby support the notion that the class base and organizational relations of a social movement are crucial determinants of its orientation, analysis, and ideology (Schwartz 1976).

As suggested in chapter 2, broad social movements are those whose ideology, goals, and program pose a wide challenge to an existing structure of domination. Having amplified this concept for the analysis of the suffrage movement, a more generalizable conception of broad social movements may now be tentatively offered.

The analysis of the early suffrage movement suggests four general indicators of movement breadth. The first may be described as a key demand, which implies that not all movement demands pose an equally great challenge to a structure of power relations. Key demands are those that most directly challenge such structures. The role of the ballot demand in the suffrage movement implies two other features of key demands. First, key demands have a universal applicability to the group on whose behalf the movement speaks. Female enfranchisement would have automatically changed the status of all otherwise eligible women; it thereby had a different character from other movement demands. Second, key demands make the accomplishment of other goals easier. If the suffrage had been granted to the early movement, it would have provided an important means to pursue other objectives in a more direct fashion. For any movement confronting any structure of power, the identification and pursuit of key demands constitutes one aspect of movement breadth.

A second indicator of movement breadth is the formulation of multiple demands. In general, movements that raise multiple demands have a broader character than those that limit their program to a single issue (Gamson 1975). Multiple demands expose different aspects of the power structure that movements confront, and such demands acquire their broad scope when considered in toto. In the case of the suffrage movement, demands for various legal rights mirrored discriminatory laws against women and cumulatively challenged the entire legal framework that reinforced women's subordination. While key demands imply broad changes all by themselves, additional breadth is acquired when movements raise multiple demands for change in an existing set of power relations.

A third general indicator of movement breadth might be called substratum demands. To the extent that legal codes rest on a more basic, material foundation of power relations (as in the sexual division of labor), substratum demands constitute the most basic dimension of a movement's orientation. If this level of social organization is not challenged, changes in the legal sphere are likely to have a limited impact on the social position of a movement's membership and constituency. At the same time, substratum demands are often easier to formulate than to actively pursue, in part because the target of the demand is less clear than in the case of legal demands. The latter must ultimately be addressed to legislatures and courts; substratum demands often do not involve such explicit targets. In any case, movement demands that address the material substratum of a set of power relations constitute a third distinct indicator of movement breadth.

The final generalizable indicator of movement breadth is the extent to which a movement sees itself as part of a broader alliance of disadvantaged groups. This indicator does not derive from the relation between a movement and the power structure it confronts, but rather from the relation between distinct movements and their constituencies. The social movement—power structure relation nonetheless remains important because movements that see themselves as allied typically perceive common features in the respective power structures they confront. The scope of a particular movement is broadened to the extent that it identifies common patterns in multiple power structures and thereby perceives itself as allied with other movements and constituencies.

In sum, the general indicators of movement breadth suggested by this analysis are key demands, multiple demands, substratum demands, and alliances with related movements and constituencies. A polar conception of narrow movements would characterize them as single-issue, single constituency movements that do not articulate either key demands or substratum demands. These ideal-typical concepts imply the corollary concept of movement transformation as involving a pattern of interrelated change in movement orientation along each of the dimensions identified. While these concepts may not be equally useful or applicable to all social movements, they appear to have a particular salience for the study of long-standing,

TABLE 6.1
General Indicators of Movement Orientation

Broad movements	Narrow movements
1. Key demands	1. Peripheral demands
2. Multiple demands	2. Single demands
3. Substratum demands	3. Superstructural demands
4. Alliances with other subordinate groups	4. No Alliances; alliances with wealthy and powerful

complex movements representing large constituencies. Examples include not only women's movements but labor, racial, ethnic, and nationalist movements as well.

A related issue involves whether this account of movement transformation can be generalized to other movements; the obvious candidates are middle-class movements and women's movements. The first tempting generalization involves other middle-class movements that were part of the same reform tradition that originated in the mid-nineteenth century and ultimately blended into the Progressive movement after the turn of the century. If the analysis of middle-class formation during these decades is valid, it would be plausible to seek similar patterns of transformation in other social movements that were primarily middle class in origin, leadership, and following. This generalization preserves the historical sweep of the present study as well as the connections it has described between broad social changes and transformations in social movements.

The other tempting generalization concerns the contemporary feminist movement in the United States. While it can be argued that this movement has undergone a process of transformation from the 1960s and early 1970s to the present, it is considerably more difficult to explain this pattern in terms of the framework that has guided our analysis of the suffrage movement.[5] Most obviously, the relative brevity of the contemporary movement has not allowed for the basic social structural changes that occurred during the course of the woman suffrage movement. The overall conceptual framework of this study would require considerable modification before it could be used to understand changes in the contemporary feminist movement.

The most useful aspect of this framework for such a task might be the focus on class and organizational factors, although how these have contributed to movement transformation is less clear. Analyzing the contemporary movement would require identifying its class composition and how that composition has changed during this second wave of feminist activism. On the surface it appears that a similar sector of professional, upper-middle-class women has solidified control of the contemporary movement and its leading organizations throughout the 1970s and early 1980s. The important questions to raise on the basis of my analysis are twofold. The first involves whether the transformations in the contemporary movement involve the same narrowing and specialization (around the Equal Rights Amendment) that was evident in the suffrage movement. The second involves whether such changes can be understood as resulting from the same dynamics of class and organizational change. This study of the suffrage movement cannot answer these questions, but it suggests the importance of raising them (see Buechler, forthcoming).

Beyond these generalizations, two principles of this analysis provide conceptual bridges to the study of other social movements. The first is that movements cannot be explained in a sociohistorical vacuum. Understanding the origin, development, transformation, and ending of social movements always requires a correlative understanding of their social context. Few would disagree with this point, but it has a particular relevance to the study of social movements because such movements seek to understand their social context in order to change or preserve it. Analyzing movements thereby requires sorting out several interrelated processes: how the context shapes the movement, how the movement perceives the context, what the movement seeks to do about the context, and how the movement alters its context. While it is a truism that everything must be understood in sociohistorical context, this applies with particular relevance to social movements.

The second principle, really a corollary of the first principle, is that when the social context changes, movements change as well. Thus the first principle becomes the second if it is set in motion over historical time. This principle directs attention away from conventional accounts of movement change (e.g., bureaucratization, opposition, etc.) and toward structural, long-term influences on movement orientation. Even at abstract levels this analytical framework is limited to phenomena that persist over some significant amount of time. While this will exclude some movements, it opens the door to the study of other social phenomena such as the growth and development of political parties.

While this study has involved a movement that narrowed its focus and specialized its program, the process of movement transformation may also involve increasing breadth over time. (See Schwartz, Rosenthal, and Schwartz 1981 for an argument that neither oligarchy nor goal displacement are inevitable outcomes in protest organizations.) At the most abstract level, this framework merely asserts a connection between social change and movement transformation; the particulars on either side of the equation may be altered to fit numerous movements and problems. As such, this framework invites comparative studies that would shed further light on the questions examined here.

The National Movement and the Midwestern Movement

Before comparing and contrasting the national and midwestern suffrage movements, a clarification of terminology is in order. The term *national movement* refers to a network of individuals and organizations primarily located in the northeastern portion of the United States (and centered in Boston and New York). In large part, this comparison thereby involves two regional branches of the same movement—the only two regions with much evidence of a women's rights movement before the Civil War. Usage of the term *national movement* nonetheless seems warranted on several grounds. First, the northeastern group always saw itself as the "vanguard" of the movement. Second, while originally responding to local conditions, the northeastern movement quickly conceptualized its target (on at least some issues) as the federal government. Finally, the northeastern group spoke for the women of the nation, and it sent lecturers throughout the nation to create a national movement in more concrete terms. Thus the term *national movement* seems conceptually warranted even if the geographical referent was primarily the movement in the northeastern United States.

The most striking pre–Civil War difference between these movements concerned their timing. The movement in the Midwest started later, progressed more slowly, and remained less organized throughout the entire antebellum period than the movement in the Northeast. At a superficial glance, activities in the Northeast during the 1840s appeared to be duplicated in the Midwest throughout the 1850s and 1860s. Consequently, no major women's rights conventions were convened in the Midwest before the Civil War. The string of conventions initiated by the Seneca Falls meeting in 1848 and continued through the 1850s in the Northeast thus had no parallel in the Midwest. The midwestern movement remained less organized in a double sense; it had fewer formal movement organizations, and it also had fewer social networks and less informal coordination than the movement in the Northeast.

Set against this difference in historical timing, the similarities between the two movements in the antebellum period were more striking. Two similarities provided the overall movement with important threads of commonality and continuity. The first was that both movements articulated grievances in a similar sequence. In both the midwestern and northeastern movements, movement participants initially expressed the same set of demands, then expanded the analysis and the demands, and ultimately debated the relative priority that each set of issues should receive in the movement's program for change.

The initial articulated issue in both cases centered around the economic status of women in a developing capitalist society. Reflecting the twin poles of that society were women's demands for the right to inherit and otherwise dispose of their own property and the right to legal and substantive control of their own wages. The next step in this sequence of demands involved family and domestic issues, including reforms in divorce laws as well as changes in laws regarding guardianship and custody of children. These demands typically originated as particular dissatisfactions in the lives of individual women; they became movement demands as they were communicated to other women in similar situations. The final stage involved a self-conscious examination of the interconnections between these various demands by movement participants themselves. At this point some women developed a broader analysis by relating economic and domestic interests in a way that led to a critique of the sexual division of labor. One of the striking similarities between the two movements, then, was the identical sequence in which grievances arose and demands were articulated.

A second similarity concerns the historical ties between abolitionism and feminism which persisted throughout the antebellum period. While it is abundantly clear that not all abolitionists were feminists, it is virtually impossible to find a feminist whose biography does not include exposure to the abolitionist movement (Hersh 1978). This is significant because abolitionism provided some of the analytical, ideological, and rhetorical building blocks of the women's rights movement; it also exposed all feminists to a common language and similar sensibilities. Indeed, the point goes even further: abolitionism ultimately confronted all feminists with a similar dilemma regarding whether, when, and how to break their ambivalent connection with abolition and establish a truly independent women's movement. In short, feminism in the Midwest and the Northeast had an important common ancestor, and the resulting family resemblance provided an important source of commonality in the antebellum period.

Finally, an analytic similarity between the two movements helps make sense of their different historical timing. From a strictly chronological viewpoint, the midwestern movement lagged behind the national movement and northeastern agitation by a decade or so. For some purposes, however, this is a superficial and even artificial method of comparing the two regional movements. Virtually all historians of the women's rights movement identify certain macrolevel social changes as important structural catalysts to nineteenth-century feminism. Among these were the processes of industrialization, urbanization, social-class development, emergence of middle-class "leisure," and the like. To whatever extent these changes were catalysts, the expectation that different regional movements will follow simultaneous chronological development makes sense only if the regions themselves underwent such changes at the same time and the same pace. The latter assumption, however, does not apply to comparisons of the Midwest and the Northeast in the mid-nineteenth century. Given the differential timing of these social changes by region, we should expect manifestations of feminist activity at a later point in the Midwest—perhaps even later than the decade interval that occurred.

For the antebellum period, this comparison reveals two regional movements following a similar sequence at different times for intelligible reasons. The image works until the outbreak of the Civil War; understanding the relation of the movements throughout the 1860s, however, requires different imagery. The image that comes to mind when considering the impact of the Civil War is one of synchronization. Whatever differences remained between the midwestern and the national movements on the eve of the war disappeared because both movements came to a virtual standstill during the war. Then in 1867 and 1868 feminist agitation began again and dramatically accelerated to the end of the decade. This time, however, the different regional branches of the movement were synchronized in the issues they addressed. Foremost among these issues for feminists everywhere were the relation of the feminist movement to the Republican party and the abolitionist cause and the changes both were seeking to introduce in the political life of the nation.

Focusing on the midwestern movement, the pattern suggested by the record is one of "accelerated development." To judge from speeches, articles, and the like, leaders of the midwestern movement acquired a new political sophistication and tactical sense in a relatively brief time; the same maturation had taken place more slowly in the Northeast in the decade before the Civil War. This accelerated development meant that certain historical possibilities were never explored. Would the midwestern movement have formulated its analysis and demands in a more politically effective way than the Northeast movement if the war had not intervened? Would the residual legacy of the frontier and its greater pragmatic egalitarianism have made the midwestern movement more effective? These questions and the historical possibilities they imply were effectively overwhelmed by the onset of the war and the resulting national synchronization of the movement.

A final contrast between the two movements in this period concerns a possible difference in the generational composition of each movement. We have seen that the midwestern movement was smaller and less organized throughout the antebellum period. Given this small size, the pattern of accelerated development, and the impressionistic accounts of movement size and growth, it appears that the midwestern movement attracted and recruited a relatively large share of its membership only after the war. If so, the midwestern movement in the immediate postbellum period would have been composed of a relatively younger generation than the northeastern movement. This younger generation would have been less involved with the abolitionist movement and its sensibilities and ideology. This hypothesized generational difference may contribute to a fuller explanation of why the midwestern movement underwent a process of transformation more quickly and more extensively than the northeastern movement during the 1870s and 1880s.

The movement synchronization of the late 1860s resulted from the possibility of a federal amendment to enfranchise women and the strenuous efforts of national leaders to build a coalition around that issue. Once it became evident that such an amendment would not be immediately forthcoming, the synchronization it had engendered dissolved. While local and state associations continued to cooperate with one another, their major activity occurred on city and state levels. This is clear in the case of Illinois and was most likely true of other regions as well. Given the differential status of the cause in the states, it is not surprising that local associations fought different battles. Some sought legal changes already won in other places. Others mobilized to exploit particular political possibilities in their own states; the IWSA's 1870 attempt to secure woman suffrage from the state constitutional convention serves as one example here.

To a large extent, the fragmentation and desynchronization that typified the 1870s and 1880s was a function of the complex political structure the movement confronted. During relatively rare moments when significant progress on the national level seemed possible, suffrage forces from around the country made a concerted effort that typically focused on the U.S. Congress. When such possibilities evaporated, the political target became a maze of subnational governmental levels. When the divisibility of the suffrage goal is added to the divisibility of governmental structure, it is easy to understand the diversity of resultant campaigns. It was not at all unusual in this period to find state suffrage associations supporting "liquor" suffrage on the state level, assisting in a county campaign for school bond suffrage, and aiding a movement for municipal suffrage in several towns and cities. While these steps were plausible at the time, with the advantage of hindsight it is clear (and was clear to some suffragists such as Anthony from the start) that such campaigns spread the meager resources of the suffrage movement so thin as to jeopardize chances for success in any one of these efforts.

This desynchronization and fragmentation was perhaps inevitable; in any case, it cannot be attributed to a lack of effort on the part of Anthony and the NWSA to forge a national movement out of a diversity of state and local organizations. It was during the 1870s and 1880s that the NWSA became a truly national organization, and its claim to speak for a national movement thereby acquired more legitimacy. This national character was exemplified in the extensive correspondence between Anthony and Harbert on matters of organization, mobilization, strategy, tactics, and affiliation, and in the fact that Anthony maintained a similar correspondence with many other state presidents. To judge from the case of Illinois, the NWSA became much more of a national organization than the AWSA.

While it is difficult to generalize from Illinois alone, two factors support such a generalization. The first is that Illinois had a strong AWSA presence via Livermore and the Bradwells; while Livermore moved to Boston in 1870, the Bradwells remained in Chicago and continued to support Stone's AWSA. Despite this, the NWSA captured and retained the allegiance of the state society, initially through the short-lived leadership of Catherine Waite and much more securely through the prominence of Elizabeth Harbert. Second, the NWSA was able to accomplish this despite its "Washington bias" and despite AWSA criticism that this bias prevented the NWSA from being a truly national organization. Given NWSA strength in Illinois despite these factors, it appears that the organization had a more legitimate claim to represent a national movement and that it was the AWSA that remained relatively isolated.

The comparable local organization that dominated the Illinois movement in this period was the IWSA. If one looks for contrasts between the NWSA and IWSA as representatives of their respective movements, two striking differences come immediately to mind. The first concerns the relative breadth of scope that each maintained throughout the middle period, while the second involves the relative autonomy they achieved as reform organizations. The comparison implies that breadth and autonomy are not isolated aspects of social movements, but in fact are integrally related and mutually reinforcing features of an organization's and a movement's orientation to social change.

While the NWSA was not immune to transforming pressures and while its orientation in the early and middle periods was not identical, there was considerable continuity in its outlook from the early period through the middle period. Relative to every other suffrage association about which there is reliable information the NWSA remained qualitatively broader in its position on the status of women and its stance toward needed social change and political reform. Most important was the NWSA's continuing critique of the sexual division of labor in its mutually reinforcing economic and familial forms.

Alongside the persistence of a relatively broad orientation was the relative autonomy the NWSA maintained in relation to other movements and organizations. In large part, this may be attributed to Anthony's sheer will and determination to maintain organizational independence and the priority of women's rights. It informed her development of movement strategy relative to political parties both big and small, it persuaded her to maintain female leadership within the NWSA organization, and most importantly it shaped her extremely cautious stance toward the WCTU and its recruitment of large numbers of women. While Anthony welcomed the partial politicization of women through such organizations as the WCTU, she consistently demanded that women come the rest of the way; she would not meet them halfway if the latter implied ideological moderation or organizational subordination.

The IWSA differed significantly from the NWSA on the dimensions of breadth and autonomy. The IWSA did as much to promote as it did to challenge the sexual division of labor and women's sphere, even as it tried to turn this into an argument for the vote. Alongside its ambiguous relation to the sexual division of labor was the IWSA's inability to maintain organizational autonomy from other movements. At different periods the IWSA either became dormant, or lost momentum to competing reforms, or voluntarily withheld its efforts for the sake of other causes, or became subordinated to other reform efforts. This failure to retain autonomy is more understandable when contrasting Harbert's positions with Anthony's arguments for organizational autonomy. In every aspect where Anthony stressed the need for autonomy—in relation to men, political parties, and other reforms—Harbert was at best ambiguous.

The most striking contrast between the NWSA and the IWSA in this period thus concerns the relative degree of ideological breadth and organizational autonomy they were able to achieve and willing to maintain. It is tempting to explain the fate of the IWSA as an adaptive response to a relatively conservative following, but this is simplistic at best. It ignores the leadership initiatives that contributed to this process in the IWSA in a way that did not occur in the NWSA. It also ignores the real data on membership proclivities, which is both extremely thin and highly ambiguous. There were cases of conservative influences on the movement coming from the bottom up (e.g., during Mary Holmes's presidency in the 1880s), but there were also cases of radical influences from similar sources (e.g., during NWSA's 1880 mass meeting in Chicago). These factors have their place in any complete account of the differences in movement transformation on the state and national levels.

While the Illinois movement was organized later than the national movement, one could say it ended earlier as well since the Illinois movement achieved its major goal before the national movement did. The significance of the Illinois victory is often underemphasized because it was not the first state to win such a victory—six western states had already granted full woman suffrage—and because it was won with a large but still limited suffrage bill. The actual significance of the victory is better appreciated when one realizes that the dynamics of enfranchisement in the West were quite different from the rest of the country and that most western victories occurred for nonfeminist reasons. Illinois, by contrast, was the first state east of the Mississippi to win a significant degree of suffrage through a concerted feminist effort; Illinois's victory was the first in a region shaped by the industrialization, urbanization, and class formation that typified the Northeast. Other midwestern states appeared equally close in the years just after 1910, but for varying reasons suffrage initiatives in the neighboring states of Michigan, Ohio, and Wisconsin all lost in the same period that brought victory to Illinois.

That the victory occurred in 1913 is significant in another respect. Accounts of the suffrage movement often read as if the First World War "gave" women the vote by making the suffrage demand effective where it had previously been ineffective. While the impact of the war is undeniable, such explanations ignore the efficacy of the initiatives of the suffrage movement itself in bringing about female enfranchisement. Without a movement that had pressed its claims before the war, altered its strategy during the war, and consciously capitalized on new opportunities, the vote would probably not have been forthcoming as some automatic result of the war.

This statement implies that the war was not sufficient for a suffrage victory; the Illinois case suggests that neither was it a necessary condition of female enfranchisement. The vote was won in Illinois before the war and the war-related social changes usually cited as contributing to enfranchisement on the national level. It was won because the movement found ways of making its demand efficacious in a prewar social context. Whether this victory could have occurred on the national level remains moot, but suffragists had won some twenty states by the time the measure passed the U.S. Congress in 1919, suggesting that this was a real historical possibility.

The case of Illinois also illustrates how the demand for suffrage was patterned by the particular state structures of power. By all accounts, the Illinois State Constitution was extraordinarily difficult to amend; thus the most typical method of state suffrage work was particularly unpromising in Illinois. Although an amendment was proposed to virtually every biennial legislature for decades, it made such little progress that even optimistic suffragists recognized this tactic as a dead end. As early as 1890, McCulloch and others actively began to seek more effective tactics. The result was the successful school suffrage bill of 1891. By distinguishing those offices for which the vote was regulated by the state constitution from those under legislative control, an ingenious way out of a seeming impasse was found. While the school suffrage bill was highly restricted, its success made it a model for later bills, including the unsuccessful township and municipal bills of the 1890s and 1900s as well as the considerably larger and ultimately successful Presidential Suffrage Bill of 1913.

The need to confront local conditions contributed to the lack of active coordination between the NAWSA and the Illinois movement throughout most of the twentieth century. From 1890 until about 1910 the Illinois movement concentrated on creating, discovering, and exploiting opportunities for female enfranchisement within the state with little NAWSA intervention. Although limited suffrage bills remained the dominant strategy, the movement was flexible enough to redirect resources to the Chicago charter proposal when that seemed to offer the best chance of some progress. For its part, the NAWSA had little to offer to these state activities. Throughout much of this period it was organizationally weak and regionally divided, and it could point to few victories and fewer strategies that fit the Illinois situation. Thus, while the organizational ties between the IESA and the NAWSA remained solid until 1910, the support that the national organization could provide to state efforts remained largely symbolic.

As of 1910 friction between the Illinois movement and the NAWSA was ongoing. In December of that year, Mary Ware Dennett of the NAWSA board wrote to all board members (including McCulloch) to complain about the lack of support for the national organization and to propose a more centralized and NAWSA-directed plan of work:

> In large places, the National is now hardly known to exist. The local Suffragists are absorbed in local work and care only for such work. They seem to utterly lack the sense of National solidarity. . . . the time has come when the methods of Suffrage work all over the country should be thoroughly discussed with the object of concentrating upon the best plan which might be made as uniform as possible in all the states, a plan which would be acceptable to every state, and would, at the same time, bind the states closer to the National. (SL, CWM Papers, Ashley/Dennett to Board Members, 1 December 1910)

As this plan took shape, McCulloch detected a specific threat to western interests: "if the contemplated plan goes through the National Association will be nothing but a New York Association and the interests will be gradually limited to the East so that the whole Western situation will receive less attention than it needs" (quoted in SL, CWM Papers, Dennett to McCulloch, 22 June 1911). Dennett defended the proposal by noting that NAWSA activities were "more and more assuming the proportions and nature of business, and business cannot be successfully administered by a scattered Board of Directors who are unable to meet frequently and act quickly and concertedly" (SL, CWM Papers, Dennett to McCulloch, 22 June 1911). By the end of September, Illinois suffragists anticipated a full-scale battle: "There is no doubt that they are going to move heaven and earth to get all the 'wild and wooley westerners' off the National Board this year, and it is very clear to me that as things are developing you will not dare to resign" (SL, CWM Papers, Stewart to McCulloch, 30 September 1911).

In 1912 further animosity developed between Chicago suffragists and the national board. The dispute revolved around the proposal of Jane Addams and others for a Mississippi Valley Suffrage Conference which would address regional concerns and exchange information and strategies among suffragists in the Midwest. NAWSA representation was invited, but Anna Howard Shaw declined, citing the "public indignities" that conference organizers had "heaped upon" the national board. In a copy of Shaw's letter, McCulloch penciled in "Mrs. Trout's statement" next to the mention of "public indignities" by Shaw (SL, CWM Papers, Shaw to Board Members, 4 May 1912). The details of this dispute are unknown, but it implies that regional differences persisted and that the conflict between Trout and Shaw predated the emergence of the Congressional Union.

Southern suffragists had their own reasons for resisting more centralized control of the suffrage movement. When the NAWSA finally rejected the Shafroth-Palmer Resolution, it dedicated itself to a national amendment strategy that could threaten de facto white supremacy at the polls in the South. Southern suffragists responded by forming the Southern States Woman Suffrage Conference, which argued that a national amendment strategy should be advocated for symbolic purposes only and that individual states should be allowed to control access to the vote within their own borders. With this strategy, southern suffragists hoped to maximize white women's votes, minimize black women's votes, and leave restrictions on black male voters intact. In 1915 Kate Gordon, a prominent southern suffragist, wrote McCulloch soliciting her legal talent in framing a bill that would maintain white supremacy (SL, CWM Papers, Gordon to Mc-Culloch, 3 August 1915). Although Gordon and McCulloch corresponded both before and after this time, there is no indication that McCulloch cooperated in any scheme to reconcile woman suffrage and white supremacy in the South.

The question of race played an insignificant role in the Illinois movement when compared to its overwhelming weight in southern politics and its tactical relevance for the NAWSA's national suffrage coalition. The Illinois movement did not confront a large black population as southern suffragists did (in an almost invariably racist way), nor did it adopt an explicitly accommodating stand toward the South as the NAWSA felt compelled to do. The midwestern movement was thus free from the more explicit

endorsements of racism that characterized the South and the national organization. On the relatively few occasions when racial issues arose, the behavior and attitudes of Illinois suffragists ranged from expressions of conventional prejudices to more honorable stances that challenged the racism
of others.

Race was just one divisive issue on the national level that had little impact in Illinois; the same was true of other issues that fragmented the national movement. In large part the Illinois movement remained untouched
because the vote was won in Illinois before many of these disputes broke
out in their most acute form. By the time the Congressional Union split
from the NAWSA, the vote was largely won in Illinois. In addition, the
CU strategy focused on Washington, D.C., and thus had little direct relevance for suffrage work in Illinois. By virtue of its timing and strategy, the
CU remained a distant issue for most Illinois suffragists.

Its major impact on Illinois came through Trout's backing of the CU and
her criticisms of the NAWSA in general and Shaw in particular. While
these disagreements undeniably alienated the IESA from the NAWSA,
they did not lead to any significant alliance between Illinois forces and the
Congressional Union. In large part the continuing split between Trout and
other suffragists rested on personality factors, for Trout was widely perceived by other suffragists as personally seeking leadership of the movement for the power and status it conferred on her.

Finally, the most lasting dispute in the closing years of the Illinois movement did not arise from the national level, but rather from competing conceptions of how best to achieve full suffrage in Illinois. This issue, and not
any national dispute, divided suffrage forces between McCulloch's Suffrage Amendment Alliance and Trout's IESA. In short, the national movement remained a fairly minor factor in the victory in Illinois and even in
the disputes that characterized the latter years of the state movement. The
factors that shaped the movement—for better or worse—were largely
endogenous to the local, state, and regional aspects of the unfolding suffrage struggle.

In one of the rare attempts to distinguish regional differences in the suffrage movement, Mari Jo Buhle and Paul Buhle have written: "In many
regions, and especially in the Midwest and West, where workers and farmers were mainly old-stock Protestants, the suffrage movement remained
democratic and open. But elsewhere, and notably among the leaders,
NAWSA became by the late 1890s a self-consciously elite movement"
(Buhle and Buhle 1978, 30). Much of the evidence reviewed here substan-

tiates this claim, especially with reference to the NAWSA and Illinois leadership in the pre-1913 period. Overall, the Illinois movement and its leadership was relatively more receptive to those groups—blacks, working women, immigrant women—that the national leadership either spurned or approached on purely instrumental grounds. If this spoke well for the Illinois movement, it should also be recalled that this is a relative claim. Without Jane Addams's suffrage work with immigrants, Margaret Robins's with working women, and Ida Barnett's with black women, the Illinois movement might well have become as insular and restricted as its counterparts in other regions and on the national level. It is worth underscoring that each of these individuals were not initially or primarily suffragists but rather were active in other spheres. Their eventual participation in the suffrage movement exerted democratizing influences in the process. While these efforts were by no means completely successful, they met with more success in the Midwest than in many other sectors of the woman suffrage movement.

NOTES

Chapter 1. *The Woman Suffrage Movement: Unresolved Questions*

1. The standard histories of the woman suffrage movement include the following: *Everyone Was Brave* by William O'Neill (1969), *Century of Struggle* by Eleanor Flexner (1975), *The Ideas of the Woman Suffrage Movement* by Aileen Kraditor (1965), *The Emancipation of the American Woman* by Andrew Sinclair (1965), *Feminism and Suffrage* by Ellen DuBois (1978), *One Half the People* by Anne Scott and Andrew Scott (1975), *The Puritan Ethic and Woman Suffrage* by Alan Grimes (1967), and *Suffragists and Democrats* by David Morgan (1972).

2. Two examples may suffice to illustrate this point. The first occurred in 1833, when the American Anti-Slavery Society barred women from joining. The women responded by forming a female antislavery society to pursue abolitionist goals (Flexner 1975). The second occurred in 1840, when female delegates to the London Anti-Slavery Convention were denied seats on the basis of gender (Sinclair 1965).

3. Woodhull's colorful character has too often obscured her contributions. In 1871 she became the first woman to speak in Congress on the issue of woman suffrage, and she is credited with persuading the House Judiciary Committee to hold hearings on a proposed constitutional amendment to enfranchise women. Given the paucity of movement accomplishments over the next several decades, these were notable achievements.

4. These events probably did not damage the immediate prospects of the movement, if only because these prospects were not good for a variety of reasons. But they did raise a legitimation problem for the movement vis-à-vis the broader public and political opponents, who periodically used similar charges to discredit the movement.

5. Though ultimately abandoned, these efforts consumed considerable movement energy in the 1870s. *History of Woman Suffrage* (1969) devoted almost two hundred pages to recounting the court cases resulting from these efforts (*HWS* 2: 586–755).

6. The seemingly simple demand for the suffrage proved even more divisible than this. In addition to the state versus federal dilemma, local jurisdictions on the county and city level provided another arena for movement demands, and in some cases, local suffrage was the first victory to be won. Further distinctions

were made on the basis of types of suffrage and partial forms of enfranchisement (school suffrage, municipal bond suffrage, etc.). Thus, the "demand for the vote" could and did decompose into literally dozens of limited and partial combinations and provided another basis for strategical dispute and disagreement within the movement.

7. The amendment, which eventually passed with no change in wording, read: "The right of citizens of the United States to vote shall not be denied or abridged by the United States or any state on account of sex" (Flexner 1975, 176).

8. Stanton served from 1890 to 1892; Anthony, from 1892 through 1900.

9. One example is provided by the NAWSA's stance toward Stanton's *Women's Bible*, which was published in 1895. In its 1896 convention the NAWSA passed a resolution disavowing any official connection with this feminist critique of the Bible, fearing that it would alienate potential supporters of the movement (see Kraditor 1965).

10. The compromise strategy was reflected in the choice of locations for annual conventions. During this period the NAWSA convened in Washington, D.C., every other year (the old NWSA strategy) and in a variety of other locations on the off years (the old AWSA preference).

11. Anthony's choice was a difficult one, for the logical successor would have been her old friend Anna Howard Shaw. However, as an older suffragist and minister, Shaw's skills were primarily oratorical, and she was not noted for the organizational abilities that distinguished Catt. In strategic terms Anthony's choice was a wise one, even if subsequent events did bring Shaw to the presidency from 1902 to 1915—between Catt's two terms of service.

12. Both had been active in the British campaign during its most militant phase and had participated in hunger strikes and been imprisoned for various forms of civil disobedience.

13. There is some debate about whether the mildly militant tactics of the CU and its offspring helped or hurt the cause, particularly in the context of the First World War. My own reading of events is that the CU tactics were beneficial on the whole, although there is no denying that they alienated some potential supporters.

14. The social histories of Eleanor Flexner (1975) and Andrew Sinclair (1965), as well as the interpretive histories discussed in this section, are notable exceptions to this pattern.

Chapter 2. Issues in the Sociology of Social Movements

1. With this change, sociological theory may be coming full circle and returning to the orientation of classical nineteenth-century theorists, for whom history and historical change were central elements in the development of sociological theory. See Zeitlin 1981 and Giddens 1971 for discussions along these lines.

2. Like all complex accounts of specific movement transformations, the Buhles refer to both internal and external processes in explaining movement change. I focus here on one part of their account because it provides a particularly good illustration of an internalist approach to change in the suffrage movement. Inter-

ested readers will find a more multifaceted explanation by consulting the Buhles' argument in its entirety.

3. This speech is remarkable in part for its anticipation of certain themes that would become crucial in Frederich Engels's analysis of women's position some fourteen years later. See Engels [1884] 1972, 88ff.

4. The first three dimensions of early movement breadth fit our conception directly for they specify the ways in which the movement posed multiple challenges to a patriarchal system of domination. The fourth aspect—involving ideological alliances with other social groups—did not deepen the challenge to patriarchal domination as much as it extended it by linking the suffrage movement, however tentatively and temporarily, to groups challenging other structures of domination.

5. This article is contained in the Elizabeth Cady Stanton Papers at the Library of Congress. It provides an especially striking example of transformation within a single individual, since it was Stanton who most forcefully articulated the orientation of the early movement some thirty years before.

6. My procedure is vaguely similar to the Weberian notion of constructing ideal types; the goal of such conceptions is not a full description of some aspect of reality but rather a "one-sided accentuation of one or more points of view . . . into a unified analytical construct," (Weber 1949, 90). One use of such ideal types is that they help to identify problems that need investigation.

7. This latter group is often classified with the working class on the basis of their form of remuneration and the nature of their work tasks, which in many cases deserves more weight than "collar color."

8. While largely accurate as a description of the woman suffrage movement in this period, the description does not encompass all the political activities of middle-class women in this period. In particular, a rather sharp and intriguing bifurcation occurred among active middle-class women in this period—between those who aligned with the suffrage movement as described above and those who sought to build consciously cross-class alliances with working women through such organizations as the Women's Trade Union League. Any analysis of this final period must come to terms with this bifurcation, the important relations between the two groups, and how those relations changed within this period. To anticipate our own investigation of the Chicago women's movement, it appears that involvement in the settlement house movement was the crucial factor distinguishing women who sought alliances with working women from those who remained confined to a middle-class view of reform.

Chapter 3. The Early Movement, 1850–1870

1. One unpublished biography of Anneke claimed that she was the catalyst for Susan B. Anthony's conversion to the suffrage cause. According to this source, when the International Council of Women met in Berlin in 1888, Anthony "testified to the fact that her first stand for woman suffrage was due to the inspiration of Madam Anneke, who in the earlier decades had braved with her the violence of popular prejudices" (SHSW, Anneke Papers).

2. It appears that Bradwell had a strong case, for she cited section 28 of chapter 90 of the revised state statutes which claimed that "when any party or person is described or referred to by words importing the masculine gender, females as well as males shall be deemed to be included." See the *Chicago Legal News*, 5 February 1870, 145.

3. Though Bradwell didn't pursue her application, members of the legal profession eventually acted on her behalf. In 1885 the Illinois Supreme Court, acting on its own motion, granted a license to Bradwell on the strength of her original 1870 petition which they had earlier denied. In 1892 the attorney general of the United States, also acting on his own motion, admitted Bradwell to practice before the U.S. Supreme Court, which had also ruled against her in 1873.

4. This provides a good example of what Kraditor has labeled an expediency orientation to the vote. Of particular interest, this orientation was evident in Livermore and others, even in the early stages of the women's rights movement and alongside its justice orientation. This suggests a modification of Kraditor's thesis, which sees a historical shift from justice orientations to expediency orientations around the turn of the century (1965).

5. The New York Sorosis was formed through a "dialectic of opposition." It was a response to the exclusion of women journalists from a meeting of the New York Press Club where Charles Dickens was speaking. When women were denied tickets on the basis of sex, plans for a women's organization began in earnest (Flexner 1975, 183).

6. Existing sources do not indicate the reasons for this original split nor are they clear about how long the Livermore group claimed the name *Sorosis*. In any case, they soon were described in newspaper accounts as an "independent" group, and the differences between the groups became clearer with subsequent events. See Pierce 1937, 2 : 456; Beldon 1913, 10; *Chicago Tribune*, 10 January 1869; and *Chicago Times*, 7 February 1869.

7. Among the accusations in the Waterman letter were charges that Livermore's group had secretly reserved the convention hall in their own name in the midst of the merger discussions and that Livermore had threatened to publish a hostile, full scale attack on the Sorosis group if they refused her "generous offer" for a merger between the groups (*Chicago Tribune*, 8 February 1869).

8. In fairness to the Sorosis organization, the *Tribune*, or both, it should be acknowledged that the newspaper described a later meeting of this group as "quite orderly." The general attitude of these two major dailies to the issue of women's rights was somewhat complex. The *Tribune* was the more liberal on women's rights issues, suggesting that the movement was raising a fundamental issue of principle that should be given serious consideration by all citizens. The *Tribune* covered both groups but was perhaps more favorable to the Livermore group. The *Chicago Times*, on the other hand, was decidedly hostile to the issue of women's rights. It editorialized about women's ingratitude to men (7 February 1869) and suggested that the predominance of clergymen at conventions demonstrated that woman suffrage was merely a ploy of the priesthood seeking to control men through the manipulation of women and the suffrage issue (13 February 1869). Despite this general hostility to women's rights, the *Times* afforded con-

siderable space to the Sorosis group in its columns and in general seemed sympathetic to their goals and activities.

9. One striking feature of the woman suffrage movement, and perhaps of all long-standing social movements, was the way it consistently used its own history as a resource in sustaining the struggle. Virtually all suffrage conventions, whether in 1868 or 1908, opened with a similar recitation of the movement's history, providing some momentum and also a sense of obligation to those present to continue the fight.

10. The resolutions were as follows:

Resolved, that a man's government is worse than a white man's government, because in proportion as you increase the rulers you make the conditions of the ostracized more helpless and degraded.

Resolved, that as the Democratic cry of "a white man's government" created an antagonism between the Irish and the negro, culminating in the New York riots of '63, so the Republican cry of "manhood suffrage" creates an antagonism between the black man and all women, and will culminate in fearful outrages on womanhood, especially in the Southern States.

Resolved, that by the establishment of an aristocracy of sex in the District of Columbia, by the introduction of the word "male" into the federal constitution in article XIV, section 2, and by the proposition to enforce manhood suffrage in all the States of the Union, the Republican party has been guilty of three successive arbitrary acts, three retrogressive steps in legislation alike invidious and insulting to women and suicidal to the nation. (*Chicago Tribune*, 12 February 1869)

11. Three months later in the ERA convention, Frederick Douglass made an identical point regarding systematic violence against blacks, albeit in more dramatic form:

With us the matter is a question of life and death. When women, because they are women, are hunted down through the cities of New York and New Orleans; when they are dragged from their houses and hung upon lampposts; when their children are torn from their arms and their brains dashed out upon the pavement; . . . then they will have an urgency to obtain the ballot equal to our own. (Cited in DuBois 1978, 187–188)

12. In addition to Anthony's awareness that their argument represented a minority position, she seems to have conceded the power of Brown's arguments in a relatively casual remark contained in a letter to the *Revolution* written in Chicago on 12 February 1869. She wrote: "William Wells Brown and Anna Dickinson enlivened the discussions of this afternoon. The former helped to annihilate 'us' of the *Revolution* on the same resolutions we discussed at Washington" (*HWS* 2:368–369). This language implied that Brown had the stronger as well as the more popular argument. Nonetheless, Stanton and Anthony did not change their position in the upcoming months, in fact arguing it even more strongly at the ERA convention.

13. The following description and analysis of the *Agitator* is based on a con-

tent analysis of the five issues I could locate in their entirety (no. 1, 13 March 1869, and nos. 10–13, 15 May through 5 June 1869). While it would be desirable to include every issue, there is enough continuity in these samples to warrant the generalizations offered in the text. These issues are available in the Chicago Historical Society.

14. The *Revolution*'s coverage of nonfeminist topics was probably due to Train's role as financier of the paper and his political interests, ranging from currency reform to Irish independence. Probably if Anthony had been granted complete editorial control, the paper would have resembled the *Agitator*'s focus even more closely.

15. These alliances were not consistent on all issues, nor were the concerns of each side mutually exclusive. For example, at least one issue at the convention— the need for a resolution repudiating any connection between the suffrage movement and the practice of free love—found Livermore arguing in favor against both Stone and Anthony. Even when they spoke in favor of the Fifteenth Amendment, Livermore and Stone did so with reservations, noting that they "deplored the backwardness of Congress in giving all rights of citizenship to women, yet welcomed with their whole heart the enfranchisement of any oppressed class" (*Agitator*, 22 May 1869, 5).

16. This letter was written—or at least dated—four days after the first organizational meeting of the NWSA. Livermore was apparently unaware at this point that such an organizational step had been taken. Thus the letter is all the more remarkable, for she advocated precisely the steps currently being undertaken but apparently unbeknownst to her.

17. Livermore described her husband in particular as "very much opposed to the plan, on the score that '. . . we Western folks do things differently from those New Yorkers and that we can't work well together'" (LC, NAWSA Papers, Livermore file, Livermore to Stone, 9 August 1869).

18. Livermore described this offer as involving a financial loss to herself, but there are numerous indications that any sale of the paper at this time would have involved a financial loss for Livermore, and further indications that the proposed transfer to the New England Association may have been her best financial option. Thus, Livermore's rationale for joining with Stone may have been primarily based on her desire to rescue a financially ailing newspaper. See the comments of Anthony and Anneke below on this.

19. Fritz Anneke had already stated his objections to the AWSA organization in no uncertain terms: "against the women's convention in Cleveland I have a strong objection, and it is that the company has chosen the infamous priest, [Pfaffe] Beecher, this arch-hypocrite, this reform-Jew—as the fat Stein used to say—this dog-common Know Nothing, who sees in the Germans only *dirt*, good enough to fertilize the ground,—that they have chosen such a fellow as president. *German women* should protest decidedly against that" (Heinzen 1940, 215; emphasis in original).

20. Briefly, the DuBois arguments are (1) suffrage was a way of directly linking women's interests to the broader public, political community; (2) the right of

suffrage in classical liberal theory had always been linked to, and implied, an independent status; and (3) the vote was perceived by contemporary participants as the most radical single demand in the program of the women's rights movement.

21. The parallel between Livermore and Stanton/Anthony weakened considerably once each group established its organizational independence. The NWSA, under Stanton and Anthony's guidance, maintained its vision of a broad reform alliance uniting many groups (while insisting on the priority of women's rights), whereas the Livermore group made few alliances with constituents other than women. In this sense, the breadth of the NWSA group was exemplary, for it both preserved the autonomy of women's demands in organizational form and simultaneously maintained its alliances with other reform constituencies.

22. The Annekes experienced "downward mobility" as a result of their immigration to the United States; Livermore was moderately upwardly mobile judging from her father's occupation; Swisshelm's status fluctuated with the uneven business ventures of both father and husband.

23. Carole Turbin has described her sample of twenty-eight nationally prominent suffragists active from 1860 to 1875 in the following terms: "Suffragists . . . came from families on the middle socio-economic levels. . . . Most suffragists whose ideas gave the movement its shape and direction came from families which were prosperous but not wealthy. . . . Most less well-known suffragists came from families which were part of the large stream of small farmers and businessmen" (1978, 62, 69, 70). Turbin further noted that although most of the women in her sample worked for a living at one time or another, they typically were not found in working-class occupations but rather concentrated in areas such as teaching, writing, and lecturing.

24. To argue that the movement offered some benefits to these women does not mean that it offered the best strategy for meeting their needs and improving their condition. Again, see Turbin 1978 for a comparative analysis of suffragist and working-class strategies vis-à-vis the situation of working women.

25. The question of organization was not really posed in Illinois until after the Civil War. Before that, there were certainly differences among Illinois women, but those differences could live in peaceful coexistence as long as the movement remained diffuse and unorganized. The differences became important when the movement sought to organize and to clarify its ideological position. One implication would seem to be that organization requires people to take their own analysis more seriously by clarifying ambiguities and acknowledging differences with others.

26. Even this data must be interpreted carefully since newspaper sources themselves were probably more attuned to figures like Stanton and Anthony than to less famous individuals.

27. Adding to the plausibility of this possibility was the previously cited letter from Livermore to Stone in which Livermore claimed that she had convinced Anthony to drop her opposition to the Fifteenth Amendment and that Anthony would make "great concessions" to unify the movement. If I read the evidence correctly, it was Stanton's intransigence in New York and Stone's resistance to her

in the Boston group which really precipitated the split. If this could have been avoided, the split itself might not have occurred.

Chapter 4. Patterns of Transformation, 1870–1890

1. The general argument in this paragraph is presented in much more detail by Leach 1980. Although I have some criticisms of Leach's book (see Buechler 1982b), one of its broader arguments about how feminism in the 1870s and 1880s complemented the bourgeois reform movement (and laid the foundation for Progressivism after the turn of the century) strikes me as a useful way to interpret the career of Harbert, if not the suffrage movement as a whole during this period.

2. These arguments contributed to a process in which the vote became "over-burdened." Once this logic became a part of movement rhetoric just before the turn of the century, feminists could—and increasingly did—cite any and all social problems as examples of phenomena that could be solved by giving women a voice in political decision making.

3. This does not mean that Harbert ignored particular class injustices; indeed, she became quite incensed over them as they affected women and children in particular. But like the reformist tradition she exemplified, she never saw them as deriving from fundamental, enduring, and structural conflicts of interest on a classwide basis. Rather she saw them as periodic and largely individual excesses that could be controlled through legislative reform with occasional help from more moderate forms of worker organization.

4. Ellen DuBois's work on the emergence of an independent suffrage movement after the Civil War (1978) might well be complemented by a parallel volume on the decades of the 1870s and 1880s. During these years, Anthony in particular made a Herculean effort to maintain the independence of the suffrage movement when many other suffragists were yielding to pleas for affiliation with—and history suggests this really meant subordination to—other reform organizations and political parties.

5. It was the rapid growth of this organization that Harbert claimed "may account for the apparent lethargy of the Suffrage Association during the years of 1877–1878" (*HWS* 3:584).

6. In addition to Harbert's speech, various persons spoke on substantive topics at this convention. This complete list serves as an index of the concerns and preoccupations of the ISSA in its founding year: foreign mission work, Chicago club work, chemistry of food, music, women's industries, appeal for the industrial school, value and dangers of personal leadership in social movements, Socrates, women in our public schools, potential mood, intemperance in eating, domestic service in the United States, evolution of ideas, domestic economy, women in history, higher education of women, and history of art (HL, EBH Papers, "Programme of Exercises of the Annual Meeting of the ISSA," 1878).

7. To provide some examples here, Kate Doggett's husband was the vice-president of the Merchant's Savings, Loan, and Trust Co. in Chicago during this

period; in the 1880s the CWC included such socially prominent and truly upper-class figures as Mrs. Charles Henrotin, Mrs. Potter Palmer, and Mrs. William Chalmers (see Pierce 1937, 3:386).

8. The CWC's contribution to the suffrage cause came somewhat later. In 1894 the CWC established the Chicago Political Equality League which grew to be the most powerful suffrage organization in the city of Chicago and, arguably, in the state of Illinois.

9. It should be stressed that this argument applies to documented ties between specific organizations. It does not imply that the general situation of working women was not part of suffragist concern, ideology, or rhetoric. In fact, there was significant and continuing concern—as well as empty rhetoric—about working women within the suffrage movement throughout this period.

10. The New Orleans conventions did not occur for several more years. When they did, under NAWSA auspices, they promoted the "states rights" politics of the NAWSA which we will examine in the following chapter.

11. The reaffirmation of the Seneca Falls resolutions occurred with the following qualification: "expunging only those that relate to conditions which society has happily outgrown" (ISHS, *New Era*, December 1885, 374). It is impossible to say whether this is a reference to relatively narrow legal changes (like ownership of property) or to broad social conditions (like conflicting interests between the sexes). However, it is certainly plausible that the reference is to the latter; if so, the qualified endorsement expresses in yet another way the transformation of the suffrage movement during this period.

12. See also "Evil Social Tendencies" by Mrs. H. A. Ware which condemned both the rich and the poor (and immigrants) for their nonconformity to the middle-class values of hard work, frugality, industriousness, and the like (ISHS, *New Era*, March 1885, 82).

13. The organized opposition of women in Illinois was just beginning at this point, largely led by Caroline Corbin and Illinois Association Opposed to the Extension of Suffrage to Women. This organization did not have its greatest impact until the turn of the century.

14. This may be seen in the snub of working women at the 1880 Chicago mass meeting, in the disjunction between movement rhetoric about working women and the lack of concrete action, in Harbert's attempts to subordinate the concerns of labor to the cause of suffrage, in Kelley's criticisms of the middle-class bias of the movement, and in the total absence of any ties between the suffrage movement and working women's organizations in the Chicago area throughout the 1880s.

15. This could be seen in Harbert's unqualified endorsement of motherhood, in her stress on the duties and obligations of wives and women, and in her consistent reinforcement of women's role in supporting and caring for men, children, and the world at large.

16. Included in this category, for example, were arguments made by suffragists about prostitution in which they pointed to the economic, political, and social advantages of men in such relationships and suggested that the real criminals in this situation were the male patrons and the economic circumstances that forced

many unwilling women into prostitution. In a similar vein, many of the arguments for raising the age of consent for girls were directed at curbing the ability of men to sexually exploit women.

17. Some qualification is necessary here because the distinction between legally defending women and socially controlling the population was often somewhat blurred. For instance, some of the arguments of the temperance movement drew direct connections between excessive drinking and specific abuses of women and cannot be categorized as either/or. Over time, however, the temperance movement was increasingly dominated by a more purely social control orientation, particularly with reference to immigrant cultural customs that these middle-class and native reformers regarded as offensive.

18. There was a curious flip side to arguments that minimized the impact of the vote in this period. While the movement argued that the vote would change little of what was desirable in the existing society, the movement also hinted that the ballot would unleash a womanly power essential to "saving the race" or "defending civilization." In this sense, the movement continued to assign massive potential power to the ballot, but I have not construed this as continuing breadth because of the shift away from women's subordination per se.

19. An important contributing and complicating factor is that justice arguments disappeared in part because of their ineffectiveness. Harbert herself commented on the irrefutable but ineffective nature of justice arguments in the 1880s. By the same token, expediency arguments did not pass the test of success either, and their new prominence in movement ideology cannot be explained simply in this way.

20. In the early period the sample of leaders revealed that three-quarters of the women wrote for the public in some form, about half were educators and/or reformers, and one-quarter were professionals; in addition, there was considerable overlap of these categories in the life of a single woman. Harbert fit this pattern perfectly; the only position she could not claim in the above list was that of educator.

21. Where it did not undermine this worldview, it altered its content in important ways. For example, ways in which the movement continued to see this kind of basic division in the world were evident in its increasing reliance on sex role stereotypes and assumptions about "natural" traits. But if the movement continued to see the world divided in this way, it did so along a different and deradicalized axis, moving from seeing a political division resulting in sexual inequality and exploitation to a moral division resting on complementary spheres and abilities.

22. A hidden question lurking throughout this account concerns whether events could have taken a different course. Specifically, could the suffrage movement, in the face of WCTU competition, have moved toward a different social base—one that might have linked it with labor and working women more solidly? It would be incorrect to dismiss this as "historically impossible" because this orientation occurred in the earlier period on the national and local level, because it continued on the national level through the NWSA even in this middle period,

and because it may have occurred in a minor way in Chicago through the Cook County Suffrage Alliance's role in the Illinois Woman's Alliance (see Tax 1980). To understand why this historical possibility was not a probability, however, requires reference to all the arguments made above about the middle-class base of the movement and the changes that class was undergoing in this period—and that Elizabeth Harbert was a particularly strong mediator of these changes and their effects on the orientation of the suffrage movement.

23. In a discussion of the contemporary feminist movement, Ellen Willis has used the term *cultural feminism* to capture some of the same dimensions I mean by the terms *moral* and *domestic* feminism. Although her discussion refers to current issues, the underlying orientation to the world is similar. She writes:

> Cultural feminists . . . redefine women's liberation as escape from the influence of corrupt "male" values and the reassertion of superior "female" values. [In cultural feminism] . . . women are often seen as "natural" pacifists whose nurturing function gives them a special responsibility to save the world. [It channels] female energy into counter-cultural projects, fantasies of restoring an alleged golden age of matriarchy, or moral crusades against male vice. It also reinforces oppressive cultural stereotypes . . . cultural feminists confuse loyalty to feminism with adherence to their conception of female values— which tends to coincide with traditional criteria of femininity. (Willis 1981, 495)

Though Willis is writing in a polemical vein as part of a current feminist debate, what she designates as cultural feminism bears some striking resemblances to positions adopted in the late nineteenth century within the suffrage movement.

24. Within obvious structural limits, it is worth underscoring the difference that individual leaders can make in the orientation of a movement, especially when they are as powerfully placed as Harbert was. Had the suffrage movement been led by a Lucinda Chandler, moralism would have been complemented with a broader sense of the underlying conflicts of interest between men and women which was so prominent in Chandler's orientation and so notably absent from Harbert's. Had the movement been led by a Mathilde Anneke, the contrasts would have been even sharper.

Chapter 5. A Specialized Movement, 1890–1920

1. It is worth emphasizing that the first suffrage bill to pass was drafted not by the IESA but by the WCTU. This is a good symbolic indicator that the temperance organization's Franchise Department was continuing to play an active role in suffrage agitation. It is also worth noting that the WCTU bill proposed a very limited form of suffrage, whereas the IESA had proposed a larger suffrage bill that this same legislature had defeated. According to *History of Woman Suffrage*, more support was found among suffragists for the larger bill than for the school bill (*HWS* 4:600).

2. As Catharine McCulloch was quick to note, the logic of this decision

meant that the state legislature was equally and identically empowered to grant municipal forms of suffrage to women; this quickly became a new focus of movement strategy and agitation.

3. According to one account, the momentum generated by suffragist speakers in the House was only overcome by some ignoble machinations on the part of antisuffragist legislators: "After the hearing the visitors were informed that it was the custom of the House, to close its afternoon session by singing patriotic airs, and all were invited to join in the singing. Taking advantage of this diversion, the committee on elections slipped away and in a secret meeting postponed the vote on the bill for a week. They feared that, should it come to a vote immediately, it might pass" (Beldon 1913, 38).

4. In the 1896–1897 list of officers and clubs, Chicago clubs ($N=35$) constituted 29 percent of the total IFWC club membership. Thus, over 70 percent of the affiliated clubs within the IFWC represented areas that did not have direct familiarity with the conditions of rapid industrialization, urbanization, and immigration so important in shaping the social, political, and reform climate of cities like Chicago.

5. The 1905 legislative session provided a good example of how club involvement contributed to the legitimacy of the suffrage cause. In the process of defeating the bill, one "senatorial joker" offered an amendment "That women and females should be at home taking care of the house and raising babies." The senator was surprised to discover that many of the bill's supporters in the audience were prominent clubwomen and senator's wives who "considered themselves insulted" by such antics and proceeded to work against the reelection of the senator. The anecdote suggests the extent to which explicit antisuffragism was out of fashion—and in direct proportion to the number of fashionable women who were taking up the suffrage cause. See SL, ESS scrapbooks, "Baby Talk Angers Women," newspaper clipping, 1 March 1905.

6. The relative priorities of the IFWC were nicely expressed in the minutes of their 18 November 1910 meeting. They responded to an impassioned appeal from the Women's Trade Union League for a resolution supporting the Chicago garment workers strike with a weakly worded response urging greater harmony. They proceeded to vigorously debate and eventually pass a resolution condemning the inclusion of comic sheets with Sunday newspapers, citing their deleterious effects on the moral character of young people (ISHS, IFWC Board Meeting minutes, 18 November 1910).

7. It should be pointed out that the ideology and program of the WTUL could and did go beyond mere organization of workers and included goals such as economic and industrial democracy. In "Self-Government in the Workshop: The Demand of the WTUL" (originally published in *Life and Labor*, April 1912 and reprinted as a pamphlet in January 1919), Margaret Robins cited the deskilling effects of certain machine production and argued that the only adequate defense was the establishment of industrial democracy within the workshop.

8. Illinois had already passed an eight-hour bill in 1893 under the careful lobbying of Florence Kelley. However, when manufacturers mobilized to oppose

the bill, it took less than two years for the Illinois Supreme Court to declare the bill unconstitutional.

9. One example was provided by events in San Francisco in 1909. In that year a cross-class suffrage organization refused to support a WTUL-sponsored streetcar conductor strike, displaying little sympathy with the strikers and annoyance at the inconvenience the strike produced. In response, wage-earning women withdrew from the suffrage organization and established their own Wage-Earners Suffrage League as an affiliate of the WTUL. Similar leagues in other cities followed shortly.

10. Organized labor in Chicago was generally supportive of the demand for woman suffrage. In 1898 almost a hundred Chicago labor organizations (representing twenty-five thousand members) signed prosuffrage resolutions (SL, CWM Papers, "Labor Organizations for Woman Suffrage," n.d.).

11. In addition to a quota, the club exercised "quality control" by requiring that prospective members be nominated in writing by several current members who themselves must have been members for at least three years, then be approved by the committee with which they sought to work, and then be approved by the club's executive board.

12. Random examples include work in the areas of protective agencies, compulsory education, industrial schools, teaching for the blind, juvenile courts, probation officers, Americanization, vocational training, employment agencies, college women's dorms, art schools, curative workshops, contagious diseases, city sanitation, mental hygiene, settlement houses, and many others. See SL, CWM Papers, "Civil, Educational, and Philanthropic Work Initiated and Supported by the CWC, 1876–1931," n.d.

13. Joining the CPEL required written nominations by three members of either the CPEL or CWC in which they stated that they had known the candidate for over one year and considered her "desirable." Candidates then had to be approved by the membership committee and receive a two-thirds vote of the board of directors; if the membership committee was unfavorable to the candidacy, a unanimous board vote was required. Finally, membership could be canceled at the written request of the Membership Committee and by a two-thirds vote of the board of directors (CHS, CPEL Collection, CPEL Yearbook, 1895–1896).

14. Another interesting chapter in Bowen's book is "Suffragists and Stockholders"; it details her efforts to use her power as a major stockholder in large corporations to advance the causes she supported (Bowen 1926).

15. Standard examples included arguments that claimed a natural or divine foundation for separate sexual spheres and sex-specific traits and abilities; that claimed women's indirect influence was already greater than men's direct influence; that suggested entry into politics was demeaning to women and added an odious obligation to their already long list of responsibilities; that men were in fact the best defenders of women's interests; and that women themselves did not desire the vote.

16. There was a distinct irony in this. The closest the suffrage movement ever came to such an orientation was in its early period. In the years under discussion,

suffrage had lost most of these implications even in the eyes of suffragists. The explanation may lie in Corbin's even more fundamental opposition to socialism and its becoming a more creditable force in the period under discussion.

17. As far as I can determine, the difference in the bills was minimal. The Progressive party bill had a blanket clause enfranchising women for all offices not specified in the constitution while McCulloch's bill specified the offices themselves. If anything, the Progressive bill might thus have been broader, but there is no reason to think the differences were very significant.

18. Governor Dunne's opposition to a constitutional measure—which was highly unlikely to pass anyway—appears to have been based on his fear that it would endanger other, non-suffrage-related legislation. See *HWS* 6:152.

19. Trout's account—by far the most thorough on this session—does not identify the suffragist. One document makes the link to McCulloch; it is in the collection of her papers at the Schlesinger Library, titled "Senate Joint Resolution" (n.d.), and carries this note in what I believe to be McCulloch's handwriting: "This is the Ill. Suffrage Amendment continuously asked for from the Ill. Legislature by the Ill. E.S.A. until in 1913 some officers of the Ill. E.S.A., asked Mrs. C. W. McC. to withdraw. The excuse was that to ask full suffrage would imperil the large 1913 suffrage bill. The bill succeeded altho the Amendment was not withdrawn." Apparently, McCulloch insisted not only on her own version of a nonconstitutional bill, but also on submitting the constitutional amendment that had traditionally been defeated by large margins in the rare cases when it even got out of committee.

20. In Illinois this revival must be attributed almost exclusively to the efforts of Catharine McCulloch. Throughout the period under discussion, she used her legal training to identify gaps in the movement's legislative progress and to push for bills that would fill those gaps. See, e.g., "Illinois Laws Concerning Women," in SL, CWM Papers, 1912. McCulloch's ability to play this role, in turn, was the result of Myra Bradwell's and Alta Hulett's prior efforts to get women admitted to law schools.

21. There was widespread agreement within the suffrage movement and among settlement house workers that the benefits of protective legislation outweighed the costs of limiting women workers' ability to compete with male laborers. Occasionally McDowell refers to "extreme feminists" who resisted differential protective legislation, but they were not further identified nor do they seem to have had a major impact in this period. Shortly after the ballot was won, this issue split the remnants of the suffrage movement into two competing factions.

22. As always, there were exceptions. One was found in Jane Addams's involvement in the international peace movement, which had a strong feminist strain reminiscent of the earlier romanticized worldview based on a distinctive woman's nature.

23. A longer list would not necessarily dilute upper-class representation in the group, for it would have to include figures like Bertha Palmer, Ruth McCormick, and others whose upper-class credentials were undeniable.

24. My best guess is that Illinois was atypical. It is useful to distinguish be-

tween upper-class women who played major organizational and leadership roles—a description that encompasses all of the Illinois women above—from socialite women who were more episodically involved when the suffrage movement was perceived as especially fashionable. When the standard literature discusses upper-class involvement, the focus is usually on the latter, as in the case of Mrs. O. H. P. Belmont in the New York association and the NAWSA. See, e.g., Flexner 1975, 260ff.

25. The point of this characterization is not to deny the importance of or the need for these changes. Rather the point is that the movement's promotion of them derived as much from a class interest in preserving the social order through moderate change as from an overarching feminist challenge to male power. This contrast serves to distinguish the final period from the first period of the movement, despite some surface similarities.

26. It is somewhat anomalous that this endorsement came from women in the movement who were able to escape these traditional roles in their own lives and assume positions in the public realm. This represented yet another axis in the social differentiation of women which divided those who remained confined to the private realm from those who participated in the public sphere. The latter, in turn, were differentiated by their class positions and occupations.

27. The fundamental dilemma described here is that of winning power from an initial position of powerlessness. At least one logical option to recruiting the broadest possible base of support is engaging in tactics of disruption that impose a greater cost on existing power structures than the cost of granting the reform itself. This was the option exercised by the militant wing of the British suffrage movement just before World War I. It is difficult to know to what extent these tactics contributed to the victory in England, but most American suffragists regarded them as inappropriate for the U.S. movement.

Chapter 6. A New View of Woman Suffrage and Social Movements

1. William Leach has recently made a related argument against the Kraditor thesis by suggesting that feminists from the earliest days of the women's rights movement argued from the standpoint of women's virtue and moral superiority and that this argument was not merely a later development in their ideology (1980, 8).

2. Carole Turbin has recently argued that the public-private distinction has often been characterized in an overly simple manner, that analysts have often confused normative prescriptions with empirical realities, and that the distinction must be seen as assuming class-specific forms (1981). I agree with these arguments, though I do not think they undermine the much more general point I am seeking to make here. In fact, they may reinforce my point in that the public-private split was of most concern to precisely the middle-class women who dominated the suffrage movement; it was in this group that the normative ideal of separate spheres was most likely to be translated into the structure of everyday life.

3. It is obvious that women have never been completely confined to the pri-

vate realm, even in the middle class where this tendency has been most pronounced. However, to the extent that women have participated in both realms simultaneously, the overall argument I am making here is strengthened. For a vaguely similar point, see Kelly 1979.

4. Of the changes identified in the table, those dealing with immigration had the least impact on the Illinois movement. During the middle period, some evidence of a nativist reaction to immigrant groups contributed to the social control imperative of the movement. In the final period, however, this became less pronounced due to the bridging efforts of the settlement house movement. This description of the relatively minor role played by factors related to immigration is region-specific; that is, the movement in other areas was more importantly affected by both ethnic and racial considerations than was the movement in Illinois.

5. Aside from this theoretical limitation, there are obvious and striking parallels. To mention two examples, feminist movements in each century originated from the involvement of women in nonfeminist movements (abolitionism and the student movement), developed through a dialectic of opposition, and eventually achieved an independent status. In addition, the parallels in the legislative battles and strategies to secure woman suffrage and the Equal Rights Amendment are uncannily similar. Perhaps a further parallel can be found in a pattern of goal transformation to the single issue of the vote and the ERA respectively, though this is not as pronounced in the contemporary movement as it was in the suffrage movement.

BIBLIOGRAPHY

Archival Sources

Collections that were especially useful to me are indicated by an asterisk.

Chicago Historical Society
  The Agitator
  American Association of University Women
  Authors and Editors
  *Louise deKoven Bowen Papers
  Chicago Legal News
  *Chicago Political Equality League
  Chicago Teacher's Federation
  Chicago Temperance Union
  *Chicago Woman's Club
  Illinois League of Women Voters
  *National Woman Suffrage Association
  *Agnes Nestor Papers
  *Woman Suffrage Collection
  *Woman's City Club of Chicago
  *Women's Trade Union League Collection
  World's Columbian Exposition, Board of Lady Managers

Chicago Public Library
  Chicago Tribune Files, 1868–1869
  Chicago Times Files, 1868–1869

Huntington Library
  *Elizabeth Boynton Harbert Papers

Illinois State Historical Society
  Jane Addams Papers
  Myra Colby Bradwell Papers
  Cornell University Collection of Women's Rights Pamphlets (microfilm)
  Prudence Crandall Philleo Papers

Debates and Proceedings of the Constitutional Convention of 1870
*Illinois Federation of Women's Clubs
Journal of the Constitutional Convention of 1869–1870
National Woman Suffrage Association Collection
New Era
J. Ward Smith Collection
Samuel Willard Papers

Jane Addams Hull House
   *Jane Addams Papers

Library of Congress
   The Blackwell Family Papers
   Carrie Chapman Catt Papers
   *National American Woman Suffrage Association Papers
   Elizabeth Cady Stanton Papers

Newberry Library
   Floyd Dell Papers
   Fortnightly Collection
   May Walden Kerr Papers
   Graham Taylor Papers

Schlesinger Library
   *Elizabeth Morrison Boynton Harbert Papers
   *Catharine Gougar Waugh McCulloch Papers
   *Ella Seass Stewart Papers

State Historical Society of Wisconsin
   Wisconsin Woman Suffrage Association
   Zona Gale Papers
   Nettie Fowler McCormick Papers
   Raymond Robins Papers
   *Mathilde Franziska Anneke Papers
   Ada Lois James Papers
   Jessie Jack Hooper Papers
   Frances Berkeley Young Papers

University of Chicago Library
   Grace and Edith Abbott Papers

University of Illinois at Chicago Circle
   *Hull House Association
   Caroline Alden Huling Papers
   League of Women Voters of Chicago

League of Women Voters of Oak Park–River Forest
Pamphlet Collection
Hilda Scott Polacheck Papers
*Lucy Tilden Stewart Papers
Temperance Collection
*Woman's City Club of Chicago
*Women's Suffrage Collection
*Women's Trade Union League of Chicago

Published Sources

Abbott, Edith. 1950. "Votes for Women in Illinois." Manuscript. Special Collections, University of Chicago Library.

Addams, Jane. [1910] 1960. *Twenty Years at Hull House*. Reprint. New York: New American Library.

Andreas, Alfred Theodore. 1884. *History of Chicago*. Chicago: Andreas Publishing Company.

Beldon, Gertrude May. 1913. "A History of the Woman Suffrage Movement in Illinois." M.A. thesis, Department of History, University of Chicago.

Blair, Karen J. 1980. *The Clubwoman as Feminist*. New York: Holmes and Meier.

Bordin, Ruth. 1981. *Woman and Temperance*. Philadelphia: Temple University Press.

Bowen, Louise deKoven. 1926. *Growing Up with a City*. New York: Macmillan.

Buechler, Steven M. 1982a. "Social Change and Movement Transformation: The Deradicalization of the Illinois Women's Rights/Woman Suffrage Movement, 1850–1920." Ph.D. diss., Department of Sociology, State University of New York at Stony Brook.

———. 1982b. Review of *True Love and Perfect Union* by William Leach and *The Rising of the Women* by Meredith Tax. *Contemporary Sociology* 11: 228–230.

———. 1985. "Social Change, Movement Transformation, and Continuities in Feminist Movements: Some Implications of the Illinois Woman Suffrage Movement." In Gwen Moore and Glenna Spitze, eds., *Research in Politics and Society, Vol. 2: Women and Politics*. Greenwich, Conn.: JAI Press.

Buhle, Mari Jo. 1983. *Women and American Socialism, 1870–1920*. Urbana: University of Illinois Press.

Buhle, Mari Jo, and Paul Buhle, eds. 1978. *The Concise History of Woman Suffrage: Selections from the Classic Work of Stanton, Anthony, Gage, and Harper*. Urbana: University of Illinois Press.

Chafe, William H. 1977. *Women and Equality*. New York: Oxford University Press.

Cole, Arthur Charles. 1919. *The Era of the Civil War*. Springfield, Ill.: Centennial Commission.

———. 1920. "Illinois Women of the Middle Period." *Illinois State Historical Society Journal* 13: 312–323.

Cott, Nancy. 1978. *The Bonds of Womanhood*. New Haven: Yale University Press.

Davis, Paulina Wright. [1871] 1970. *A History of the National Woman's Rights Movement For Twenty Years with the Proceedings of the Decade Meeting Held at Apollo Hall, October 20, 1870.* Reprint. New York: Source Book Press.

DuBois, Ellen. 1974. "The Radicalism of the Woman Suffrage Movement: Notes toward the Reconstruction of Nineteenth Century Feminism. *Feminist Studies* 3:63–71.

―――. 1975. "A New Life: The Development of an American Woman Suffrage Movement, 1860–1869." Ph.D. diss., Department of History, Northwestern University.

―――. 1978. *Feminism and Suffrage.* Ithaca, N.Y.: Cornell University Press.

―――. 1979. "The Nineteenth Century Woman Suffrage Movement and the Analysis of Women's Oppression." In Z. Eisenstein, ed., *Capitalist Patriarchy and the Case for Socialist Feminism,* 137–150. New York: Monthly Review Press.

Dye, Nancy Schrom. 1973. "Creating a Feminist Alliance: Sisterhood and Class Conflict in the New York Women's Trade Union League, 1903–1914." *Feminist Studies* 2:24–38.

―――. 1975. "Feminism or Unionism? The New York Women's Trade Union League and the Labor Movement." *Feminist Studies* 3:111–125.

Eisenstein, Zillah R., ed. 1979. *Capitalist Patriarchy and the Case for Socialist Feminism.* New York: Monthly Review Press.

Engels, Frederick. [1884] 1972. *The Origin of the Family, Private Property, and the State.* Reprint. New York: Pathfinder Press.

Flexner, Eleanor. 1975. *Century of Struggle.* Cambridge: Harvard University Press.

Frank, Henriette Greenbaum, and Amalie Hofer Jerome. 1916. *Annals of the Chicago Woman's Club, 1876–1916.* Chicago: Libby Company.

Gamson, William. 1975. *The Strategy of Social Protest.* Homewood, Ill.: Dorsey Press.

Giddens, Anthony. 1971. *Capitalism and Modern Social Theory.* London: Cambridge University Press.

Gilman, Charlotte Perkins. [1890] 1966. *Women and Economics.* Reprint. New York: Harper & Row.

Grimes, Alan P. 1967. *The Puritan Ethic and Woman Suffrage.* New York: Oxford University Press.

Gutman, Herbert G. 1977. *Work, Culture, and Society in Industrializing America.* New York: Random House.

Harbert, Lizzie Boynton. 1871. *Out of Her Sphere.* Des Moines, Iowa: Mills & Company.

Heinzen, Henriette M. 1940. "Biographical Notes in Commemoration of Fritz Anneke and Mathilde Franziska Anneke." Anneke Papers, State Historical Society of Wisconsin.

Hersh, Blanche Glassman. 1978. *The Slavery of Sex.* Urbana: University of Illinois Press.

History of Woman Suffrage [*HWS*]. 1969. Vol. 1, ed. Elizabeth Cady Stanton, Susan B. Anthony, and Matilda Joslyn Gage, 1881; vol. 2, ed. Stanton, Anthony, and Gage, 1882; vol. 3, ed. Stanton, Anthony, and Gage, 1886; vol. 4, ed. Anthony and Ida Husted Harper, 1902; vol. 5, ed. Harper, 1922; vol. 6, ed. Harper, 1922. Reprint. New York: Arno Press.

Jacoby, Robin Miller. 1975. "The Women's Trade Union League and American Feminism." *Feminist Studies* 2:126–140.

Kelley, Florence. [1905] 1969. *Some Ethical Gains through Legislation.* Reprint. New York: Arno Press.

Kelly, Joan. 1979. "The Doubled Vision of Feminist Theory." *Feminist Studies* 5:216–227.

Kraditor, Aileen S. 1965. *The Ideas of the Woman Suffrage Movement, 1890–1920.* Garden City, N.Y.: Doubleday.

Leach, William. 1980. *True Love and Perfect Union.* New York: Basic Books.

Livermore, Mary A. 1897. *The Story of My Life.* Hartford, Conn.: Worthington.

McCarthy, John D., and Mayer N. Zald. 1973. *Trends of Social Movements in America: Professionalization and Resource Mobilization.* Morristown, N.J.: General Learning Press.

———. 1977. "Resource Mobilization and Social Movements: A Partial Theory." *American Journal of Sociology* 82:1212–1241.

McDowell, Mary. 1937. *Mary McDowell and Municipal Housekeeping: A Symposium.* Springfield, Ill.: Illinois State Historical Society.

Marx, Gary T., and James L. Wood. 1975. "Strands of Theory and Research in Collective Behavior." *Annual Review of Sociology* 1:363–428.

Marx, Karl. [1852] 1963. *The Eighteenth Brumaire of Louis Bonaparte.* Reprint. New York: International Publishers.

Michels, Robert. [1915] 1962. *Political Parties.* Reprint. New York: Free Press.

Morgan, David. 1972. *Suffragists and Democrats.* East Lansing: Michigan State University Press.

Notable American Women [NAW]. 1971. Three volumes ed. Edward T. James, Janet Wilson James, and Paul S. Boyer. Cambridge: Harvard University Press.

Oberschall, Anthony. 1973. *Social Conflict and Social Movements.* Englewood Cliffs, N.J.: Prentice-Hall.

O'Neill, William L. 1969. *Everyone Was Brave.* Chicago: Quadrangle Books.

Pierce, Bessie. 1937. *History of Chicago.* New York: Knopf.

Piven, Frances Fox, and Richard A. Cloward. 1977. *Poor People's Movements.* New York: Pantheon.

Riegel, Robert. 1963. *American Feminists.* Lawrence: University of Kansas Press.

Rosenberg, Rosalind. 1982. *Beyond Separate Spheres.* New Haven: Yale University Press.

Rosenthal, Naomi, Meryl Fingrutd, Michele Ethier, Roberta Karant, and David McDonald. 1985. "Social Movements and Network Analysis: A Case Study of 19th Century Women's Reform in New York State." *American Journal of Sociology* 90:1022–1054.

Rowbotham, Sheila. 1976. *Hidden from History.* New York: Vintage.

Schwartz, Michael. 1976. *Radical Protest and Social Structure.* New York: Academic Press.

Schwartz, Michael, Naomi Rosenthal, and Laura Schwartz. 1981. "Leader-

Member Conflict in Protest Organizations: The Case of the Southern Farmer's Alliance." *Social Problems* 29:22–36.

Scott, Anne F., and Andrew M. Scott. 1975. *One Half the People.* Philadelphia: Lippincott.

Sinclair, Andrew. 1965. *The Emancipation of the American Woman.* New York: Harper & Row.

Spector, Robert M. 1975. "Women Against the Law: Myra Bradwell's Struggle for Admission to the Illinois Bar." *Illinois State Historical Society Journal* 68:228–242.

Stanton, Elizabeth Cady. [1895] 1974. *The Woman's Bible.* New York: Arno Press.

Strasser, Susan. 1977. "Never Done: The Ideology and Technology of Household Work, 1850–1930." Ph.D. diss., Department of History, State University of New York at Stony Brook.

———. 1982. *Never Done: A History of American Housework.* New York: Pantheon.

Tax, Meredith. 1980. *The Rising of the Women.* New York: Monthly Review Press.

Thompson, E. P. 1963. *The Making of the English Working Class.* New York: Random House.

Tilly, Charles. 1978. *From Mobilization to Revolution.* Reading, Mass.: Addison-Wesley.

Trout, Grace Wilbur. 1920. "Side Lights on Illinois Suffrage History." *Transactions of the Illinois State Historical Society* 1920:93–116.

Turbin, Carole. 1978. Woman's Work and Woman's Rights. Ph.D. diss., Department of Sociology, New School for Social Research.

———. 1981. "Issues and Questions Concerning the Interrelationship between Work and Family Life among Workingwomen in the 19th Century in the U.S." Manuscript.

Useem, Michael. 1975. *Protest Movements in America.* Indianapolis: Bobbs-Merrill.

Weber, Max. 1949. *The Methodology of the Social Sciences.* New York: Free Press.

Wertheimer, Barbara Mayer. 1977. *We Were There.* New York: Pantheon.

Wheeler, Adade Mitchell, and Marlene Stein Wortman. 1977. *The Roads They Made: Women in Illinois History.* Chicago: Kerr.

Wiebe, Robert H. 1967. *The Search for Order, 1877–1920.* New York: Farrar, Straus, and Giroux.

Willard, Frances E., and Mary A. Livermore. [1893] 1967. *A Woman of the Century.* Reprint. Detroit: Gale Research Company.

Willis, Ellen. 1981. "Betty Friedan's 'Second Stage': A Step Backward." *Nation* 233:494–496.

Wilson, John. 1973. *Introduction to Social Movements.* New York: Basic Books.

Wolfe, Alan. 1977. *The Limits of Legitimacy.* New York: Free Press.

Wood, James L., and Maurice Jackson. 1982. *Social Movements.* Belmont, Calif.: Wadsworth.

Zald, Mayer N., and Roberta Ash. 1966. "Social Movement Organizations: Growth, Decay, and Change." *Social Forces* 44:327–341.

Zeitlin, Irving. 1981. *Ideology and the Development of Sociological Theory.* Englewood Cliffs, N.J.: Prentice-Hall.

INDEX

Abolitionist movement: women's participation in, 3–4, 62, 64, 65; and women's rights movement, 4, 40, 50, 57, 218–219

Addams, Jane: and Hull House, 158, 161, 167; and international peace movement, 242n.22; and middle-class consciousness, 158; and Progressive party, 176; and woman suffrage movement, 152, 169–170, 176, 186, 226, 228; and Women's Trade Union League, 159; and working-class women's perspective, 194

Affirmative action, 74

Age of consent, 151, 238n.16

Agitator, 76–83, 85–86, 89, 98–99, 234n.14

Alliances, 40, 213

American Anti-Slavery Society, 4, 229n.2. *See also* Abolitionist movement

American Social Science Association, 122–123

American Woman Suffrage Association (AWSA): formation, 7, 86–88; and IWSA, 104, 221–222; and Mary Livermore, 77, 84, 221; and NWSA, 32–33, 85–88, 98; state-by-state strategy, 9–10, 11. *See also* National American Woman Suffrage Association

Anneke, Fritz, 60–61, 234n.19

Anneke, Mathilde Franziska, 60–62, 83, 87, 88, 89, 92, 231n.1, 239n.24

Anthony, Susan B.: and Elizabeth Boynton Harbert, 221–223; and *History of Woman Suffrage*, 10; and Illinois movement, 57, 70–76, 83–88, 98, 233n.12; and priority of woman suffrage, 6, 71–72, 83, 147, 221, 222, 223, 233n.12, 236n.4; and *Revolution*, 6, 7–8; and Lucy Stone, 98; and temperance movement, 119–120; and working-class women, 130

Anthony amendment, 10, 16, 19, 230n.7

Antisuffragism: as ideology, 20–21, 241n.15; as popular sentiment, 103, 116, 127, 133; as social movement, 153, 168, 172–173, 178. *See also* Caroline Corbin; Illinois Association Opposed to the Extension of Suffrage to Women

Ash, Roberta, 32, 34

Aveling, Edward, 172

Barnett, Ida, 228

Bebel, August, 135

Beecher, Henry Ward, 8, 79

Black women, 96, 228

Blackwell, Alice Stone, 12

Blackwell, Henry, 6

Blatch, Harriot Stanton, 14

Bowen, Louise deKoven, 166–167, 176, 186, 194, 241n.14

Bradwell, James, 71, 72, 74–75, 86, 105–106, 221